AGES OF WOMAN, AGES OF MAN
Sources in European Social History, 1400–1750

D0061264

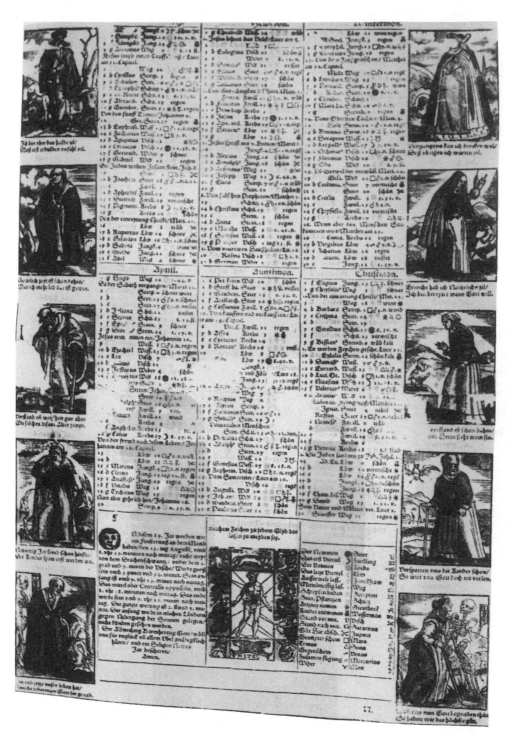

German calendar for the year 1589 showing the ages of woman and ages of man. Reproduced with permission.

AGES OF WOMAN, AGES OF MAN

Sources in European Social History, 1400–1750

Edited by Monica Chojnacka and Merry E. Wiesner-Hanks

Contributor/Translators:
Darlene Abreu-Ferreira, Pernille Arenfeldt, Grethe Jacobsen, Eve Levin, Carol Loats, Leslie Peirce, Allyson Poska, Katharine Swett

With additional translations by: Agnes S. Arnórsdóttir, Louis Grijp, Hermina Joldersma, Hilary Marland, Jeffrey Merrick, Helmut Puff, Elizabeth Rhodes, David Vassberg

Longman

An imprint of **Pearson Education**

London • New York • Toronto • Sydney • Tokyo • Singapore • Hong Kong • Cape Town
New Delhi • Madrid • Paris • Amsterdam • Munich • Milan • Stockholm

PEARSON EDUCATION LIMITED

Head Office:
Edinburgh Gate
Harlow CM20 2JE
Tel: +44 (0)1279 623623
Fax: +44 (0)1279 431059

London Office:
128 Long Acre
London WC2E 9AN
Tel: +44 (0)20 7447 2000
Fax: +44 (0)20 7240 5771
Website: www.history-minds.com

_____

First published in Great Britain in 2002

© Pearson Education, 2002

The right of Monica Chojnacka and Merry E. Wiesner-Hanks
to be identified as Authors of this Work has been asserted by them
in accordance with the Copyright, Designs and Patents Act 1988.

ISBN 0 582 41873 9

British Library Cataloguing in Publication Data
A CIP catalogue record for this book can be obtained from the British Library

10 9 8 7 6 5 4 3 2
07 06 05 04 03

Set in 10/13pt Garamond
Typeset by Graphicraft Limited, Hong Kong
Printed in Malaysia, KVP

The Publishers' policy is to use paper manufactured from sustainable forests.

CONTENTS

CONTENTS

GEOGRAPHIC TABLE OF CONTENTS

GEOGRAPHIC TABLE OF CONTENTS

INTRODUCTION

When we think about the past, many of us imagine it as rather monolithic, short on variety and slow to change. Compared to the changes of the twentieth and early twenty-first centuries, earlier centuries seem to merge into a single image of grueling labor, archaic institutions, and poor hygiene. When we look at artistic renderings from the past, we see people with solemn faces and heavy, uncomfortable clothes. Often when we read about their lives, they seem overwhelmingly laden with hardship and oppression, or else (for a select few) extreme luxury and decadence.

Such perceptions are not entirely groundless, of course. Compared to the present, life was often very hard in pre-modern times. Travel and communication, so important to our own age, were unwieldy and undependable. Luxuries included regular baths or more than one outfit to wear; for most people these were scarce, and life expectancy was much lower than it is in the modern west. But that is not the whole picture. In many ways, women and men moved to rhythms strikingly similar to our own. Then as now, people worked hard to support their families, and rejoiced at the birth of a healthy child. They chafed at social injustice and challenged institutions they perceived as unjust. Young people worried about their future prospects, and often looked forward to having their own homes. Virtually everyone looked forward to parties, where drinking and dancing were favorite pastimes.

We can explore the differences and similarities between people's lives in the past and our own by reading non-fiction studies or historical novels, but it is often more interesting to go directly to the historical sources themselves, that is to written and visual records produced in the period. One of the problems with this is that these records, particularly those that concern the lives of ordinary people rather than intellectual or political elites, are housed in archives around the world and written in languages wo may not understand. Of course, for any period before the invention of the typewriter, records are all hand-written, which means we need to learn how to decipher them – a skill called paleography – before we know what they contain.

1

INTRODUCTION

This collection seeks to overcome some of these problems, and presents a wide variety of sources concerning the lives of ordinary people in Europe for quite a long period of pre-modern history, roughly 1400–1750. Most of the sources are drawn directly from archives, and are printed here for the first time. The vast majority were originally written in a language other than English, and have been translated by our many contributors, who have also written the introductions to the sources. They range geographically from Europe's farthest outposts in the west – Iceland and the Azores in the Atlantic – to its eastern reaches in Russia and the Ottoman Empire.

This collection has been organized around two main principles: stages of life and gender. In the western tradition, since the time of the ancient Greeks, people talked and wrote about the 'ages of man', dividing people's life-course into specific stages. Some writers argued for four stages, corresponding to the four seasons; some twelve, corresponding to the months; and some any number in between. The number that was increasingly accepted was seven: infancy, childhood, adolescence, young adulthood, mature adulthood, older adulthood, and old age. These stages were often depicted artistically as a stepped pyramid, with the individual standing on each step and growing in size and responsibilities to mature adulthood, and then shrinking again with old age. Other artists and writers counted off the ages by decades, in which case they often settled on eight or ten stages in order to have a round number. The illustration that appears as the frontispiece to this book is an example of these, a calendar, designed to hang on people's walls, by the German printer Michael Manger, showing the ages of man on the left and the ages of woman on the right. Death, depicted as a skeleton, accompanies the final figures on both sides.

This collection is similarly divided into eight chapters. The first three follow the classic stages: childhood, youth, and young adulthood, with the third focussing particularly on the process of finding a spouse. The next four chapters investigate aspects of adult life – marriage, work, religion, and social networks – and the final chapter explores widowhood and old age. Each chapter contains between twenty and thirty sources from at least ten different countries, and ends with a series of questions for discussion.

The second organizing principle of this collection is gender, and the sources address the numerous and varied ways in which women's and men's notions of themselves affected their lives and explore how normative concepts of masculine and feminine – i.e., what those terms actually mean – influenced social and political developments. This is the issue at the heart of gender studies: the examination of how definitions of what is feminine (for example, submissive, emotional, weak, nurturing) and what is masculine (for example, dominant, stoic, strong, detached) are shaped. For over two decades, scholars have explored such definitions and concluded that they are not simply the natural outgrowths of biological realities, but are in fact created to a significant degree by social exigencies. Historians of gender presume a close relationship between notions of 'masculine' and 'feminine' and concrete social, economic, and political agendas. We study how these agendas depended upon traditional stereotypes of men and women and their respective roles in society and worked to reinforce them.

The chronological focus of this collection is the period 1400–1750, for which historians use a variety of names, some of them contested. Part of this period is often termed the Renaissance, though the dates of that designation vary depending on whether one is talking about Italy (where the Renaissance 'happened' from 1400 to 1550), or England (where it happened from 1500 to 1620), or Scandinavia (where it happened from 1550 to 1650). This chronological uncertainty, combined with the sense that the word 'Renaissance' (rebirth) describes the experiences of only a small group of elite individuals, has led some scholars to avoid this label entirely. The sixteenth century is often called the 'Reformation' though some scholars avoid this label as they feel it over-emphasizes religious developments. Recently the phrase 'early modern' has become more popular, though scholars debate both *when* European society became 'modern' enough to be designated as such, and *whether* the label is appropriate at all, considering the many continuities with the previous centuries. Conversely, others argue that calling this era 'pre-modern' seems to put too much emphasis on a later break, and that there are, indeed, 'modern' elements clearly evident in European society as early as the fourteenth century. As you read the sources in this collection, you will no doubt find evidence to support all of these points of view – some things will seem very 'modern' (however you choose to define that term), while others seem foreign and archaic.

Whatever we may choose to call this period, this was a time in which many notions that we take for granted were in flux. Religious revival, reform, and conflict dominated the age. An especially tumultuous period was the flowering of the Protestant and Catholic reform movements. These developments in turn led to violent wars, fueled both by religious passions and political ambitions. Against this backdrop of brutality and spirituality, ideas about the essence of things were hotly contested, women accused of witchcraft burned by the tens of thousands, and Europeans who battled against bouts of war and plague searched their souls and bibles for an explanation for their distress.

But even as natural catastrophes and religious conflict seemed to plunge Europeans into a miasma of suffering, these centuries were among the most exciting and productive of Europe's history. Cities were growing and offering men and some women a host of new professional and economic opportunities. Civic and regional governments began developing new programs to encourage growth and stability and to help the poor. Europeans encountered other peoples on a new scale, in the East, Africa, and the Americas. These encounters were often destructive for the non-Europeans, but enriched the European continent both culturally and economically. This was also a period of state and empire building, as central authorities, from Henry VIII and Elizabeth I of England to Suleiman the Magnificent of the Ottoman Empire, consolidated and expanded their power through the establishment of institutions and through force.

All of these developments were shaped by the gender norms and gender structures in European society, and, conversely, shaped the opportunities and situation of men and women. One example of such shaping can be seen in the profession of midwifery in the early modern period. Midwives had functioned as healers and medical authorities for centuries, often with the sanction of local governments. But by the seventeenth century they were coming under increasing fire, and their right to practice healing was systematically challenged throughout the continent. This occurred in tandem with the rise of the (male) physician, whose professional status rose as that of the midwife declined. Midwives, once respected members of society, now found themselves accused of practicing folk magic or, at best, 'old-fashioned' and dangerous medicine. Why were midwives the target of such attacks? The answer is complicated, but we can look in part to broader developments in science and society in this period. As the scientific academy grew in stature, it became increasingly important to its members to control all aspects of science, including medicine. This could only be done by establishing irrefutable definitions of acceptable scientific methods and practice, and excluding those whose practices differed from institutional ones.

The history of midwifery provides just one example of a particular early modern development that constrained women's activities, and other such constraints were long-standing. Women's ability to hold property, run a business, participate in religious worship, engage in political activity, or even rear children was severely circumscribed by both law and custom. This was true throughout Europe, though the degree to which such strictures were implemented varied from region to region.

The laws and customs that dictated a specific, restrictive role to women – an entirely private existence, focused exclusively on rearing one's children and obeying one's husband – also limited men, though less severely. While men were obviously the beneficiaries of the limitations placed on women in the public arena, they too were bound by notions of 'masculine' honor and duty. Like women, men usually had to accept the path chosen for them by their parents, in both marriage and occupation, a path determined by social status and familial interest. This patriarchal society had been constructed by men for their own advantage, yet individual men sometimes paid a price for this as well.

Early modern definitions and expectations of women and men were in many ways fluid, and shifted across time and place. Expectations and legal restrictions surrounding young unmarried women were different from those surrounding an elderly widow. The married woman was supposed to live up to a particular ideal,

4

the nun another. The ambiguity of some of the categories of difference between men and women conflicted with volumes of writings, dating back centuries, about the sexes that asserted innate, biological differences with clear social implications. The reality was not so neat.

Thus, despite the vast array of forces brought to bear on circumscribing men's and especially women's opportunities, the real world allowed for more mobility and agency than official policy implies. The documents assembled here make that clear. If the Catholic and Protestant churches asserted the preeminence of the man in religious instruction and guidance, women in fact actively participated in the lively debates about salvation. If the father was the putative head of household according to both church and state, in reality wives and mothers managed their families in ways that reached far beyond the four walls of their homes. If marriage was viewed as a social union by the state and a procreative one by the churches, marital love and companionship could still thrive between husband and wife.

The documents in the chapters that follow reflect the forcefulness of gender stereotypes and the complex reality that sometimes challenged them. Some themes run throughout all or most of the chapters. These include definitions of power, relations between men and women, the breadth and depth of patriarchy's reach, and the range of options women and men might exercise. Questions appear at the end of each chapter, but here are some more general ones to ask yourselves throughout:

1 In what ways are the conditions described in these documents different from similar conditions today? For example, how has the relationship between work and home life changed?
2 Are contemporary expectations of children or couples radically different from early modern ones? How so?
3 How would you describe the range of options that women and men possessed In this period?
4 What sorts of geographical differences do you find? How about class differences?
5 Look at the documents themselves. Does the type of document (i.e., will, letter, court testimony) affect the sort of information we scholars can glean from it?
6 In what ways were gender stereotypes reinforced? In what ways might they be circumvented?

1

CHILDHOOD

Childhood was a perilous stage of life in early modern Europe. Many children died young – about half before they reached the age of five – and many also lost one or both parents, so that families frequently contained half-siblings, step-siblings, and foster children. It began with an event that could itself be dangerous – childbirth. Using English statistics, it has been estimated that the maternal mortality rate in the early modern period was about 1 percent for each birth. Most women experienced multiple childbirths successfully, but all of them knew someone who had died in childbed. Thus women took care to be tended by experienced friends and relatives, or to use the services of professional mid-wives where these were available. Male physicians took little interest in delivery, and were generally called in only if the child or mother or both were dead or dying, so their presence was dreaded. In the middle of the seventeenth century, a few male barber-surgeons in France and England began to advertise their services for childbirth, and having a 'man-midwife' became fashionable for wealthy families. Female midwives continued to handle the vast majority of, and in eastern and southern Europe all, births, however.

The actual techniques of delivery varied widely, even within the same town. Some midwives and mothers preferred to use a birthing stool, a special padded stool with handles which tipped the mother back slightly; other mothers lay in bed, kneeled, stood, or sat in another woman's lap. The level of intervention also varied from midwife to midwife. Some tried to speed the birth along by making the mother change positions or pulling on the child as it emerged, while others might wait for days during a very difficult labor before attempting to interfere. The most skillful and best-trained midwives took a middle route, intervening only when they thought it necessary. Midwives were responsible for the spiritual as well as the physical well-being of the children they delivered, for they were allowed to perform emergency baptisms on children they thought might die.

Just as women recognized the dangers of birth, parents recognized the dangers of childhood and tried to protect their children with religious amulets and pilgrimages to special shrines, made toys for them, and sang them lullabies.

Even practices which to us may seem cruel, such as wrapping children tightly with bands of cloth (termed 'swaddling'), were motivated by a concern for the child's safety and health at a time when most households had open fires, domestic animals wandered freely, and mothers and older siblings were doing work which prevented them from continually watching a toddler. Paintings from the period show small children in wheeled walkers which kept them safer until they learned to walk securely, and women's diaries inform us that they led their toddlers on 'leading-strings' attached to their clothing to prevent them from falling or wandering.

In most parts of Europe, boys inherited family land while girls generally did not, and in all parts of Europe, men were regarded as superior to women. These practices and attitudes led parents to favor the birth of sons over daughters. Girls significantly outnumbered boys in most orphanages or foundling homes, as poor parents decided their sons would ultimately be more useful; infants had a much poorer chance of survival in orphanages than they did if cared for by their parents. Occasionally parents who could not care for their children killed them outright, but these cases are quite rare and generally involve desperate unwed mothers; we cannot tell from the records whether girls were more likely to be killed than boys, for the court records generally simply refer to 'child' or 'infant'.

It is difficult to know whether boys and girls were treated very differently when they were infants and small children. Children were all dressed alike in long dress-like garments for the first several years of their lives, rather than put into pink or blue outfits as is often common in contemporary Weslem culture. Until they were about seven, children of both sexes were cared for by women, generally their own mothers if they were poor and servants or nurse-maids if they were wealthy. It was when children began their training for adult life, at the age of four or five, that clear distinctions became evident. Girls of all classes were taught skills that they would use in running a household – spinning, sewing, cooking, care of domestic animals; peasant girls were also taught some types of agricultural tasks. Boys also began to learn the skills they would use later – assisting fathers in their work or working in the fields. If parents themselves could read, they might begin teaching their children to read along with teaching them practical skills, or send them to a primary school if one was available. The vast majority of people in early modern Europe did not learn to read, however; they were not necessarily uneducated, for they may have been very highly skilled in a trade and astute about the world around them, but this education came through oral tradition and training, not through books.

Many children began to work when they were very young; boys as young as seven might be apprenticed to a man other than their father to learn his trade, and girls at that age sent to another household to be a domestic servant or, more rarely, an apprentice in a trade. Arrangements for apprenticeship or foster care were generally made with legal documents, many of which have survived. The young age at which children were often sent away from their parents in these documents has been used as evidence of parental coldness, but can also be used as evidence that parents cared about their children's future, and tried to improve their prospects. Though poor children and orphans were most likely to be sent away, wealthier children often left home at a young age as well. In northern Europe in particular, even noble children might be sent at eight or nine to the homes of even wealthier and more prominent people, with the expectation they would learn good manners and make acquaintances and contacts that would later lead to favorable marriages or help them in their careers.

BIRTH AND INFANCY

1 Ordinance regulating midwives, Germany 1522

Women in early modern Europe, like those in most of the world's cultures in most periods, generally gave birth assisted by female relatives and friends. Women who had particular talents or inclination were often called to assist more often, and gradually such women began taking payment for their work, evolving into professional midwives. Midwives were trained by watching and helping more experienced midwives, but beginning in the sixteenth century in some parts of Europe city governments began to regulate midwifery and require midwives to swear an oath if they wished to obtain a license. This is the first midwives' ordinance from the south German city of Nuremberg, which served as a model for many other cities. (Nuremberg Staatsarchiv, Amts-und Standbücher Nr. 100, fs. 101–105. Translated by Merry Wiesner-Hanks.)

Every midwife should give her oath and swear she will conscientiously care for and stand by every expectant mother in her time of need to whom she is called, whether she is rich or poor, to the best of her abilities and understanding. She should proceed to whomever she is called first, immediately and without opposition, and make absolutely no excuses or delays, as has often been the case, but faithfully stand by her. Also no woman is to be hurried or forced to deliver before the proper time; she should wait and hold out until the appropriate time.

If the thing [the delivery] looks like it will be dangerous, she should call one or two of the women who oversee midwifery and proceed with the emergency according to their advice. In no case is she to wait or delay to call them until the need is so great they cannot handle it, or she will warrant serious punishment.

If it happens that the birth takes so long and the first midwife has a pressing need to rest or sleep for a while, she should call another sworn midwife and not an apprentice, who will then be just as responsible to appear immediately without opposition. She should then steadfastly and helpfully care for the woman in labor just as if she had been called at first. If it happens that this second midwife is caring for another expectant mother at the time she is called, she should stay with this one and send another midwife to the other birth.

If any midwives show themselves to be disobedient or disagreeable, the city council will not only remove them from office, but will also punish them severely, so that all will know to shape up and watch their behavior.

The council has certainly experienced that the midwives deal very deceitfully and for their own profit with the *Arme Kindbetterin Almosen* [a city fund for poor expectant mothers] running back and forth to respectable women, who do not need the alms, promising them bedding and lard and other things if they will agree to call them as midwives. These lucrative operations are leading to a decline and breakdown of the *Almosen*. Because the council sees this with no little displeasure, from now on the midwives will be sworn by their oaths not to run after these women, or promise them the *Almosen*, but to refrain from this completely. If the council discovers any further incidents, she [the midwife] will be let out of her office, and will be punished in each case according to the severity of the deed, however the council decides.

From now on no midwife will be allowed to take on an apprentice who has begun with a different midwife and left her without justifiable cause, but every apprentice shall stay with the woman with whom she started. Justifiable and legitimate cause for leaving may be proven to the council or to those appointed by it. In such cases, the apprentice will not be forbidden to complete her training years with another sworn midwife. In this case, the woman that caused the apprentice to leave through her unfairness and unreasonableness will not be allowed to take on another apprentice until the end of the training years of the first.

They should not take on any flighty, young apprentices, as it so often happens that they marry during the course of their training and that all sorts of injuries result from their inexperience. They should rather take on apprentices well advanced in years and preferably living alone, from whom one expects more diligence than from younger ones.

They should also not allow themselves to drink wine in excess, as all kinds of injury and harm have been inflicted on the pregnant women because of this. The council has decided to punish severely any who break this restriction.

The honorable council has discovered that the midwives often send their maids (who have not completed their instruction or who have just completed it and have no experience yet) alone to women who are giving birth for the first time, through which these women are often neglected and deplorably injured. Therefore the honorable council orders that from now on no maid, whether she has half-completed her training or not, is to attend alone any woman bearing her first or second child, whether she goes with the knowledge of her instructor or not. After the passing of the normal years of training, the apprentice shall carry out her first birth in the presence of her instructor. In the case that the instructor is dead or not there, another sworn, experienced midwife should be present. Anyone who is convicted of this will be punished to the extent that the council's displeasure with the deed can be felt.

The high honorable council has also had enough of midwives taking their proper salary for poor women not only from the established overseer of the charity [the *Arme Kindbetterin Almosen*] but also from the women themselves, and therefore receiving double payment. This gives the honorable council great displeasure. Because of this the midwives are to swear that when they receive their proper salary (that, due to persuasive reasons, has been set at 20 kreuzer for each birth) from the overseer for caring for a poor woman, they are not to demand or want anything more, but let themselves be completely satisfied with their established salary. All of this is liable to punishment, which the high honorable council will set each time according to the crime and opportunities of the case.

Recently evil cases have taken place, that those women who live in sin and adultery have illegitimate children, and during birth or before purposefully attempt to kill them by taking harmful, abortion-causing drugs, or through other notorious means. Some of these cases never come to the attention of the authorities, and proper punishment for them cannot be carried out. This the high honorable council, because of the God-given authority it carries, can no longer tolerate. Therefore they have made the recommendation that the midwives' oath be added to. They are to swear yearly, that when one of them is called to deliver a baby for such a woman, one who is carrying an illegitimate child, she [the midwife] is obliged to ask with intent what the name of the child's mother is, and who the child's father is. As soon as she has brought the child into the world, she is to report to the Lord Mayor whether the child is alive or dead, who its mother and father are, and where the mother is lying in bed. Also no dead illegitimate children are to be carried to the grave before she gives her report to the Lord Mayor. At least three or four unsuspected female persons are to go with the child to the grave. If one or more of the midwives act against this, and will not comply with what has been sent forth above, the high honorable council will deal with them as perjurers with corporal punishment. Then they will finally know to conform to this.

[Changes in and additions to the regulations were made fairly regularly, and in 1579 were codified and reissued along with the original 1522 ordinance:]

On the request of the sworn midwives to the high honorable council to improve their ordinance in several various points, this further pronouncement is to be published, to bring the following improvements to their ordinances.

First: The midwives have sworn in their oaths not to send or use an apprentice during her normal training years to a woman having her first baby, but have requested to have this limited to only the first quarter-year. The high honorable council believes this to be much too short a time, and will set the limit at one year. Therefore from now on no midwife should send a maid to a woman having her first child unless she has completed one year of her training program.

Second: It has often come about that some midwives who were with women during their labor run away from them and to others, without caring that this is utterly and completely against their sworn duties. Through this running away many births are hurried, and it should be severely punished. Therefore, when, from now on, one or more midwives leave a woman in need, without calling another sworn midwife to come in their place, they will be required to pay the high honorable council a five gulden fine, without exception.

Third: Some women have allowed their little children to be carried to holy baptism by strange people when the midwife was too busy, although such small children are easily harmed and injured. Therefore, the high honorable council orders that from now on all new-born children are to be carried to holy baptism by their sworn midwife or her apprentice. Any midwife will be fined two gulden if she breaks this ordinance.

Fourth: No midwife is to send her children or servants to a baptism, nor ask for anything to take home to them, with a fine of two gulden.

Fifth: No midwife is to take on a maid-apprentice without the knowledge of the overseers of midwifery. No maid-apprentice is to be accepted who is married or has her own household, but only those who are single or widowed, so that these persons are not called away from their instructors to their private business or housework, and will always be available. They should not live in the midwife's house, but in the neighborhood, and should keep themselves occupied at all times.

Sixth: Some maid-apprentices have been wantonly leaving their mistresses and continuing their training with others, which is not only not to be tolerated but specifically forbidden in the midwives' ordinance. In order to deal with this the high honorable council has decided that from now on no maid-apprentice who has left her mistress before the completion of her proper training period without justifiable cause may be taken on or instructed by another midwife. These maids have forfeited the office [of sworn midwife] with this action. However, if a midwife treats her maid so unreasonably that she cannot stay with her, it will not be forbidden for her to complete her training with another mistress. The overseers of midwives should make note of this. If they cannot decide the case, it will be the responsibility of the high honorable council, and their decision will have to be awaited. The high honorable council also wants the midwives, when they accept maid-apprentices, to take on the children of citizens before any foreigners.

The high honorable council has discovered that some of the midwives are taking all or half of the tips that have been given to their maid-apprentices by people, which leads to all sorts of lack of diligence and care among the maids. In order to prevent this, the high honorable council has demanded that from now on all that a maid receives for herself from a child's mother, father, relatives or others, that has been given willingly above the normal payments, should remain the maid's and she is not to be required to give any to her mistress. She should, however, give the house-maid five gulden a year from this, as she is doing her housework [i.e., whenever a maid-apprentice is serving at a birth].

The high honorable council has also discovered that some midwives have no maid-apprentices, with the result that when the old midwives die no qualified people may be appointed to their posts. In order to improve this, the high honorable council seriously asks all midwives who have completed the training period with one or more maids to take on another capable one in their place a quarter or at longest a half year later. Also, if they are with pregnant women, they are not to send their maid alone to another to whom they've been called, but go there themselves, so that all kinds of dangers may be prevented.

2 Memoirs of the midwife Catharina van Schrader, Netherlands 1734

There are many more sources available about the way births were supposed to proceed, such as the ordinance printed above or published instruction books for midwives, than about how births actually happened. Catharina van Schrader (1656–1746), a professional midwife in Frisia, part of the Netherlands, is unusual in that she kept notebooks of all her cases for more than fifty years. When she was in her eighties, she extracted the most complicated cases from her notebooks and put them all into a single book, dedicating it to the women she had helped. She was often called in when other midwives had given up on a case, and this book thus contains gruesome examples of difficult births.
(Excerpt from *Mother and Child Were Saved: The Memoirs (1693–1740) of the Frisian Midwife Catharina Schrader* (Amsterdam: Rodopi, 1984), pp. 63, 64. Translated and annotated by Hilary Marland. Reprinted by permission.)

On 27 September fetched to Antje, wife of the brewer, Aate Schoyeles. By The Lord's decree, delivered her two daughters. The first came forth sitting. Broke the water of the other . . . I had to look for the feet. Got them with great difficulty, though delivered it with its feet. Still all well, by God's blessing, for mother and children. (The diary states that the first child came with its bottom first, the second back first.)

1710, been fetched on 18 October to Hantum to the wife of Pitter Bockes, who had been in heavy labour for two whole days. And assisted by the midwife from Hantum and surgeon Nicklas, who both gave it over [to Schrader]; I found the arms born to the shoulder. Placed her backwards and not without great difficulty brought the shoulder and arm inside. Looked for the feet. The child was dead when I came. I had heavy work before I could get the feet. But The Lord be thanked. It progressed quickly. And the mother does well.

1711 on 20 March fetched to Maykc, wife of Cornelis Jans, Mennonite preacher and thread winder. I was with her three days and nights doing everything which art allowed. The child came presented right, but was grown in fast. Have drawn off her water through a catheter; also given an enema. And everything in the presence of doctor Eysma. It was caused by all that heavy bearing down and the presentation of an arm. That was not good. The child was then already dead. I had to cut off an arm, and delivered it with terrible difficulty. And stuck the hook in the back of his head and got it like this. The Lord be praised, honoured and thanked. The woman does well. A healthy childbed. It is a woman who had always been very crippled in her lower body. Such [women] have heavy births and deliveries in general. [The fuller notebook account of this birth adds that the woman retained her water. After the delivery the arm Schrader cut off was put in her sleeve, because she did not want anyone to see it. The woman was healthy and unharmed after the birth. The child was a boy.]

1711 on 28 April to Mayke, the wife of master Watse, a boat builder. The child came [presented] with his back sideways. She had a heavy flooding. With very great difficulty I pulled the child with its bottom to the birth canal. It was hard for her and myself. And had almost given it up, but the Lord gave deliverance. And had to be born doubled up with his bottom [presenting]. However the child and the mother lived. A healthy childbed.

3 Illustration of birthing stool and child in the uterus, England 1545

Manuals for midwives were published throughout Europe in the early modern period, which suggests that some midwives could read, because there was clearly a market for such books. As was common in this era, many of them copied text and illustrations from earlier books, usually without attribution. These are illustrations from Thomas Raynalde's *The Birth of Mankynde*, published in London in 1545, though they had originally appeared in a German midwives' manual. Women commonly gave birth on stools like this one, gripping the handles on the side; the midwife would sit on a smaller stool in front of the mother. The lower illustrations are rather fanciful depictions of the child in utero, showing the standard head-first and the less common feet-first presentation.

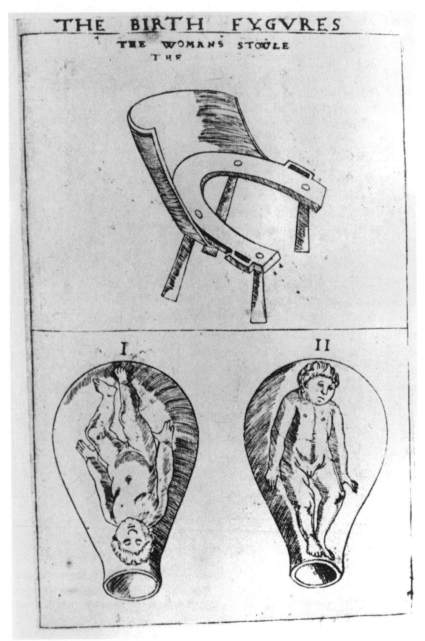

4 News sheet showing conjoined twins, Germany 1565

Printers in many parts of Europe regularly published single-page broadsheets covering current events and other things they thought would be interesting enough to cause people to buy them. Many of these focussed on unexplained natural phenomena, often viewing them as a sign of God's pleasure or anger. Conjoined human and animal twins, and other types of birth defects, were common subjects for such broadsheets; with the rumor of such a birth, a printer or the local authorities might send out an artist, and then publish the illustration. This is a very typical example, published in Augsburg by the printer Hans Zimmermann. The text below explains who saw the baby (who had died and was buried), notes that the parents were honorable and hard-working, and comments that God alone knows why such things happen and that pregnant women and their husbands should understand them as a warning to put their trust in God.

(Walter L. Strauss, *The German Single-Leaf Woodcut, 1550–1600* (New York: Abaris Books, 1975). Reprinted by permission.)

5 Letter from a woman to her father regarding breastfeeding, Wales 1618

The vast majority of women nursed their own children, often until they were more than two years old, but middle- and upper-class children were often nursed by wet nurses, either within their own home or the home of the wet nurse. Wet nurses were chosen with care, often by the father of the child, who made a contract with the husband of the wet nurse. (Such contracts stipulated the wet nurse would not have sexual relations with her husband, as this was viewed as harmful to the milk.) Sometimes women objected to being overruled in the choice of the wet nurse, or described other problems they had in hiring and retaining such women.
(National Library of Wales (N.L.W.), 9056E, f. 80, February 4, 1618. Excerpt from a letter by Elizabeth Bodvel to her father Sir John Wynn at Gwydir. Excerpted by Katharine Swett.)

Loving father my duty most humbly remembered:

The first nurse that came to my child was an Anglesey woman not liked by any here but only by your son Bodvel [Elizabeth's husband], who would needs have her to be the nurse and none else, as my mother can tell you; whether it was her missdieting of herself [i.e., not eating enough or eating the wrong food], or her dogged nature that dried up her milk, I protest I know not, being neither angered by me nor any of the house. The other which came to be the nurse was a tenant's daughter of yours who had milk sufficient for two children until she heard that her love had gotten one of your maids with child. I persuaded her what I could that it was not so but nothing did prevail, for she went away unknown to me her haste was such to be gone. I thank god my child thrives well although it was my hard fortune to meet with such as I did, but it shall be a warning for me how I take a nurse at anybody's preferring. I humbly thank you for your care of me and my child which I hope will prove like his pretty uncles of Gwydir . . .

6 Bishop's ruling about children and parents sleeping the same bed, Spain 1583

In order to keep them safe and warm, infants normally slept with the parents in the same bed. Unfortunately, some children were smothered by the bedding or by their parents' bodies. During the sixteenth century, authorities grew increasingly concerned with the problem of accidental infanticide. In this excerpt from a sixteenth-century diocesan synod in northwestern Spain, the bishop, Juan de San Clemente, attempted to solve the problem.
(Libro de Visitas, Santa Eulalia Bouses, Archivo Histórico Diocesano de Ourense, 27.2.5, May 16, 1583. Translated by Allyson Poska.)

We mandate to the priests and the curates that they admonish their parishioners to put their infant children in crib and cradle, because we have seen

16

and we see the enormous and grave sins which the mothers and the fathers cause the children, and we place upon the penalty of four ducats . . . They have been advised to make cribs and cradles quickly in which to put the children because some have not complied, and sleeping with their children has resulted in many asphyxiations and deaths that the parents cause their innocent children as we see almost every year with such pain . . . and we mandate to said priests and curates that as soon as they hear that some woman in their parish is pregnant they mandate that within 15 days they [the parents] make a crib and cradle in which to put the child, and if the woman and her husband do not comply, prohibit them from the mass and divine offices.

7 Prohibition of bringing children to church, Spain 1697

During the Protestant and Catholic Reformations, religious leaders attempted to make church ceremonies more solemn and orderly, bringing decorum to what had earlier often been a noisy atmosphere. Fidgety and crying children frequently disrupted religious ceremonies, and in this excerpt from an Episcopal visitation to a parish in northwestern Spain, the parishioners are told to stop bringing small children to the church. Such mandates had serious consequences for female parishioners who were then obligated to miss the service and its accompanying administration of the Eucharist and catechism lessons in order to stay home with their children.
(Libro de Visitas, Santiago Amuidal, Archivo Histórico Diocesano de Ourense, 3.2.6, f. 21, November 18, 1697. Translated by Allyson Poska.)

Item, as his Honor is informed that the women of this parish bring young children to the church and that they are troublesome to the priest during the Mass, he mandates that henceforth they should not be so bold as to bring them to the said church.

8 Baptismal records, Portugal 1588–1592

One of the first ceremonies in a child's life in early modern Europe was baptism. The intricate details found in baptismal records can tell us much about local customs. In the case of a child born out of wedlock, the loss of status to its mother is evident with the omission of her last name, a practice that was used to identify single people in general. Many early modern people were known locally by their nicknames, or identified by the part of town or village in which they lived. Emergency baptisms could be performed by lay persons, including women, though in Catholic parts of Europe if the child survived it went through a second baptism in the church conducted by the parish priest. (Protestant areas differed in their handling of emergency baptism.) Baptisms were a means to celebrate the birth of a child, to confirm its Christian faith, and to enhance allegiance and support networks through the system of godparents for the newborn. Most children were given a godmother and a godfather, but some had four godparents, two of each sex.

17

(Arquivo Distrital de Aveiro, Concelho de Ovar, Freguesia de Esmoriz, Baptismos, Livro 1, f. 1, f. 2, f. 7 (1588–1669); Concelho de Arouca, Freguesia de Tropeço, Baptismos, Livro 1, f. 4 (1564–1617). Translated by Darlene Abreu-Ferreira.)

[f. 1] On the fourth day of the month of February in the era of one thousand five hundred and eighty-eight years I baptized Maria daughter of Maria a young unmarried woman with the nickname *a toia*. She was given for father Bastiam a young unmarried man son of João Fernandez from the outskirts. Godparents were Pero Gonçalvez *do augro* and Antonia Pirez wife of João Alves from the outskirts all from this parish. With authority I signed here today above mentioned day month and year. Balthasar Jorge.

[f. 2] Domingas daughter of João Nunes from Lameiros and of his wife Maria Dominges born Christmas day in the year eighty-eight and was baptized on the first day of January in the year eighty-nine. Godparents were Bastiam son of João Fernandez from the outskirts and Caterina Fernandez wife of Antonio Gonçalvez of the village all from this parish *des moris* and in truth I signed here today said day month and year. Balthasar Jorge.

[f. 7] Domingos son of João Fernandez from the village and his wife Antonia Gonçalvez born on the thirtieth of August in one thousand five hundred and ninety-two years was baptized at home by Catherina Fernandez wife of Antonio Gonçalvez mother of the said Antonia and on the sixth day of September of said era was brought to this church of *Sancta Maria dos Moris* where the exorcism was performed and the Holy oils were applied by me Balthasar Jorge abbot of the said church. Present Isabel Gonçalvez wife of Matheus Fernandez *das pedras* and Matheus Fernandez the younger *do campo* all from this parish. In truth I signed here today day and era *ut supra* [as above]. Balthasar Jorge.

[f. 4] Saturday XV of the month of July 1564 I Francisco Mendez curate baptized a daughter of Jurdão Pirez *de fundo de villa* and his wife Madalena Jorge with the name Isabel. Godparents were Sebastião Jorge *de fontão dabbades* and João Alvarez *da cella* and Catherina Anes wife of Joam Jorge *de trepeço* and Maria Jorge wife of João Dominguez *do pereiro de lamas* and in truth I signed here. Francisco Mendez.

9 Medical guide for women and children, France ca. 1535

While medical works for physicians were written in Latin, those for ordinary people were written and published in the vernacular. This is the title page of a very popular medical work, *Weiber und Kinder Apotek*, published in Strasbourg in about 1535, and attributed to a botanist from Strasbourg, Otto Brunfels, but actually written by an anonymous compiler. It is addressed to all mothers, future mothers, midwives, and wetnurses, and includes one section on diseases of women and a second on diseases of children. The title page shows a physician carrying a flask – most likely of urine, for inspecting urine was a common way for physicians to diagnose disease – two children playing with whirligigs, and a middle-class married woman, identified as such by her head covering and bunch of keys. This was a relatively small book and probably affordable for middle-class families to use as a reference.

EDUCATION AND TRAINING

10 A father's instructions for the education of his children, Denmark 1654

Middle- and upper-class fathers (and occasionally mothers) oversaw the education of their children and sometimes left detailed instructions about this, especially if they were ill and thought they might die. The following instructions were composed by the Danish nobleman Mogens Sehested (1598–1657), who was a member of one of the most prominent, wealthy, and influential families within the Danish realm at the time. Mogens Sehested and his wife, Lisbeth Gyldenstjerne, had six sons and nine daughters, of whom five boys and seven girls survived their first years. The following instructions were aimed at the education of the seven youngest children. At the time the document was written the oldest of these, Sophie, was about sixteen years old, and the youngest, Jens, was eight or nine years old. The document clearly reveals the different emphasis on the education that sons and daughters were to receive. As was common among nobles throughout Europe at the time, it was sufficient for the girls to acquire reading and writing skills and to be taught Christian virtues and the meaning of the Holy Scriptures, whereas the boys were subject to a much more varied and thorough education comprising foreign languages, mathematics, geography, and other subjects. Only two years after compiling these instructions, the sons were sent to the town of Viborg to continue their education as their elder brothers had done before, embarking upon their 'grand tours' throughout Europe. Christian Schmidt, to whom the following instructions were given, accompanied them to Viborg. At the same time, the daughters most likely were sent to the households of relatives for their further upbringing, and at the age of eighteen to twenty-two years they could expect to be married into other, preferably prominent, noble families.

(The original document is lost but a contemporary transcription is preserved in the Danish National Archives, Copenhagen. It has previously been published in *Personalhistorisk Tidsskrift*, ser 7, vol. III (Copenhagen, 1919) and in Birte Andersen, *Adelig Opfostring. Adelsbørns opdragelse i Danmark 1536–1660* (Copenhagen, 1971). Translated by Grethe Jacobsen and Pernille Arenfeldt.)

Instructions for [the Preceptor of] Mogens Sehested's Children (1654)

As I, in the name of Jesus, have employed the honest and much learned person Christian Valentinson Schmidt to be the preceptor of my children, he is hereby given instructions and orders as to how he shall behave and act in this service.

1. Firstly, he himself must above all fear and love the almighty God and diligently practice prayer and invocations and devoutly respect and heed the word of God.

2. Secondly, he must with the greatest diligence and gravity maintain the fear of God in my children, have them read the explanations of their prayers and catechisms evening and morning as they have been used to, and when they come from the church [he must] be informed of what they learned from the sermon.

3. Thirdly, he must teach and instruct the boys in the fundaments and practices of the Latin language according to the manners and ways which were urged upon all of them yesterday and hereafter will be repeated in a manner most suited to them. And if the children are found to be negligent or indifferent to learning when they are asked and commanded, he must diligently and seriously admonish them, so

that they mend their ways and improve; if they do not respect such admonition, he has the authority to punish them with the switch in moderation, and not with paddle, rod or fist, which are not suited for children. If, against all expectations, some of the children should prove reluctant or obstinate the school master shall at once let me know that they may be properly punished further.

4. He must also continue to teach Jytte Sehested to read and write and have Sophie and Margrete Sehested write on Wednesday and Saturday afternoons when the boys are free from school.

5. He must diligently pay attention to the children's manners and conduct, especially when we are not at home, [he must ensure] that they maintain proper table manners and do not go to the farm buildings or any other place outside of the house when he is not with them, and accompany them both going outside and returning.

6. He must live soberly and properly and not cause any offence or indignation neither by words nor by actions and not go anywhere in town without prior notice and permission.

7. During the summer, the children must read their morning prayers in the school for the schoolmaster at six o'clock in the morning, and then together with him come down to read and sing to the servants in the hall. Afterwards they shall immediately be given their breakfast, and as soon as they have eaten it they must return to the school and remain there to do their lessons until it is nearly ten o'clock, so that they can get some exercise before the meal. When it is one o'clock after the noon meal they shall return to school and remain there with their lessons until it is nearly five o'clock so that they again can get some exercise before the [evening] meal.

8. When we are at home, the children are permitted to go to the sitting room to play and move about when they are not in school, while when we are not at home, they must remain in the school or in the small room next to it to play and the houseboy must be with them and look after them, or they can walk with the schoolmaster on the earthwork or in the field, although they cannot knock at the door of anyone's house here in town, except when we are at home and they are granted permission to do so.

9. The schoolmaster must also pay diligent attention to the children's houseboy so that he keeps their clothing and shoes clean and that [the houseboy] pays attention to what is lacking and that nothing disappears. Similarly, every morning and evening he [the houseboy] must properly dress and undress the children and properly fold and lay their clothing in an appropriate place, in the same way he must build

21

the fire in the school when it is needed. If the boy is found to be negligent or obstinate, the schoolmaster has permission to punish him with the braided leather whip or rod, as [it] is appropriate [punishment].

10. For his service, the aforementioned Christian Schmidt shall be given an annual pay of forty rigsdaler to be paid twice a year as he wishes and needs. And his salary shall commence from the first of July of this year to the same day the following year and then yearly as long as he remains in this service. That this will be kept in this manner and complied with, I sign with my own hand. At Ribberhus 4 July anno 1654.

11 Fostering contract for a daughter, France 1610

Most families were not well-off enough to have a tutor for their children, nor even to send them to school. Children generally began work at an early age, either in their own household or in the household of others, and learned skills by watching or informal instruction. In urban areas, these arrangements were sometimes formalized by contracts, drawn up by a notary, between the parents and the head of the household in which the child would be living. While we might wish to distinguish between arrangements made primarily for the care of a child and arrangements made primarily to provide labor to another household and gain vocational training for the child, these arrangements were quite similar as formalized before notaries. The emotional and practical vulnerability of children in these processes is not explicit in contracts such as these. In the following arrangement for foster care, a young daughter is placed into another household, for the remainder of her childhood, by both of her parents. She would be well provided for in her new circumstances, but during the sixteen years of the arrangement, she would also serve in the new household and learn the trade of her 'foster' father. (In another document recorded on the same day, similar arrangements were made for a son of this same couple. He was placed into service and apprenticeship with the same man, but for only three years, and without any payment.)
(Paris, Archives Nationales, Minutier central, Étude CXXII/389, June 4, 1610. Translated by Carol Loats.)

Present in person were Vincent Cervet, farm worker living at Mortayne, parish of Saint Malo, in Preche, and Marie Poigne, his wife, whom he authorizes for this transaction. Together they acknowledge and affirm that, for the benefit of, and to avoid losses to Marguerite Cervay, their daughter, they have given and left her, from today for the next sixteen years, to and with Francois le Peletier, *merchant plumassier* [maker of plumed hats], bourgeois [citizen] of Paris, living there on the bridge of Notre Dame in the building with the sign of the shield of Brittany, present and accepting.

[Le Pelletier] has promised and promises to show and teach his art of plumassier, the merchandise and all in which he is involved to the said Marguerite Cervay; to have her instructed in the Catholic apostolic and

Roman faith and religion; to provide and deliver what she needs in terms of drink, food, fire, bed, home, light; and to treat her gently, as is appropriate; to have her lanced, medicated, and treated in case of sickness providing that the sickness does not last more than fifteen days each time; and to maintain her with clothes, linen, footwear, and other necessary clothing honorably, as her status warrants, during the said time of sixteen years; and at the end of that time leave to her all the clothing and worn clothes that she then may have in use; and further to give her the sum of 100 livres tournois, one time, to contribute towards her portion in marriage, or otherwise to use at the discretion of the said father and mother, in consideration of the services that she will have provided to him domestically during that time.

To do this, present was the said Marguerite Cervet, aged eight and one half years or so. [She] finds these [arrangements] acceptable and promises to learn the said art to the best of her ability; to serve the said Pelletier and his wife well and faithfully in it, and in all other things lawful and honorable that are commanded of her and as a servant is obliged to do; to work toward their benefit, avoid losses to them, and warn them of problems if they come to her attention; without taking flight nor serving elsewhere during the said time.

And in case of flight or absence, the said father and mother will be obliged to search for her in the city and outskirts of Paris and bring her back to the said Peletier to finish the said service if they are able to find her; and [they] pledge her to complete loyalty and faithfulness.

As thus etc., promising, obligating, each in his own right, etc., the said Cervet and his wife and their daughter, the one for the other and each of them alone for all without dispute or division, renouncing body and goods, etc., Cervet and his wife renouncing any benefits of division or dispute. Done and passed at the offices, etc., the year 1610, the 4th day of June in the afternoon; and the said Pelletier has signed and as to Cervay and his wife and their daughter, they declare that they do not know how to write or sign.

12 Fostering and apprenticeship contract for a son, France 1610

Children who had only one surviving parent were particularly likely to be placed into service in the household of others, both for care and training. In this document, a woman who was involuntarily single because her husband deserted her places her son into another household as an employee and to learn a trade. Although the son would receive no wages, the mother would receive financial assistance, the stated purpose for which was to allow her to fulfill her obligations in the contract (to provide his clothing during the three-year contract). It was customary in service and apprenticeship documents for the notary to specify that the young person entering another

household was renouncing body and possessions, that is, that he or she was devoting body and possessions to the employer.
(Paris, Archives Nationales, Minutier central, Étude X/15, December 22, 1610. Translated by Carol Loats.)

Marie Frevel, wife but deserted for the last nine years, she says, by Mahis Deslandres, master *tissutier rubannier* [ribbon and trim maker] in Paris, [she] living there in the rue du Gravilliers, parish Saint Nicollas des Champs, affirms that, for the benefit of Adam Deslandres, son of the said Mahis Deslandres and of the said Frevel, aged 11 years or so, whom the said Frevel has pledged to complete faithfulness and loyalty, she has given and placed him in service and employment for the next three years. [She has placed him] with the respectable Henry Camue, master of the said trade *tissutier rubannier* in Paris, living there, rue du Ruetal, parish Saint Leu Saint Gilles, present here.

[Camue] has taken and retained [Adam Deslandres] in his service for the said time, during which he will be obliged and promises to show and teach him [Camue's] trade and all in which he is involved because of it; supply and deliver what he needs in terms of fire, bed, lodging, and light, and treat him gently, as is appropriate.

And [Frevel] placing him will maintain him during the said time with all clothing, linen, footwear, and other respectable clothing, according to his status.

In consideration of this service, the said parties remain in agreement on the sum of 18 *livres tournois* that the said Camue promises and guarantees to pay to the said [Frevel] or someone on her behalf, to assist in the said support of the employee her son, that is six *livres tournois* one year from today, another six *livres tournois* one year later, and the other six *livres tournois* at the end of the said three years.

To make this [agreement], present [is] the said employee, who has promised to serve his said master faithfully, work to his benefit, and warn him of losses as soon as they should come to [the boy's] attention; and not to run away nor go to serve elsewhere during the said time.

And in case of flight or absence, the said [Frevel] promises to search in the city and outskirts of Paris and bring him back if she can find him, to complete the time of his said service.

As thus promising, obligating, each in his own right, even the said employee renouncing body, etc. Done and passed in Paris at the offices of the notaries signed below, the year 1610, Wednesday, the twenty-second day of December in the afternoon. The said [Frevel] has said that she does not know how to write or sign.

13 Apprenticeship contract for a priest's son, France 1610

Though fathers normally had legal authority over their children, in the case of children born outside of marriage this authority was held by the mother. This was the situation for the children of Catholic priests, who could not legally marry. Though it is difficult to say exactly how many priests fathered children, the tendency of some priests to maintain sexual relations, sometimes long-term ones, with women is well documented. In the rural setting, a priest might have a long-term companion whose services were indispensable to the maintenance of his household, while in the cities some priests had either short- or long-term relationships with women. Circumstances sometimes required the priest to assume responsibility for his offspring, as in the following contract in which a priest places his son into apprenticeship with a merchant jeweler after his mother had died.
(Paris, Archives Nationales, Minutier central, Étude VIII/577, October 2, 1610. Translated by Carol Loats.)

Was present in person master Jehan Le Conte, priest established in the church of Nostre Dame de Paris, living in the cloister of the said church, who acknowledges and affirms, for the benefit of Pierre Le Conte, his son, and [son] of the late Catherine Le Plie, aged 14 years or so, present and consenting, [that Jehan Le Conte] has placed and given [Pierre Le Conte] in service and apprenticeship, from the first day of this present month of October for the next three years.

[Jehan Le Conte has placed his son] with the honorable François Le Prestre, merchant jeweler, bourgeois of Paris, living in the rue de la Vieille Drapperie, in the parish of Saint Croix en la Cite, here present and accepting, [who] has taken and retained, takes and retains the said Pierre Le Conte as his apprentice.

And during the said three years [Le Prestre] promises to show and teach, to the best of his ability, the commerce of his said merchandise of jewelry and all in which he is involved in practicing it; and to supply and deliver what he needs in terms of drink, food, fire, bed, lodging, and light; and to treat him gently and courteously, as is appropriate.

And the said [Le Prestre] has promised to maintain him honorably with all clothing, linen, breeches, shoes, and other things necessary to him; without the parties being obliged to pay any money on one part or the other because of the said present service and apprenticeship.

And therefore the said apprentice has promised and promises to learn the said commerce of the said merchandise of jewelry, serve his said master in [the trade] and in all other things lawful and honorable, work to his benefit, avoid losses to him, and warn him of problems if it should come to his attention, without absenting himself during the said time.

And in case of absence, the said father, placing him, promises to search for him in the city and outskirts of Paris to bring him back to his said master, if he can be found, to finish the time of this present service; and further pledges [the apprentice] to complete loyalty and faithfulness.

Because thus, etc. promising, obligating, each in his own right, the said apprentice renouncing body and possessions. Done and passed in duplicate in the offices of the notaries signing below, Saturday afternoon, the second day of October, the year one thousand six hundred and ten, and [all parties] have signed this present record with the said notaries.

14 Apprentice contract of a young girl, France 1542

Usually a child's parents or parent made apprenticeship arrangements, but sometimes this task fell to an older sibling if the parents died. In the following document, a young man places his sister into service and apprenticeship; the parents are not mentioned, which probably means that they are deceased. Jean Brou's youth is suggested by the fact that the notary records Brou's assertion that he was legally capable of acting in this matter. Thus not only did children often begin their working lives at a young age, but they also were required to take over other adult responsibilities as well. (Paris, Archives Nationales, Minutier central, Étude XXXIII/27, May 5, 1542. Translated by Carol Loats.)

Jehan Brou, scholar studying in the university of Paris, living in the rue de Porte Bordelles, exercising and in possession of his rights, as he says, affirms that he has given and placed as servant and apprentice Noelle Brou, his sister, from today the day of this document for the next two years.

[He has placed her] with Cleophas Frizon, embroiderer, living in Paris at the boulevard de la Porte Bordelles, and Jehanne le Bethe, his wife, authorized, etc., hoodmaker, here taking and retaining the said Noelle as their servant and apprentice during the said time. And they have promised and promise to show and teach [Noelle] the said trade of hood maker and all, etc.; and with this [those taking the apprentice] promise to provide and deliver what she needs etc.; and the said [Jehan Brou] will maintain her with all her clothing and other necessities whatsoever, honorably, according to her standing.

Present here [was] the said Noelle, apprentice, aged 16 years or so, who has found the said arrangement quite agreeable, [and] promises to learn the said trade, serve her said master and mistress in it and in all other things lawful and honorable, etc., work to their benefit, avoid losses to them, and warn them of problems as soon, etc.; and without taking flight, etc., wishing, etc.; and in case of flight, the said [Jehan Brou] promises to search, etc., and bring her back, etc., and so pledges her to loyalty, etc.

Promising, obligating, etc., the said Noelle seized, etc., renouncing, etc. Done in duplicate, the year 1542, Friday, the 5th day of May.

15 Letter from Sir Edwin Sandys of the Virginia Company requesting authority to coerce children to go to Virginia, England 1620

Apprenticeship was not always a possibility, particularly for very poor children, for apprenticeship contracts often required a payment on the part of the parents or family member. Poor children often simply hung around on the streets of Europe's cities, begging, stealing, or hoping to make a little money carrying packages and messages or doing odd jobs. City authorities worried that these loitering children would spread disease or cause disruptions, and made various suggestions about how to solve the problem. The following is a letter from Sir Edwin Sandys, an official of the Virginia Company, to a member of the King's highest group of advisors, the Privy Council. (Susan M. Kingsbury, ed., *The Records of the Virginia Company of London: The Court Book, from the Manuscript in the Library of Congress*, vol. III (Washington, 1933), p. 259.)

Right Honorable [Sir Robert Naughton of the King's Privy Council]:

Being unable to give my personal attendance upon the Lords [the Privy Council], I have presumed to address my suit in these few lines unto your Honor. The City of London have by act of their Common Council, appointed one hundred children out of their superfluous multitude to be transported to Virginia; there to be bound apprentices for certain years, and afterward with very beneficial conditions for the children. And have granted moreover a levy of five hundred pounds among themselves for the appareling of those children, and toward their charges of transportation. Now it falleth out that among those children, sundry being ill disposed, and fitter for any remote place than for this City, declare their unwillingness to go to Virginia, of whom the City is especially desirous to be disburdened, and in Virginia under severe masters they may be brought to goodness. But this City wanting authority to deliver, and the Virginia Company to transport, these persons against their wills, the burden is laid upon me, by humble suit unto the Lords to procure higher authority for the warranting thereof. May it please your Honor therefore, to vouchsafe unto us of the Company here, and to the whole plantation in Virginia, that noble favor, as to be a means unto their Lordships out of their accustomed goodness, and by their higher authority, to discharge both the City and our Company of this difficulty, as their Lordships and your Honors in your wisdom shall find most expedient. For whose health and prosperity our Company will always pray. . . .

16 Letter from George C. to Sir Anthony Ashley Cooper of the House of Commons, England 1668

Suggestions such as those made by Sir Sandys were actually followed in England, and children arrested on the streets of London for various minor crimes were sometimes subject to deportation and transportation to the colonies. Sometimes children were detained for nothing at all, and freed only if their parents could pay a fine to the arresting officials. The following letter is from a private citizen of London to a member of the House of Commons, asking that such practices be prohibited; such a bill was introduced and debated in Parliament in 1670/71, but was not passed. (London, Public Record Office, CO 1/22. no. 56, quoted in Robert H. Bremner, *Children and Youth in America: A Documentary History, Volume 1: 1600–1865* (Cambridge, MA: Harvard University Press, 1970), p. 12. Reprinted by permission.)

I have inquired after the child that was lost, and have spoken with the parents. His name was John Brookes. The last night he was after much trouble and charge freed again, and he relates that there are divers other children in the ship crying, that were enticed away from their parents, that are kept and detained in the ship. The name of the ship is the Seven Brothers and as I hear bound for Virginia; and she is now fallen down to Gravesend, and, if a speedy course be not taken to stop her she will be gone. I heard of two other ships in the river that are at the same work, although the parents of the children see their children in the ship, yet without money they will not let them have them. The woman and child will wait on you, where you approach and when to give you this relation and 'tis believed there are divers people and others carried away that are strangers come from other parts, so that it were good to get the ships searched, and to see who are against their wills carried away. Pray you move it in the House to have a law to make it death. [i.e., to end this practice] I am confident your mercy to these innocent children will ground a blessing on yourself and your own. Pray let not your great affairs put this good work out of your head to stop the ships and discharge the children.

Your most humble servant
George [last name torn away]

ORPHANS

17 Plan for handling the problem of orphans, Portugal 1655

All poor children were vulnerable to exploitation, but orphans were particularly at risk. Schemes suggesting children be sent overseas such as that of Sir Edwin Sandys often specified that the children should be orphans to avoid problems like those detailed in the previous source. Manoel Severim de Faria, chanter and capitular of the cathedral in Evora in Portugal, describes the general condition of seventeenth-century Portugal in his work *Noticias de Portugal*, and among his many concerns is what he calls a depopulation problem. To solve this problem he proposes a regimented and regulated system of raising orphans so that they can best serve the nation. Boys will work in merchant ships, and possibly settle in overseas colonies

and increase the Portuguese presence there; girls will marry and have more babies. The selection translated here outlines his plan, and he warns his readers that the situation is grave indeed, for if his solution is not adopted the number of those pretending to be poor and of thieves in Portugal will continue to grow.
(Manoel Severim de Faria, *Noticias de Portugal*, Third edition (Lisbon: Na Offic. de Antonio Gomes, 1791 [1655]), pp. 57–63. Translated by Darlene Abreu-Ferreira.)

In this regard it is convenient and of great value to Portugal given the great multitude of foundlings, and [male] orphans, that exist in this Realm, who raised in proper doctrine, until placed in trades, will be of great utility to the Republic. It is more expedient to use this remedy in maritime regions, such as Lisbon, Setúbal, Porto, Viana, and in the Algarve; for with these orphans and the abandoned once taken into custody could supply ships with cabin-boys, and swabbers for vessels, and mariners, people of whom there is a great shortage in this Realm, and with the proper doctrine, and training would be of great profit to our navigations; for there is a common lack of breeding geared toward men of the sea, as we have seen in so many shipwrecks, and losses, of which stories are full of these complaints. Wherein with this remedy we will impede a large part of the fictitious poor, and vagabonds, that exists in this Realm, and they will occupy themselves in honest work, and be of benefit to the Republic, and with this the number of residents in those locations would increase, and the population in the Realm.

This way of recruiting the orphans is so well-known that already in 1641 the members of the *Cortes* [the Portuguese parliament] asked His Majesty cap. 53 with these words: 'It would be greatly advantageous that in the amassing of young orphans, or what is known of *Santo Antonio*, that we recruit many boys, and that an amount be applied for their sustenance, for there they will be taught the art of seafaring, with which there will always be an abundance of mariners, of whom there is a great lack in this Realm.' In this chapter the example is given of the hospital that the Queen of Castile set up in Madrid to train boys to be mariners due to the existing shortage of them. And the response from His Majesty is that he will order that which this chapter asked of him.

The same that has been said for the relief and remedy of orphaned boys can be said of orphaned girls, or better yet much more care must be given to them, for lack of support is a greater danger to them, for women have much less means to make a living than men. Thus it behooves that a remedy for them be found, by applying all the means that can exist to have these [female] orphans of the people get married: for besides the great service to Our Lord by removing the occasion for them to disgrace themselves, we will attain the intent of increasing the number of people with the multiplication of matrimonies. The City of Milan serves as an example of

29

this, which is the most populous in Europe; and one of the reasons for its growth is the dowry it provides each year to 800 [female] orphans. The same can be seen in the increase that the City of Seville had for some years; for whereas much of it was caused by the commerce with the Indies, we can also attribute it to the marriages that take place each year of a great number of [female] orphans, for in that city there are the chapels of Micer Garcia de Gibraleon, and of the Archbishop D. Fernando Valdès, and of the Canon D. Fernando de Menchàca, founded exclusively with the large revenues they have to marry many [female] orphans: besides having many hospitals, as the Deos padre, the Santo Isidro; of S. Clemente, of S. Hermenigildo, and the Misericordia, that each marry many young women, there are many more that with the surplus from their revenues they carry out this act of charity.

To put this means to work; we say that some portion of municipal revenues could be used, where abundances exist, or assign some revenue from the head tax, which income be used solely for this pious work. We would also ask that all municipal purveyors that wherever they find money, or bequests left to spend on pious works; that were not named by the testators, be spent entirely on these weddings. And likewise could be regulated other similar things, for this intent to take effect.

18 Individual care for orphans, Spain 1650

Very young children could not be sent to sea, and before the widespread establishment of orphanages, an abandoned child's only hope for survival was to be left at a local convent or monastery or taken in by a good samaritan. In some towns, like the city of Ourense in northwestern Spain, the city council then paid individuals some compensation for the care of the child.
(Acuerdos del Ayuntamiento, City of Ourense, Spain, libro 24, f. 248, November 5, 1650. Translated by Allyson Poska.)

And in as much as an abandoned child was found in the convent of Santo Domingo and the city gave it to a woman who lives in the city so that she might care for it, this city council sends her a bank note worth exactly one ducat.

19 Wetnursing arrangements for an orphan, the Azores (Portugal) 1570

Because there was no way to feed infants artificially, care for orphaned infants, as with other infants, involved finding a wetnurse. In the following, town officials of Velas,

a town in the island of S. George in the Azores, reconsider the hiring of a wetnurse for a foundling for whom no parents had been found.
(António dos Santos Pereira, ed., *Vereações de Velas (S. Jorge) 1559–1570–1571* (Ponta Delgada, Universidade dos Açores, 1984), p. 183. Translated by Darlene Abreu-Ferreira.)

In this meeting it was resolved by the distinguished officials Manoell Afomso ordinary judge and Pero Louremso and Lopo Diaz town councillors and Gaspar Gonçallvez council procurator that at the time when they entered and started serving their offices they found that the previous officials had given to raise a foundling who was left to the council not having found her a father nor mother. And at the time that they entered [their offices] the wetnurse who had her came to council with the said foundling because her contract had terminated. And, respecting the necessities, they resolved that the same wetnurse take her another year. For what she asked, for her work and to maintain the said foundling, one thousand and five hundred *réis* paid in portions, worth noting: they gave her fifty [sic] *réis*; and the thousand *réis* they will give her: at the end of April, another five hundred *réis*; at the end of August, the other five hundred.

The said wetnurse Barbora Jorge pledged to take care of the said baby girl foundling, and requested Mateus Gonçallvez the porter for the city [to sign on her behalf]. And they signed.

I Francisco Vaz notary public wrote this. I state and declare that the procurator for council paid the said five hundred *réis* as ordered by the said town councillors. Pero Louremso, Lopo Diaz, Manoell Afonso, Mateus Gonçalvez.

20 Adoption of an orphan, France 1540

Orphans who were abandoned or had no relatives willing to care for them could be formally adopted in early modern Europe. In this contract, a couple adopts a very young boy whose parents had died in one of Paris's poor relief institutions, the Hôtel Dieu. The adopting couple's stated intention to make him their heir indicates that they probably had no other children. Notice that the young child had other relatives who freely agreed to the adoption, but they apparently could not or would not take him in. (Paris, Archives Nationales, Minutier central, Étude XXXIII/25, November 11, 1540. Translated by Carol Loats.)

Guillaume Percheron, day laborer living on the rue de Copeaulx in the dwelling of the Carmelites [an order of friars] of Paris, and Jehanne Goret, his wife, she authorized in this matter, affirm that, for the great love and attachment that they have and declare for Batiste Bernard, aged three years or so, they have taken and retained him and by this contract take him in their custody, to raise him.

[Batiste Bernard is] the minor son of the late Symon Bernard, who while living was poor and a day laborer living in the said street, and [the late] Catherine Corbillon, his wife, the two previously the father and mother of the boy, who were natives of Saint Martin d'Étampes, and who died, it is said, at the [poor relief hospital of] Hôtel Dieu of Paris after Saint Jehan Baptiste past.

[Percheron and Goret] have promised and promise to supply and deliver what he needs in terms of drink, food, fire, bed, lodging, and light, as much in health as in sickness; to instruct him in good morals; and to maintain him in all his clothing and other necessities whatsoever, all well and duly as appropriate and as if he were their own child.

And [they also promise] to provide for him in marriage or otherwise as appropriate to his standing and according to the ability and property of the said Percheron and his wife.

And in consideration of the things said here, they give him all and each of their possessions that they may have at the time of their passing on, to take as if he were their own child and rightful heir.

Present for this [was] Estienne Papillon, plowman of vines, living at Bonyeres les Cellees, near the said Étampes, uncle of the said minor through Martine Bernard, his wife, who was the sister of the deceased [father] of the said minor; and Audrye Papillon, wife of Jehan Gaillard, living at Saint Michel in Paris, rue du Puys de Fer, cousin of the said minor, who have given and give the said minor to the said Percheron and his wife as is stated; and they affirm clearly that this is for the benefit and welfare of the said minor, who has no possessions or kin who are able to provide for him.

Promising, etc., obligating, etc., each in his own right, etc., renouncing. Done in duplicate and passed, that is by the said Percheron and Estienne Pappillon and Audrye Papillon on Thursday, the 11th day of November, the year 1540, and for the said Jehanne Goret, wife of the said Percheron, on the day of [blank], 15 [blank].

21 Orphan's petition outlining his mother's troubles, Italy 1564

Children as well as adults were often confronted with immense hardship because of wars and other types of political and religious conflicts in early modern Europe. They were forced to flee from place to place, becoming refugees, and sometimes appealed to the political authorities in their new locations for support. The following is an excerpt from a petition to the Venetian High Court of Appeals [Pien Collegio]. During the late fifteenth and sixteenth centuries, Venice fought a largely losing battle against the Ottoman Turks, who were extending their empire westward from their capital of Constantinople. The Venetian colonies on the Greek islands were the site of bloody battles which ended in Ottoman victory and occupation. Here a young man, Luca, is pleading for government assistance for him and his older sister, and outlines his family's woes, which had begun before he was born.

(Archivio di Stato di Venezia, Pien Collegio, Suppliche di Dentro, filza 1, no. 73, September 1564. Translated by Monica Chojnacka.)

The mercy and compassion of Your Serenity [i.e., the Venetian state] have always consoled and relieved the miseries and calamities of your poor and humble subjects. Thus we, Luca Mosua and my sister Lucia, have not hesitated to appear at your feet to recount with reverence [the story of] our poor mother Todara. Her husband and the father of my sister, named Zuan Mosua, from Nauplia [a city of the Peloponnese] served Your Serenity in those days for a long time, in the role of captain, and died in the line of duty . . . having been killed by a Turk. Realizing that her husband was dead, and that she had no means of sustaining her family, [my mother] left Nauplia to harvest her grapes and other possessions to support herself, but the poor woman had bad luck and ended up in the hands of a Turk along with her daughter Lucia, and they were enslaved in captivity for seven years, and after that Turk made dishonest use of my mother, he impregnated her with me, poor Luca, and it happened that one day when the Turks were all at their religious services, our mother saw a chance, and because she greatly desired to return to live among Christians, she escaped with Lucia and with me her little son, who was still in swaddling clothes [i.e., a baby], and she walked for eight straight days and eight nights until God brought us to the coast and the city of Zante, where we found a frigate that took us from that island, and then we came to Zaffa, where I was baptized, and a little while after that our poor mother was killed by some houses that fell during an earthquake. . . .

22 Orphanages for non-Christian children, Italy 1576

Adoptive homes could not be arranged for every child, and churches and city governments began to establish orphanages in the fifteenth century; some of these were for all children orphaned or left as foundlings in an area, though others had specific purposes. The Catecumeni, established in Venice in 1557, housed men, women and children of Jewish or Muslim origins with the primary aim of converting them to Christianity. This institution was the delivery point for non-Christian children who had been either orphaned or captured in a war. Once at the home, they were converted, given religious instruction, and sometimes adopted by Christian families. Some petitions for adoption have survived, including one by Bortholo and Madalena, a couple who eloquently expressed their desire for a little girl named Caterina.

(Istituzioni di Ricovero e di Educazione (IRE), CAT, c.1, Catastico di Catecumeni, 1576, pp. 34–35. Translated by Monica Chojnacka.)

Finding themselves, Bortholo of . . . the parish of San Vido, and . . . the modest lady Madalena, husband and wife, without children, and at an age at which they are unlikely to have them, and desiring to adopt a little girl for consolation and comfort in their old age they have insistently requested the . . . governors of the house of the Catecumeni to grant them as an adopted daughter Caterina who at one time was Turkish, raised in the above-named house . . . the said couple will accept her as an adopted daughter, treating her and governing her and instructing her in good behavior, and persevering with her in good faith, as if she had been conceived and born of the couple themselves . . . (The governors) of the above-named house of the Catecumeni . . . have granted, and grant, to said sr. Bortholo, and Madalena, husband and wife . . . said Caterina, who is 7 years of age.

23 Guardian's defense of an orphan's interests, Ottoman Empire 1541

Poor orphans might be sent to orphanages or the colonies, but wealthier orphans were often given guardians. In Muslim societies, Islamic law made it the duty of the local judge to appoint a fit guardian for orphan minors and, when necessary, to draw on the public treasury to support indigent orphans. In the following case from the court records of Aintab, the woman Gulshah, guardian of the orphan girl Halimeh, is summoned to court by Ahmed, who claims a vineyard in Halimeh's possession; Gulshah's counterclaim prevails when Ahmed cannot provide proof of ownership. Women often served as guardians of orphans, suggesting that they were assumed to to be knowledgeable about the management of property as well as the legal status of orphans.

(National Library, Ankara, Gaziantep Sicili 2, f. 323c. Translated by Leslie Peirce.)

Ahmed son of Mevlana Nureddin came to the court and summoned [the defendant] Gulshah daughter of Mustafa, who was the legally appointed guardian of Halimeh, daughter of the deceased Haji Sundek. He said: 'I demand the vineyard of 250 vines that is located in the agricultural area known as Tashgun and bounded in the direction of prayer [the south] by Arab's vineyard, on the east by Merchant Ahmed's property, on the north by Ibrahim's vineyard, and on the west by a stream. This property is a family trust that used to be cultivated by my father Mevlana Hamza.' Whereupon the defendent said, 'The aforementioned vineyard belongs to my ward Halimeh as a legal inheritance from her father. It is her property.' When the aforementioned Ahmed was unable to provide proof of ownership, the vineyard was judged to belong to Halimeh. The foregoing was recorded at the request [of the defendants]. Dated September 28, 1541.

24 Apprenticeship of orphans, France 1542

Once orphans had reached a certain age, many cities in early modern Europe tried to arrange apprenticeship placements for them so that they would be fed, housed, and taught a trade. In the following document, a young girl whose parents had died is placed into apprenticeship by the officers of the poor relief system in Paris. The woman taking her as an apprentice may in this way also be receiving poor relief in the form of labor and a stipend for care of the child.
(Paris, Archives Nationales, Minutier central, Étude VIII/474, July 25, 1542. Translated by Carol Loats.)

Jacqueline Parisot, hosier [maker of stockings] and wife of Anthoyne Gougneulx, day laborer, the said Jacqueline living in the rue Anemairet in the building whose sign is the seal of France, in Paris, affirms that the Commissioners appointed on the matter of the poor of this city of Paris have given her, as apprentice, from today for two years, Marguerite Massarpe, impoverished child aged 8 or 9 years, orphan without mother or father.

Jacqueline has taken [Massarpe] as her apprentice, to whom she has promised to show and teach her the profession and trade of hosier well and duly; and during the said time will well and honorably provide her with what she needs in terms of drink, food, fire, bed, lodging, light, clothing, footwear of linen, body linen, and similarly all her other necessities whatsoever; however, she will be paid by the said Commissioners 100 sous tournois for each of the said two years.

To do this is present the said Marguerite, apprentice, who has promised, promises, and guarantees to serve the said Jacqueline in the said profession and learn well and duly the said trade, obey all [Jacqueline's] lawful and honorable commands, work to her benefit, avoid losses to her; without fleeing or serving elsewhere during the said time.

Promising, etc., obligating, etc., even the said Marguerite renouncing body and possessions, etc., Done and passed in duplicate in the year 1542, Tuesday, the 25th day of July.

INHERITANCE

25 Inheritance by children, Denmark 1556–1559

Orphans were not the only children whose inheritance rights needed affirmation, and courts in many parts of Europe contain records regarding the inheritance by children. The following notices are taken from the records of the City Council Court of Malmø, Scania, Denmark, which also functioned as a probate court. According to Danish law from the early Middle Ages until the nineteenth century all siblings received an equal share of their paternal and maternal inheritance – equal in the sense that everybody received a share, but brothers received a double share, sisters a single. However, this was not always followed (see first notice). The records also reveal the different career patterns that boys and girls were expected to follow.

(*Malmø stadsbog 1549–1559. Rådstuerettens, bytingets og toldbodrettens protokol*, Einar Bage, ed. (Copenhagen: Selskabet for Udgivelse af Kilder til dansk Historie, 1972), pp. 324, 441. Translated by Grethe Jacobsen and Pernille Arenfeldt.)

The paternal inheritance of the children of Erik Knudsen

Monday after Trinity Sunday [June 1, 1556] Jep Laage, Tyge Tolfsen, Hans Nielsen, Niels Samsing, Hans Skinder and Laurits Tækkere guaranteed with raised hand for this child inheritance which Oluf Willumsen, who married Gertrud, Erik Knudsens' widow, put forward for his stepchildren, Oluf Eriksen and Bodil Eriksdaughter, to him 100 mark and to her 90 mark to be handed over when he comes of age and in the meantime [Oluf shall] keep him with clothes, meals, learning and food, and the girl when she has entered into honest service and then in addition help her with clothes and wedding expenses and in between also clothe and feed her and pay no other rent of the said money. But the house shall remain undivided between the mother and the children.

Determining the maternal inheritance of Rasmus Hesse's children

Monday after St. Lawrence [August 14, 1559] Rasmus Hesse appeared with his brother-in-law Hans Fickeson and his wife's brothers, Hans Matsen, Laurits Matsen and Christoffer Matsen, and he allotted his children, Mads, Jens, Johanne, Elline and Margrete all together 150 mark as their maternal inheritance in all movables as well as debt and demands, excepting the house which they will keep as common property. The aforementioned sum will be paid to the children when they come of age and are provided for. In the period in between he will be obliged to keep the children honest and well with clothing, food and discipline.

The maternal inheritance of Jørgen Væver's children

The same day Jørgen Væver appeared and with him his wife's mother's brother Peder Mikkelsen of Vintrie and the mother's brother's son Rasmus Jensen of the same place and aforementioned Jørgen allotted his children Hans, Margrete and Inger as their material inheritance each 10 thalers and each girl 1 pound of cobber and the boy free board, lodging and schooling until he is 12 years and also to keep the girls honest and well. Niels Erlandsøn and Rasmus Hans Lollike set surety for him with raised hand.

26 Royal ordinances regarding inheritance, Portugal sixteenth century

National and local governments in early modern Europe all had rules regarding inheritance, which differed widely; local traditions added even more complexity to this picture. In some areas, the eldest son inherited almost everything (primogeniture), while in others all the children or at least all the sons divided the landed property and goods (partible inheritance). The ability of girls to inherit also varied widely, particularly if the inheritance included a family estate. Portugal was one of the areas with somewhat egalitarian inheritance regulations; royal ordinances from the sixteenth century state that daughters and sons had equal rights of inheritance, though some stipulations were made that were clearly gendered. The example highlighted here emphasizes the greater control parents had, or were expected to have, over the sexual and marital conduct of daughters than of sons. Although Article 1 of Titulo LXXII mentions sons or daughters, the section begins with a specific reference to daughters, as does Article 2. Some of the grounds for disinheriting children of either sex are also noted, thus revealing some of the concerns of the period, including children's involvement in witchcraft, or children's lack of diligence in releasing their parent(s) from captivity.

(*Ordenações do Senhor Rey D. Manuel, vol. IV* (Coimbra: Na Real Imprensa da Universidade, 1797), pp. 183–188. Translated by Darlene Abreu-Ferreira.)

Titulo LXXII. If any daughter before the age of twenty-five years sleeps with any man, and gets married without permission from her father, or from her mother, for that very act she shall be disinherited, and deprived of all the goods and property of the father or mother, even if by them she is not explicitly disinherited.

1. And if at the time of death of the father or mother there is another legitimate child, or children, who have not committed the same error, the father or mother cannot bequeath the daughter, who erred thus, against the will of the legitimate son, or of the legitimate daughter who did not make a similar error, the legitime [i.e., inheritance] that by right would come to her. And if at the time of death of the father or mother there is no other legitimate son or daughter, or grandchildren, or legitimate descendants from both sides, in this case they can, and each one bequeath an inheritance on the daughter that erred against them, as and in the amount they consent; because whereas the said injury was done solely to them, with just reason they can forgive her, since there is no other son, or daughter, or grandchild to whom that would be prejudicial.

2. But if the said daughter married a person who is notably known for having married better, and more honourably than what her father and mother could have her marry, in this case the said daughter is not disinherited, and deprived of all goods and property, as noted above: but the father or mother can only disinherit her, if they wish, of half of the

legitime that lawfully belongs to her from the death of each of them; and not having disinherited her explicitly of the said half for the said reason, she shall freely have the entire legitime, as if the marriage had been consented by the father or mother, and this is so whether at the time of the death there is another legitimate son or daughter, or grandchild of each of them, or not.

And the other reasons, for which a father or mother can disinherit a son or daughter, are as follows:

3. First if a son or daughter violently lay their hands on their father, or on their mother.

4. Likewise if they insult them with grievous and injurious words, and especially in a public place where the father or mother with reason will experience more shame; and it is up to the arbiter to appraise if the injurious words were grievous, or trivial.

5. Likewise if the son or daughter criminally accuses the father or mother of some crime, that does not concern Our State.

6. Likewise if the son or daughter use witchcraft, communicating with the witches.

7. Likewise if the son or daughter give poison to the father or mother, or undertakes to give it to them, and if it was not given by him [or her], or gives the opportunity, favour, or advice, or consent to someone else to purposely give it.

8. Likewise if under any other guise or manner by him [or her], or by another, he [she] seeks his [her] death.

9. Likewise if the son had affection, or carnal union with the wife of his father, or with his [female] concubine, that with him he had at home maintained, and governed; and thus we say of the daughter that similarly had affection for the husband of her mother, or her [male] concubine that she had with her at home maintained.

10. Likewise if the son or daughter gave notable information of the father or mother to the Justice for which the father or mother received some dishonour of their person, or damage to their goods and property.

11. Likewise if the father or mother are imprisoned for some debt, and the untrustworthy son did not wish to pledge to release them from prison having the credit, and the wealth with which to release them from it, and having it requested of him.

12. Likewise if the son or daughter impede the father or mother from doing their will as they wish; for in such a case the father dying at this time without a will, that son or daughter shall be deprived of their inheritance, and if after they outlive they can freely disinherit that son or daughter, that prohibit them thus.

13. And if any father or mother loses their natural judgement, and the son or daughter, or any other their creditors . . . be negligent in caring for their infirmity, this [son or daughter] can be disinherited by that father or mother, or grandparent, they regaining their judgement, and discerning understanding, in such a manner that they can freely make their wills.

14. And dying either intestate [i.e. without a will], or with a will that they made before losing their judgement, the inheritance will not be gotten by those heirs, that were remiss, and negligent in serving them, and seeking their health; for it can be presumed, that if they return to their full understanding they will not leave them their inheritance due to the ingratitude, that against them they committed.

15. And losing any man or woman their judgement and understanding, and he whose inheritance was entitled to inherit, either from a will or intestate, was remiss or negligent in serving him and taking care of his infirmity, and some other outsider appealed to him to look after the health of that insane person, if not he [the outsider] would attend to and care for his health, and this one to whom this request was made, was remiss and negligent regarding the said request, and this petitioner attended to the insane person, and worked for his health as well as he reasonably could, in such a case he will have the inheritance from the insane person upon his death, having died without understanding, and the other who should have had the said inheritance shall be wanting due to the ingratitude, and thus as unworthy shall be deprived of the said inheritance.

16. Moreover if the father or mother are placed in captivity, and the son or daughter are negligent in rescuing him, and liberating from the said captivity, and this father or mother from their own good diligence are free from the said captivity without the help, or advantage of the son or daughter, the father or mother thus rescued from the said captivity can disinherit freely that son or daughter, that thus were negligent in redeeming their liberty; and if the father or mother thus put in captivity die in it due to the blame or negligence of their son or daughter, this son or daughter, thus negligent in the redemption of liberty of their father or mother, shall be totally deprived of all their inheritance, for the blame and negligence that they thus committed in not redeeming their liberty.

17. Likewise if the father or mother are Catholic Christians, and the son or daughter are heretics, who completely does not believe in our Holy Catholic Faith, digressing from the precept of the Holy Mother Church, in that case the father or mother can freely disinherit that son or daughter.

18. And all that is said regarding the father or mother is applicable to the grandfather and the grandmother, on the part of the father, as of the mother.

27 A father's will, Wales 1642

Parents often stipulated the inheritance that would be coming to each child in their wills, for which many survive from the early modern period, especially for the upper classes. This is the will of a man from the landed gentry in Wales, and is very similar to English gentlemen's wills, with provisions made for servants and (small) donations to various parish churches. Note that the daughters' dowries are larger than the younger sons' cash inheritances. The cost of the sons' education and training in a livelihood, such as the law or trade, figured in their parents' allocation of resources, whereas the daughters' status could only be maintained through marriages. The daughters are financially rewarded if they agree to their parents' choice of spouses, though they are not completely disinherited if they choose someone of whom their parents disapprove. William Anwill's oldest son Lewis had died, and William had to pay the very large dowry payment of 1200 pounds for Lewis's daughter Katherine. (Public Record Office, Prerogative Court of Canterbury Will, 80 Cambell 1642. Transcribed by Katharine Swett.)

[William Lewis Anwill, esquire, of Park, Merioneth. 19 December 1641. buried parish church Llanvrothen.] To my son Evan Anwill 500 pounds. 100 pounds each to my sons Moris and Richard Anwill. To my two daughters Jane and Lowrie if unmarried at my death 800 pounds each provided they follow the advice and counsel of their mother Elizabeth my wife and their brother my son and heir Robert Anwill, but if they marry of their own head without such advice and consent then that daughter to have 200 pounds and no more. I give to every one of my 6 daughters Mabel Elizabeth Anne Gwen Jane and Lowrie 10 pounds each to buy silver plate, which my executors are to buy for them, which is to be a salt cellar and 2 silver bowls or a cup to everyone of my daughters, whereupon I will that my name and the name of such of my daughters as shall severallie enjoy the said 10 pounds worth of plate given her be stamped. Also to Katherine Anwill my grandchild my son Lewis Anwill's daughter 10 pounds of plate whereupon my will is that my and her name be stamped, also I give and bequeath to my daughter Elizabeth wife of John Evans 5 pounds to buy her some plate. A milkcow and calf to my servant Rowland Owen. 20 shillings to the cathedral church of Bangor. 20s each to Llanvrothen and Dolgelley church. 10s to Malloys. 20s to the church of Lewes in Montgomeryshire. 10 pounds for the poor of Llanvrothen. And whereas I am bound to discharge my lands of 1200 pounds being the portion of Katherine Anwill my son Lewis Anwill's daughter if she shall be married, my will is that those 1200 pounds be paid out of the money I have in mortgage upon lands and out of the debts due me. I nominate and appoint as my executors my son and heir Robert Anwill and my wife Elizabeth his mother, they to be residuary legatees. Every child of my daughters Mabel

Anwill and Gwen Anwill to have 6 heads of beasts of 2 year old meat. To my sons in law William Wynn esquire and David Lloyd gentleman, each a gold ring worth 5 pounds. Witnesses William Wynn, William Prichard ap William, Gruffith ap William Prichard, Rowland Owen, Robert John Griffith, Gruffith ap Howell, John William, William Mathew, Rowland Lloyd.

Questions for discussion

1   What were the chief concerns of authorities regarding childbirth and the activities of midwives?
2   What religious issues were important in early childhood?
3   What did parents view as essential in children's education? How was this different for boys and girls?
4   What were the normal stipulations in apprenticeship contracts?
5   What particular dangers faced poor children and orphans?
6   How did inheritance regulations and practices differ depending on gender?
7   How would you compare the treatment of children in the early modern period with that advocated – or practiced – today?

2

YOUTH, SEXUALITY, AND THE SINGLE LIFE

Opportunities for school attendance for most young people ended before they reached adolescence. A very small number of young men were able to continue their studies at the universities, which began to develop in Europe during the Middle Ages, or at academies and other types of schools begun by humanists interested in classical learning. Study at European universities was conducted in Latin, with a student determining his own pace; examinations were held to gain a degree, not to pass a course. Students lived together in dormitory-like arrangements (called 'colleges') and younger students sometimes brought tutors with them from home to oversee their activities.

For the majority of early modern Europeans, adolescence and young adulthood was a time of work, not study. In southern and eastern Europe, marriage was often between people in their late teens, with the young couple then living with one set of parents for a long time, or between a man in his late twenties or thirties and a much younger woman, with households again containing several generations. In northern and western Europe, people did not marry until they were in their mid twenties, long after they were sexually mature, and they immediately set up an independent household. This meant that both spouses spent long periods as servants or workers in other households, saving money and learning skills.

Political and religious authorities approved of this pattern of late marriage, on the one hand, as they felt older couples would be better able to support themselves and their children, but, on the other, they also worried about it, for they viewed unmarried young people as a source of disorder. Unmarried men were regarded as more likely to get drunk and engage in fights than married men, and unmarried women risked getting pregnant out of wedlock. Laws were passed forbidding unmarried people to move into cities and ordering them to find a place of residence with a married couple. (Such laws were also passed, and enforced, in colonial New England.) Many employers and masters – and some parents – complained that the boys and young men under their supervision were very difficult to control, and that they frequently engaged in rowdy or disruptive behavior, drinking, fighting, and swearing. According to court records, gangs of young men frequently roamed the streets of many towns in the evening, fighting with one another, threatening young women, and drinking until they passed out; in university towns these groups might be made up of students. These activities were frowned upon and punished if they got out of hand, but were also in some ways expected as a normal part of achieving manhood.

While a certain amount of wild behavior was tolerated in young men, it was not in young women, and punishments for sexual misconduct by unmarried women, particularly premarital intercourse and pregnancy out of wedlock, could be quite sharp. It was often very difficult for unmarried women to avoid sexual contacts. Many of them worked as domestic servants, where their employers or employers' sons or male relatives could easily coerce them, or in close proximity to men. Female servants were sent on errands alone or with men, or worked by themselves in fields far from other people; though notions of female honor might keep upper-class women secluded in their homes, in most parts of Europe there was little attempt to shield female servants or day laborers from the risk of seduction or rape.

The consequences of unwed motherhood varied throughout Europe, with rural areas which needed many workers being the most tolerant. Once an unmarried woman suspected she was pregnant, she had several options. In some parts of Europe, if she was a minor, her father could go to court and sue the man involved for 'trespass and damages' to his property. The woman herself could go to her local court and attempt to prove there had been a promise of marriage in order to coerce the man to marry her. Marriage was the favored official solution, and was agreed upon in a surprising number of cases, indicating that perhaps there had been an informal agreement, or at least that the man was now willing to take responsibility for his actions. Marriage was impossible in many cases, however, and young women often attempted to deny the pregnancy as long as possible, hoping for a miscarriage, or they even attempted abortion. Desperate women gave birth in outhouses, cowstalls, hay mounds, and dung heaps, hoping that they would be able to avoid public notice, and took the infant to one of the new foundling homes which opened during the fifteenth or sixteenth centuries in many cities. A few did kill their children, a crime that carried the death penalty, often specified as death by drowning.

Along with extra-marital pregnancy, other sexual activities were also regulated and punished during this period. During the Middle Ages, most European cities allowed prostitution in licensed city brothels; the city leaders justified this by saying that it protected honorable women and girls from attacks by young men. During the fifteenth century, many cities began to feel increasingly uneasy about permitting prostitution, and began to require the women to wear distinctive clothing or not to appear in public at all. By the sixteenth century, cities in central and northern Europe began to close their houses of prostitution, and southern European cities, especially those in Italy, licensed prostitutes and restricted their movements. Church and state authorities during the early modern period also attempted to suppress homosexual activity. After about 1250 they increasingly defined homosexual actions as 'crimes against nature', seeing them as particularly reprehensible because they thought they did not occur anywhere else in creation. Homosexual activity, usually termed 'sodomy', became a capital crime in most of Europe, with adult offenders often executed by being burnt alive. The number of actual sodomy cases was quite small, however, and persecution was sporadic. Homosexual subcultures began to develop in a few large cities, such as London, Amsterdam and Paris, with special styles of dress, behavior, slang terms, and meeting places, but historians disagree about whether such individuals (or anyone in early modern Europe) thought of themselves as having a life-long 'sexual identity.'

ADVANCED EDUCATION

1 Regulation of teachers, France 1494

Universities first developed in Europe during the Middle Ages, and offered advanced training in specific subjects for male students only. One usually began a university career as a teenager in a faculty of the arts, then progressed into more advanced courses in law, medicine, or theology and philosophy; this education was not limited in terms of time, and many young men were university students well into their thirties, although they were forbidden to marry as long as they remained students. Cities in which a university was located also often had preparatory academies for students planning on attending the university later, and students at these academies were taught by advanced students from the university. The following are regulations for teachers at academies associated with the University of Angers in France.
(Lynn Thorndike, *University Records and Life in the Middle Ages* (New York: Columbia University Press, 1944), pp. 367–368. Reprinted by permission.)

And first it was decreed that one wishing to hold a school should be a master of arts, mature, prudent and discreet.

Also, it was decreed that every schoolteacher compel his scholars speak Latin both at play and work, and especially in commonplaces. Also, that no one be allowed to hold a school unless he has scholars who can dispute together and make a satisfactory exercise.

Also, that in every school, disputations be held twice a week with daily reviews and other exercises.

Also, that in every school there be at least two teaching masters, one in logic and the other in philosophy, who in the aforesaid exercises and disputations may offer the scholars a model and guidance.

Also, that the headmaster accustom his scholars to rise and salute the masters and humbly obey them.

Also, that no teacher fraudulently steal away the scholars of another either by his own or another's action.

Also, that no breach of discipline be permitted among the scholars, but the teacher, without dissimulation in the sight of all, shall take note of offenders as the case requires.

Also, let teachers beware lest their scholars be truants or leave the house without permission, and see to it that they do not soil their clothing or books in untimely and superfluous feasting and games, but stay indoors especially as it grows dark.

Also, that on Sundays and holy days the teacher send them in order to low mass in the morning before breakfast and then to high mass, if the feast calls for this.

Also, that on the chief feasts of the year, and especially at Easter, Pentecost, Assumption, All Saints, Christmas, and the beginning of Lent, he exhort and induce them to confess their sins and send them to church to confess.

Also, it was decreed that, when there shall be a sermon to the clergy in the faculty of theology, they shall be required to send them there in order by themselves or with some one of their masters, and likewise to solemn actions of the faculty of arts, and that on such occasions they shall be seated and walk two by two going and returning.

Also, it was decreed that scholars of this sort should not be sent to the fields without a master to lead them and bring them back, to keep them together and control them and keep an eye on them all, and they should go and return two by two especially through the town.

Also, that these teachers should not permit any scholar of theirs undergo an examination for any degree, unless they believe him sufficiently prepared and able to obtain the degree, but should exhort and warn him not to subject himself to such an examination lest he chance to be failed and so brought into disrepute.

Also, it was decreed that in points not here specified we should follow the statutes of the university of Paris as far as possible.

Also, it was decreed that no teacher or instructor in arts or even in grammar may receive the scholars of another instructor or teacher whether they are students in arts or even in grammar, for any reason without the consent of the headmaster of the house or school, which consent he shall be required to manifest to the person to whom said scholar shall go by a note signed with the sign manual of preceding master.

Also, it was decreed that no master or instructor should receive anyone as a student in grammar by making a deal for less than usual price, which is twenty solidi of Tours, unless there be several of the same family or a case of evident poverty.

Also, it was decreed that no master of any school shall receive the guide or tutor of young students or those in arts, unless the tutor himself is studying in the faculty of arts or has the degree of master in the said faculty and is of its bosom.

Also, it was decreed that whoever of the teachers shall have contrary to the aforesaid should *ipso facto* be deprived of all honour and emolument as a teacher.

2 The day of a university student, Belgium 1476

Though many of the books that university students studied are well known, documents that describe a normal day in the life of a university student are not common. The following is an ordinance for the University of Louvain in 1476, issued by the duke who had jurisdiction over the university and indicating the way in which the student was supposed to work at that institution.
(Hastings Rashdall, *The University of Europe in the Middle Ages* vol. II, pt. II.
(Oxford: Clarendon Press, 1895), p. 766.)

The tutors shall see that the scholars rise in the morning at five o'clock, and that then before lectures each one reads by himself the laws which are to be read at the regular lecture, together with the glosses. . . . But after the regular lecture, having if they wish, quickly heard mass, the scholars shall come to their rooms and revise the lectures that have been given, by rehearsing and impressing on their memory whatever they have brought away from the lectures either orally or in writing. And next they shall come to lunch . . . after lunch, each one having brought to the table his books, all the scholars of the Faculty together, in the presence of a tutor, shall review that regular lecture; and in this review the tutor shall follow a method which will enable him, by discreet questioning of every man, to gather whether each of them listened well to the lecture and remembered it, and which will recall the whole lecture by having its parts recited by individuals. And if watchful care is used in this one hour will suffice.

3 Statute against oaths and blasphemy, Germany 1398

Despite the hopes of those in charge of universities, students did not spend all their time studying, and many sources remain regarding their extra-curricular activities. This is a decree issued by the faculty of the University of Heidelberg, one of the largest and most prestigious universities in Germany.
(Lynn Thorndike, *University Records and Life in the Middle Ages* (New York: Columbia University Press, 1944), pp. 260–261. Reprinted by permission.)

At a meeting of the doctors and masters it was agreed harmoniously and enacted by oath, among other matters, to make penal statute against persons of the university swearing beyond measure, as follows: Since it has often been brought to our notice by persons worthy of faith that some members of our university not only do not fear to blaspheme by the name of our Savior Jesus Christ, of the glorious virgin Mary and of the saints, taking them in vain and repeating them without reason in oaths, but also by the parts of the very body of the Lord and so by the humanity of God and in other far-fetched ways which we grieve to record, setting a pernicious example to simple persons, to the great shame and scandal of the clergy of our university, and since all oaths and blasphemies of this sort are quite contrary to the divine precept and to the institutions of both laws, canon and civil, and likewise by moral standards are undoubtedly forbidden, therefore we, Nicholas de Cuba, the rector, and the doctors and masters aforesaid, having held mature deliberation and counsel concerning this, to restrain the aforesaid insolences for the honor of our Lord Jesus Christ, the glorious virgin Mary, his mother, and the saints, have decided to order and enact, and do order and enact, and furthermore under obligation of obedience in so far as we can prescribe, that henceforth no person of our university, of whatever grade, status, or condition, presume to swear, or rather blaspheme, by the forbidden sacred members, namely of Christ, blessed Mary or the saints, that is, by head, hair, viscera, blood and the like, or in any other farfetched or unaccustomed or enormous manner, under penalty of two pounds of wax to be paid irremissibly each time he shall have so sworn to excess, of which one pound shall be applied by this our orders to the church of the Holy Spirit, the other to the chapel of the university, for lights. But if, which God forbid, any person shall be found continuing oaths, or rather blasphemies of this sort, he shall be punished more severely, according to our pleasure and according to the quality of his excess. Given and enacted in the congregation held in our chapel, in year of the Lord 1398, on the very day of blessed Peter *ad vincula*.

4 Royal proclamations regarding universities, Portugal 1538–1552

Universities were under the control of a variety of different types of authorities, often including the king in many parts of Europe. Kings and other rulers thus often issued proclamations regarding university life, generally at the request of a university official concerned about a certain issue. The three royal proclamations below all deal with events at the University of Coimbra in Portugal. The first two concern activities of the students that were to be forbidden; note that in the first one, the students were not punished, but only the women. The third entry reveals a great deal about the intricacies of early modern Portuguese society as well as university life. Most positions in high office were inherited and kept in the family for generations. Typically the eldest son was given the inherited position, but, in the absence of sons, daughters could also inherit these offices and pass them on to their future husbands or sons. The case highlighted here illustrates that daughters were not left out of the family's inheritance. The brother got the university post, but he was required to give each of his two sisters a dowry of 100,000 réis, not an insignificant amount. To put this amount in some perspective, a survey of Lisbon conducted in 1552 stipulates that 2,000 réis was equal to one year's salary for domestic servants.

(Mário Brandão, ed., *Documentos de D. João III* (Coimbra: Universidade de Coimbra, 1937), vol. I, pp. 114, 153–154; vol. IV, pp. 145–146. Translated by Darlene Abreu-Ferreira.)

I, the King, make it known to whom this charter reaches that it is right and pleases me to have it so for the service of God and me, and for the good of the University of Coimbra, that every student of the said university who has a concubine or a woman of ill-repute in his house that woman be imprisoned and in jail pay one thousand *réis* half for the one who accused [her] and the other half for the coffer of the university. Thus I notify the curator of the said university and demand that he enforce the said penalties on the women who are apprehended in such an error. And this my charter shall be announced in the said university that it be known by all. Done by Amrique da Mota in Lisbon on the xix day of September of one thousand bcxxxbiij years [1538].

Reverend Bishop Rector Friend: I, the King, send you many greetings. I have been informed that some students of that university not respecting what amounts to the service of God and me and the honor of their persons go about at night with weapons making music and other acts not very honest through that city from which results in scandals for its citizens and residents and little authority and honor to the university. And since I get grief from such things occurring, I order that you inform yourselves of this and reprehend those who do this according to the quality of the person and have the bailiff of the university called and tell him on my behalf that he keep a watch for this and comply with my ordinances. And thus the ordinances that I have made about this, for [if] not done in this manner I will attend to the situation [so] that it is right as it pleases me and you write to me about what is happening in this situation, documented well. [Done by Amrique de Meta in Lisbon on the xx day of June of 1539]

I, the King, make it known to whom this charter reaches that it is right and it pleases me that on the death of Bento Taborda, Knight of my House [and] bailiff of the University of Coimbra, [I] do reward the said office to his eldest son that when this becomes a deed to serve with such declaration that the said son give two hundred thousand *réis* to his two sisters, daughters of the said Bento Taborda . . . one hundred thousand *réis* to each to assist with her wedding or to become nuns in a monastery according to the better wishes of their father. And for his trust and my memorial I had this charter given him that I ask him to fulfil entirely as we count on him [to do so]. Done by Jorge da Costa in Lisbon on the xxix day of the month of June of jbel and two [1552]. Manuel da Costa had it written.

5 Letter to a university student from his brother, Wales mid seventeenth century

As the previous sources make clear, students did not spend all their time studying. This letter from one young man to another is of a type more usually penned by worried fathers to sons who were carousing instead of studying while away at university; then, as now, the relative freedom of university might go to young heads, and their college tutors were left to report their behavior to their parents. Richard had apparently been doing well until recently. Notice that Thomas appeals to his brother's self-interest in advising Richard to abandon his new friends and return to his books for, first, his own happiness and personal advantage, second, his personal honor, and, not till last, for the sake of his friends and relations.

(N.L.W. Chirk MS f. 6426, July 30, no year but is mid seventeenth century. Thomas Myddelton to his younger brother Richard. Excerpted by Katharine Swett.)

Dear Brother Dick, I am much troubled & concerned that after so many letters of your commendations I should now be informed of the contrary which cannot but afflict an affectionate Brother. Idle, loose debauched company . . . I ever dissuaded you even to converse with, much less to make an intimate acquaintance; as you love therefore your happiness abandon all such people whose chiefest wit consists in abusing Superiors, and slighting all things as well sacred as civil, nor have they a greater itch after anything then to inveigle youth into the like practices whereby they may be as well ruin'd as themselves. O Shun and avoid such subtle insinuating persons, for you shall ever find that as sober ingenious discourse is the most commendable, so it is likeways (without all contradiction) the most advantageous; tis now you are to receive the ground of learning which by your care and improvement will be of inestimable worth hereafter the result will be then to the honor of yourself the comfort and satisfaction of your friends and relations nor do I doubt but you will yet apply yourself to study and take a resolution against all impediments that may [hole in page] least seem to hinder your progress, pray let me hear from you. My service to your tutor, who you are beholding to for his singular care of you, and the good character he ever gave of you. No more but that you shall ever have the wishes of, your affectionate brother Thomas Myddelton.

6 School for young women, Germany 1785

Universities and academies were for male students only, and throughout most of the Middle Ages and early modern period the only way that girls or young women gained an education beyond basic reading and writing was by studying on their own or with a private tutor or governess hired by the family, or in a convent. In the eighteenth century this began to change, and in a few urban areas schools for girls from upper-class or wealthy middle-class families were opened. The following announcement of the opening of such a school in Frankfurt makes clear what type of curriculum was envisioned as appropriate for young ladies of these classes. Speaking French was regarded as genteel and refined, and much of the rest of the curriculum consisted of 'accomplishments' that would improve a girl's chances in the marriage market. (Frankfurt newspaper quoted in Anna Maus, *Von Philathropien zur Mädchenschule 1782 bis 1957. Die Geschichte der Karolinenschule zu Frankenthal/Pflaz* (Trautheim, 1958), p. 24. Translated by Merry Wiesner-Hanks.)

Mr. Fontanesi has recently opened an educational establishment for young ladies of the Protestant religion here in Frankfurt. The Elector [the ruler of the area around Frankfurt] donated the building for this, and also donated 1400 gulden. There are two head teachers in this establishment, Madame Moissonnier and Madame Degelieu, and three governesses, the Mademoiselles Moissonnier, Price, and Breguet, all of them from French-speaking Belgium.

Every young lady pays an eleven gulden entrance fee, and then fourteen gulden per month for her education and room and board. Every one of them must bring with her: silver tableware, two pairs of linen tablecloths, a dozen napkins and just as many handtowels. Those who stay longer than a year in the educational establishment must leave these behind [when they go], but those who stay only one year must leave only half of them.

Every day they receive: in the morning bread and milk, at noon soup, meat, vegetables and condiments, at four o'clock fruit and bread, and in the evening soup and broiled meat. All those who are used to drinking wine receive wine. In addition they also get heat, light, medicine for minor ailments, and their washing. In terms of instruction various masters are hired by the school to teach religion, morals, geology, history, natural history, writing, figuring, and also knitting, sewing, embroidery, bleaching, lacemaking, fashion, cosmetics, hair-arrangement, and household skills. All of this for fourteen gulden per month. Dancing, music, and drawing lessons, as well as lessons in speaking English and French, will cost extra. French is spoken continually. The number of students has already grown to forty.

RESTRICTIONS ON SINGLE PEOPLE

7 Laws requiring unmarried people to register or leave, Denmark 1549

Most young people in early modern Europe did not attend universities or academies, but worked in their parents' households, or as servants, apprentices, journeymen, or wage-laborers. Political and religious authorities often regarded young, unmarried people as sources of disorder, and passed laws requiring them to live with older adults or otherwise restricting their behavior. In Malmø, for example, the second largest city of the Kingdom of Denmark, the city council issued a new set of ordinances in 1549 that restricted activities and individuals viewed as upsetting morality and public order.

(*Malmø stadsbog 1549–1559. Rådstuerettens, bytingets og toldbodrettens protokol.* Udg. v. Einar Bager (Copenhagen: Selskabet for Udgivelse af Kilder til dansk Historie, 1972), p. 35. Translated by Grethe Jacobsen and Pernille Arenfeldt.)

Anno domino 1549, December 14th, the Mayors, the City Council and the Royal Reeve decided to issue this bylaw, which is as follows:

First it was gravely determined, decided and agreed upon that no one should be sitting and drinking alcohol during the sermon on Sundays or other holy days, nor should anyone wander around in the street or in the chapel behind the choir during the sermon. Nor should any cellar be opened on aforesaid days before the noonday sermon is over, unless it is done for the sake of strangers and travellers who arrive and want to leave at once. Whoever breaks this rule will be punished accordingly.

Similarly, all single men and unemployed menservants should at once appear at the City Hall and swear an oath to the Mayors and the Council acting on behalf of His Royal Majesty and the city of Malmø or they should at once be expelled from the city.

Similarly, all girls who are self-supporting [lit. self-feeding] should enter into service again or be expelled from the city at once.

Then about those whores and poor women of the city, it was decided that whoever is found in the city after New Year's Day and has not been provided with an honest man and she is caught wearing a cape or a head-dress while she keeps up such a life, she will lose this clothing and be punished according to the law.

8 Unmarried woman's registration as an honorable woman, Denmark 1554

In the years following the issuing of these ordinances, several single women ap-peared in court to obtain a written testimony, confirming that they were honest and decent maidens. Notice that the woman is not accused of any specific act, but must swear to her honorability simply because she is not married.
(*Malmø stadsbog 1549–1559. Rådstuerettens, bytingets og toldbodrettens protokol.* Udg. v. Einar Bager (Copenhagen: Selskabet for Udgivelse af Kilder til dansk Historie, 1972), p. 193. Translated by Grethe Jacobsen and Pernille Arenfeldt.)

18th June 1554 the bearer of this letter, Anne Pedersdatter, our burgheress [female citizen] was (in court) and brought with her these aftersaid honest men and women, her neighbours: [the names of ten men and seven women] whom she has summoned to appear in front of us and asked and urged them for God's and justice's sake that they would give her a true and honest testimony concerning how she had lived and behaved herself among them and whether she had consorted with wicked people or loose company with drink, bad behaviour, been a tapster [woman who sold beer] or in any other way led an evil life or stayed in any unsuitable house or in any way heard or learned anything about her, in secret or in public, except that which was honest and suitable in every way.

Which aforesaid honest men and women all and each in agreement stepped forward and with the proper oath swore by God and the salvation of their souls that they had never at any time heard or learned, secretly or publicly, any dishonour, dishonest lifestyle or loose behaviour nor (that she had) stayed in a disreputable house but (that she had) always as a maiden and a women behaved and led a life and associated with neighbours and everyone honestly, modestly, suitably and early as well as late in every way. To further witness that thus has been recounted, sworn and testified in front of us, we have sealed this our open letter with the seal of our city, given and written year and day and place as said above.

9 Episcopal decree regarding several single women, Spain 1571

Though the Danish ordinances regarded both unmarried men and unmarried women with suspicion, women who did not marry received the most intense scrutiny. In this excerpt from the decrees of an Episcopal visit to a small parish in northwestern Spain, a representative of the bishop condemned the actions of a number of single women and admonished their parents to control their behavior.
(Libro de Visitas, Santa Maríía Amarante, Archivo Histórico Diocesano de Ourense, 24.1.13, f. 17r, July 23, 1571. Translated by Allyson Poska.)

Item: His Honor ordered that as he has discovered information against some single women of this parish whose way of living is so bad and who are bad examples . . . that from now on Margarida, daughter of Vicente Asiana, and Catalina, daughter of Olinda de Dacon, María de Negrellas, single, María dos Casares, blind and single, Herena de Dacon, and Luzia de Amarante, from here forward live honestly and chastely, not being bad examples, under the penalty of one silver mark . . . he orders that henceforth, if they do not comply, the fathers and mothers of the aforementioned should punish them so that they might live properly.

10 Episcopal decree about foreign women, Spain 1610

Independent unmarried women of all types were frequently seen as disruptive to community social and sexual norms, and in border areas, significant tensions often accompanied the foreign, single women who migrated to other jurisdictions for work

and love. In Spain, Portuguese women had a reputation for turning to prostitution, but, as this passage indicates, they were believed to cause physical as well as moral damage. In this mandate from an Episcopal visit to a Spanish parish on the border with Portugal, the episcopal official, known as the Visitor, warned parishioners of the dangers of their Portuguese neighbors, particularly women who ventured over the border into their community.
(Libro de Visitas, Santa Eulalia Bouses, Archivo Histórico Diocesano de Ourense, 27.2.5, f. 95 (1610). Translated by Allyson Poska.)

The Visitor, continuing his visit, found that this place is on the frontier with Portugal and that often women, both married and unmarried desiring to live in the said place, succeed in coming from the Kingdom of Portugal. For the most part, they come excommunicated by their prelates and their lives and customs are bad examples. They cause damage to the homes of the inhabitants of this place as well as in the groves, vineyards, meadows, turnip fields, and other places. In order to remedy this, the said Visitor orders the said parishioners . . . do not give shelter nor rent nor sell to any such persons.

11 Ordinance prohibiting girls from living with their mothers, France 1665

Restrictions on unmarried women usually focussed on the women themselves, but sometimes also on those who gave them room and board. This might even include their own mothers, as this ordinance from Strasbourg in 1665 makes clear.
(Strasbourg, Archives Municipales, Statuten, vol. 33, no. 61 (1665). Translated by Merry Wiesner-Hanks.)

Numerous complaints have been made that some widows living here have two, three, or more daughters living with them at their expense. These girls go into service during the winter but during the summer return to their mothers, partly because they want to wear more expensive clothes than servants are normally allowed to and partly because they want to have more freedom to walk around, to saunter back and forth whenever they want to. It is our experience that this causes nothing but shame, immodesty, wantonnness and immorality, so that a watchful eye should be kept on this, and if it is discovered, the parents as well as the daughters should be punished with a fine, a jail sentence, or even banishment from the city in order to serve as an example to others.

12 Punishment of a young thief, Germany 1742

The worries of authorities about 'shame' and 'immorality' among young people were sometimes realized. Young people without skills or stable living situations did sometimes turn to crime, particularly to petty crimes involving property. In this case from the German city of Freiburg, a young woman is sentenced to a variety of punishments for her theft.

(Georg Schindler, *Verbrechen und Strafen im Recht der Stadt Freiburg im Briesgau von der Einführung des Neuenstadtrechts bis zum Übergang an Baden (1520–1806)*, Veröff. a.d. Archiv d. Stadt Freiburg im Breisgau 7 (Freiburg, 1937). Translated by Merry Wiesner-Hanks.)

Freiburg 1742

The jailed Maria Fargashin, eighteen or nineteen years old, is to be considered nothing less than a vagabond without any honorable life, because she stood watch recently in the Loreten chapel for the thieves who were stealing the clothes from [the statue of] the holy Mother of God, and took the goods from this theft and sold them. It would be appropriate for the city executioner to punish her with the dust-broom [a euphemism for the whip]. However, because of persuasive reasons she is given a milder punishment this time, and graced with the following sentence: she is to be exhibited to the people on the pillory wearing a sign detailing her crime and holding a switch in her hands for one hour, to be given 24 lashes on the calves of her legs, to swear an oath that she will not appear in this city for the rest of her life, and then to be banished. She is to be firmly warned that if she appears or is seen again in this city or the area governed by this city, she will be punished much more harshly and with no mercy shown to her because she will then be an oath-breaker.

SEXUALITY

13 Confession questions, Russia seventeenth century

The restrictions on single people often indicate that sexual activity by unmarried people was a great concern of early modern authorities, an issue that also emerges in a variety of other types of sources. Catholic and Orthodox Christians were expected to confess their sins to a priest periodically, and the priest would pose questions to them, taken from standard lists, termed penitentials or confessional manuals. The purpose of the questions was twofold: to identify sins parishioners might have committed, and to teach them to avoid improper conduct. Most lists emphasized first and foremost sexual misconduct, and secondarily behavior disruptive to religious and community life. The following list, dating from the seventeenth century, was designed for young, unmarried women, and indicates the types of sins the writers of the confessional manuals – usually a priest – expected them to be most likely to commit.

(A. Almazov, *Tainaia ispoved' v pravoslavnoi vostochnoi tserkvi*, vol. III (Odessa, 1894), p. 169. Translated by Eve Levin.)

Did you break any vow that you promised to God?

Did you laugh in God's church during the holy liturgy, or exchange idle words with your girlfriends?

Did you enter God's church when you were unclean from the flow of blood, until the eighth day? [Russian Orthodox observance forbade women from going to church during or after their menstrual period.]

Did you play with your girlfriends inappropriately, as though with a man, or did you kiss youths with desire?

Did someone defile you by force, either while asleep or while drunk?

Did you look at someone of the male sex with anticipation?

During Lent and on Wednesdays and Fridays, did you eat either milk or cheese? [In Russian Orthodox observance, believers are required to abstain from meat and milk products during fast periods and on Wednesdays and Fridays.]

Did you quarrel with your parents, with your father and mother, or brothers and sisters, or did you strike them with something, or did you condemn them for any reason or tell them to go to the devil?

Did you steal any things or money or anything else from your father and mother, or from your relatives or your girlfriends?

Did you receive holy communion and then vomit?

Did you swear falsely and kiss the cross or icons? [Kissing the cross was a ritual to confirm the veracity of an oath.]

Did you recite maledictions and spells, or have your girlfriend do so for any reason?

Did you drink until you lost your memory, or dance and sing devilish songs?

Did you curse yourself out of some need or from heartache, or did you long for death for yourself?

Did you wash yourself with some drink or with anything else, and give it to somebody? [In Russian folk belief, a person could inspire sexual attraction by bathing in water or milk and then giving it to the object of their affection to drink.]

14 Lawsuit regarding a pregnancy out of wedlock, France 1548

Despite the best efforts of political and religious authorities, women did get pregnant out of wedlock, and formal legal arrangements were sometimes made to support the child. These arrangements were recorded by notaries. In this document from Paris in 1547, a single woman and a man go on record to settle a lawsuit in progress regarding the woman's pregnancy and the subsequent birth of a child by the man. The woman's economic circumstances and means of earning a living are not specified. The man, as a legal practitioner given the title 'master', was probably comfortably well off, though not rich.

55

(Paris, Archives Nationales, Minutier central, Étude XI/27, January 25, 1548. Translated by Carol Loats.)

Were present in person master Jherosme Honys, legal practitioner at the Palais in Paris, on the one hand, and Mathurine de Marville, living in Paris, rue Alexandre Langloiz, on the other hand, who have made and now make the agreements, compromises, and arrangements which follow.

That is to say that the said de Marville has promised and here promises to raise and support, well and duly, from this point on, a young girl named Claude, to whom she previously gave birth, child of the said Honys; in return for which the said Honys will be obliged and obliges himself to give and pay her, each month for the next two full years, one *écu soleil*, the first term of payment falling due the last day of February coming up.

And in addition to this, [Honys] has given four *écus d'or* in cash, and has promised and promises to pay her six *écus soleil* by the day and feast of Easter coming up, for maintenance and clothing of the said child; without Honys being in any way obliged to give anything else for the support of the said child, from this point on, if not of his own goodwill.

In consideration of the things above, the said Marville has released and here releases the said Honys of all things whatsoever, equally for what she is able or might be able to ask in original amount as for expenses in the legal process pending before whatever judges there might be, and of all other things whatsoever for which she could make demands and take legal action in whatever cause or way that might be, from the past up to now.

Thus etc., promising, etc., obligating, etc., each in his own right, etc., renouncing, etc. Done and passed in duplicate in the year 1547, Wednesday, the 25th day of January.

15 Trial regarding a birth out of wedlock, France 1540

Another much more complex notarial document similarly settles a lawsuit in progress regarding a pregnancy and promises of marriage. Marriage was one of the sacraments of the Roman Catholic church, and in Catholic parts of Europe, church courts had jurisdiction over disputes regarding many issues related to marriage. In this case, a woman – Gillette Blanchyen – claimed to have had sexual relations with a man – Jehan Luyrette – for whom she had worked as a servant for several years. She claimed that she had borne a child from the relationship, and that Luyrette had promised to marry her. The legal proceedings had apparently been extensive prior to the time the two agreed to settle before a notary, which may be one of the reasons two other men, Pierre Luyrette (most likely a relative of Jehan Luyrette) and Marc Nouel, are required to guarantee Jehan Luyrette's payment. Female servants were particularly at risk of becoming pregnant outside of marriage. They frequently worked or were sent on errands unchaperoned, and their employer or their employer's sons could easily put pressure on them. Pressure on a young woman to engage in sex often involved promises of marriages, and cases such as this were common in courts all over Europe.

(Paris, Archives Nationales, Minutier central, Étude XXXIII/17, June 18, 1540). Translated by Carol Loats.)

Present and appearing personally were on the one hand, Gillette Blanchyen, living at Victry sur Seyne, exercising and in possession of her rights, as she says and affirms as the truth, [here acting] for herself and in her own name; and on the other hand Pierre Luyrette, farm worker, and Marc Nouel, court clerk [bailiff] at the said Victry, in their own names and acting as agents in this matter for Jehan Luyrette le Moyen, called *le Menu*, also farm worker living at the said Victry, by whom they have promised and will be obliged and promise to have ratify, consent, approve, and find acceptable the contents which follow, in total and whenever, etc.

The parties, including the said Gillette, say that she had had the said Jehan Luyrette summoned, as regards marriage, before Monseigneur the official of the Archdiocese de Jezas in the church of Paris. [There] the said Luyrette had refused to acknowledge the jurisdiction of that court, and as non-religious, demanded a transfer before monsieur the *prévôt* of Paris [an officer of the French king] or his *lieutenant criminel*; and defenses were presented to the said official not to handle the said Luyrette before him. [Gillette and Luyrette are here disputing who has jurisdiction over the case, the church courts of the archbishop of Paris or the secular courts of the king.]

And since then, *provision* [an advance on the damages she was expected to receive] had been awarded by the said *prévôt* of Paris or his said *lieutenant criminel* to the said Gillette in the sum of 20 *livres tournois* which had been paid as security by the said Gyllette.

And the said Luyrette had been made prisoner in the prisons of the Châtelet of Paris [a prison run by royal officials] at the request of the *gens du Doyen*; since then he had been released, on paying bail.

And also, [Gillette] had requested another *provision* in the sum of 10 *livres parisis* from the very day that the said Luyrette had been taken prisoner, and this as much for the original amount of the expenses and damages that she could have claimed and could claim and for which she could have and could bring legal action against the said Jehan Luyrette – as much for reason of the defloration and fleshly copulation that she is maintaining she experienced from the person of the said Luyrette, from which she is saying she had given birth to a child who has died, as for the promises of marriage that she is maintaining had been made to her by the said Luyrette.

And [the two parties] had proceeded by many and various writs and summonses. So that they avow they are fed up with the said legal process, and to put an end to it and avoid the costs and outlays that might ensue, by this means to nurture peace and affection between them, the parties, in the said names, have affirmed and affirm, in regard to all that is stated, that they have negotiated, compromised, and together come to terms, as follows.

That is to say, the said Gillette, in the presence and with the advice of Geneviefve Quetart, her mother, Nicolas Blanchien, her brother, and other kin, here present, has released and relieved, releases and relieves the said Jehan Luyrette, called Le Menu, and his possessions and heirs, etc., in so far as it relates to herself only, forever and without recall, completely and absolutely, of any obligation for all and each of her said expenses and damages that she had claimed, has claimed, and could claim against him for all this that is said above and related matters, including the copulation and fleshly company and promises of marriage above mentioned, if there were any of these things.

This release from obligation made in return for, among other things, the value and sum of 35 *livres tournois* that for this [matter] the said [Pierre] Luyrette and Marc Nouel, in the said names and each of them for the whole without division or dispute, have promised and will be obliged, promise and guarantee to give and pay to the said Gillette, or someone on her behalf, etc., one half at the next [feast day of] Saint Remy [October 1] and the other half one year later. And Jehan [sic- clearly the scribe was confused and should have written 'Pierre' here] Luyrette and Marc Nouel pledge their own acts and debts and undertake this obligation towards the said Gillette, as is stated, on their own.

And in doing this, the said sum of 20 *livres tournois* of *provision* so awarded to the said Gillette will be given and forwarded to this Gillette and by this [action] her security payment is and remains discharged.

And further it has been agreed between the said parties that the said sum of 10 *livres parisis* of the other *provision* will be similarly paid to the said Gillette if it is found that this provision should be given or awarded to her.

And therefore the said Gillette consents and agrees also as it relates to her that the said Luyrette should be completely freed.

And the said parties in the said names withdraw and abandon the said process and differences which could be between them, whether in the church court or in the Châtelet of Paris, because of this and related matters, and also as it relates to her, without any other expenses or damages on one part or the other, and each will pay his own counsel and agent.

Also the said Gillette consents that, as it relates to her, the bail paid by the said Jehan Luyrette in leaving the said prisons will be and remain finished and discharged, without affecting the sum of 25 *livres* 5 *sous tournois* that she claims is due to her from the said Luyrette for the remainder of her wages and compensation for her having served and lived with the said Luyrette for the duration of 7 to 8 years, except however deducting for what she might have [already] received toward these wages and compensation. Pierre Luyrette and Mark Nouel have promised and will be obliged and promise to have the said Jehan Luyrette accept this obligation to the said Gillette completely, within 8 days, to pay her this amount within three weeks starting today.

Thus, etc., promising, obligating in the said names, each in his own right, etc., and further the said Pierre Luyrette and Marc Nouel each for the whole without division or dispute, etc., renouncing, etc., and similarly these two, Pierre Luyrette and Marc Nouel, [renouncing the] benefits of division and process of dispute.

Done and passed in duplicate, the year 1540, Friday, 18th day of June.

[According to a related document, Jehan Luyrette appeared before one of the notaries, agreed to all the terms of the previous document, and relieved Pierre Luyrette and Marc Noèl and their possessions and heirs of the obligations they had taken on. This second document is dated Tuesday, June 29.]

16 Death sentence of a woman accused of infanticide, Germany 1740

Many women who had children out of wedlock could not get the father to agree to support the child, or in some cases even acknowledge that the child was his. Pregnancy outside of marriage was disastrous for many women, and they tried to hide the pregnancy as long as possible, or to abort this child with herbs or other methods. If they could not induce a miscarriage, they might give birth as secretly as possible, and then abandon the child or attempt to kill it. During the sixteenth century, governments in many parts of Europe became very concerned about infanticide, and required unmarried women who became pregnant to report their pregnancies; those who did not might be charged with infanticide if the baby died, even if there was no proof that it had been killed. Medical personnel often had great difficulty telling if a child had been born dead or had died shortly after birth, but the more stringent laws were enforced; more women were executed for infanticide in early modern Europe than for any other crime except witchcraft. The following case from Frankfurt is typical of this uncertainty in terms of proof.
(Criminal court records from Frankfurt, quoted in Wilhelm Wächterhäuser, *Das Verbrechen des Kindesmordes im Zeitalter der Aufklärung* (Berlin, 1973), p. 11. Translated by Merry Wiesner-Hanks.)

Anna Maria Rauin admitted, concerning her child that was conceived in immorality, that as soon as it was born she shook it back and forth by the head so that it would not cry and no one would discover it or learn about it, and that she grabbed it around the throat under the face and held it very firmly. But she denied having murderous intentions or having handled the child in a way to murder it. The examination of the body by the doctors and surgeons was inconclusive in terms of determining the cause of death or whether the lungs had drawn breath, despite their best medical understanding. The accused herself was not certain, but only thought that the child was born living into the world and was then strangled by her. Because her confession may have been motivated by fear of torture, and because of the absence of a clear corporis delecti and complete certainty that the child lived, the death sentence might appear not to be proper, and it might appear as if the accused should be given an unusual punishment [i.e., not the death sentence], or should be forced into making a more complete confession through firm handling on the part of the city executioner. However, it appears from the circumstances, and is fully demonstrated without a doubt through the confession of the accused . . . that it was the intention of the accused to keep the child from crying by pressing in on its throat so that no one would know anything about this birth. This is indeed premeditated murder, that is, an intent to kill the child, and the accused, who as any reasonable person would, clearly understood that holding it by the throat and neck would cause this gentle little child to strangle and die. . . . Thus she is sentenced to death by the sword.

17 Inquisition punishment of a statement about sexuality, Spain 1692

Though laws and religious doctrine forbade sexual intercourse outside of marriage, many rural people did not accept this idea. Sexual intercourse was a regular feature of peasant life, and frequently the guarantor of marriage promises. In conversations like this one recounted to the Inquisition in 1692, peasants presented their own pragmatic, but heretical versions of Catholic belief and practice.
(Relaciones de Causas, Archivo Histórico Nacional, Sección Inquisición, legajo 3861, no.18, f. 24 (1692). Translated by Allyson Poska.)

Domingo de Quintana, farmer, from Santa Eulalia de Budian . . . fifty two years old . . . in a vineyard with six or seven companions in a conversation about the son of Luis de Borja . . . and a lawsuit that was being litigated in the Audiencia about the pregnancy of a young woman, he had said that it was a greater sin for a married man to have intercourse with an unmarried woman than for an unmarried man to have intercourse with an unmarried woman and that intercourse between single people was only a venial sin . . . He was given a grave warning, admonished, exiled from this city and the town of Budian for four leagues and two years, and required to get instruction in our holy faith.

18 Regulations of a city brothel, France 1500

One of the reasons rural (and many urban) people may have had difficulty regarding sexual relations outside of marriage as a sin is that in many parts of Europe prostitution was tolerated or even legal. Prostitutes were often regulated beginning in the fifteenth century; the following are the ordinances of a city brothel in Strasbourg, passed in 1500 by the city council. During the sixteenth century, brothels in many Protestant areas were ordered closed by city authorities, but illicit prostitution continued. In Catholic areas, such as Italy, prostitution was regulated and licensed, but not prohibited.
(Strasbourg, Archives Municipales, Statuten, vol. 3, fs. 4–5 (1500). Translated by Merry Wiesner-Hanks.)

How the brothel manager, his wife, and their servants should treat the whores.

In past times and still today wanton knaves often take women and daughters from other areas and put them in or sell them to the city brothel. Then such persons are kept in the brothel against their will by the brothel manager and his wife, so that they can not leave the brothel, although some of them would willingly turn away [from this life] and do penance. This is difficult to tolerate, so the mayors and the city council and the 21 [a smaller city council] have decided that from henceforth this shall be handled in such a manner:

That is, that no brothel manager nor his wife nor his servants shall sell or pawn a woman, whether for a large sum or a small sum. If they have sold or pawned any women, these persons should now be free. If any brothel manager, his wife, or his servants do this in the future, they shall pay the city five pounds each time this happen. Those that disdain this and will not follow it shall be banished from the city of Strasbourg under threat of corporal punishment. Those who want to carry out this sinful work [i.e., prostitution] may take women in and maintain them for a relatively small weekly sum for room and board, a sum which both parties agree to in good will.

If the brothel manager, his wife, or his servants give the whores clothing, linens, food, or drink, the women are to pay for this by the week so that the debts are repaid. They are not to use this to keep the whores in their debt or pawn them, but the whores are to have the free will to decide whether to stay or to go without being forced by the brothel manager, his wife, or his servants, by the pain of the aforementioned fine.

The brothel manager, his wife, and his servants are not to claim a part of the money that the poor whores earn with their bodies, nor force them to do such work, for it should be up to them whether they earn money or are idle.

At all times, the whores are to be free to go to church, to sermons, to hear mass and to other church services, whenever and wherever they want, and not stopped by the brothel manager, his wife, or his servants, by the pain of the aforementioned fine.

All brothel managers, their wives, and their servants are to be summoned and ordered to swear an oath to obey this ordinance.

The two officers who assist the mayor, the three tower guards, and the two bailiffs are also to take an oath, that if they experience or learn that this ordinance is not being followed, they are to punish and report this. The seven officers of morality are also expected to enforce this ordinance according to their oath, with one-fourth [of the fine] going to the officers who carry out the punishment for their troubles.

19 Punishment of a woman for theft and prostitution, Germany sixteenth century

The life of prostitutes and courtesans has often been romanticized, and some women who were the mistresses of powerful men were themselves quite influential. Most women who sold sex combined this with other types of work, and sometimes with criminal activity. (This is one reason that 'whores' and 'poor women' were linked in the Danish ordinances regarding single people included above.) They were imprisoned and received beatings or other corporal punishments for their actions, and one senses how desperate these women could become in cases like the following from Nuremberg, taken from the city executioner's diary.
(Albrecht Keller, ed., *Meister Franntz Schmidts Scharfrichters inn Nürnberg all sein Richten* (Leipzig: Wilhelm Helms, 1913). Translated by Merry Wiesner-Hanks.)

Barbara Wissnerin, a very base, lewd whore: who due to great unchastity, multiple theft and breaking and entering has already been in the *Loch* [the city jail] eight times. She was banished many times, and has perjured herself [i.e., and come back into Nuremberg] and was beaten in the *Loch*. She was publicly burned through the cheeks, and her first two fingers were chopped off. But all warnings have not helped. As she was recently arrested again, and made herself a large belly out of rags, as if she were pregnant, so that the officials would hold back, and not use the necessary severity. She was let out of the city after swearing an oath, and warned under penalty of death not to come in to the city again. Whereupon she came in again and was caught at theft. Now on her own confession her day of execution is set for next Thursday, the first of March. For the said punishment she will be taken from life to death in water [i.e., drowned].

20 Police report of a man arrested for sodomy, France 1723

Early modern theologians, jurists, and doctors applied the word 'sodomy' to a variety of non-procreative sexual activities: bestiality, masturbation, and oral or anal intercourse involving any combination of individuals. Under this umbrella they condemned sexual relations between men and between women, but male 'sodomites' were arrested and punished for sodomy much more commonly than female 'tribades' were. The repression of sexual relations between men was sporadic and selective throughout Europe. In Paris the police entrapped hundreds of 'infamous' men in parks during the first half of the eighteenth century. Reports like the following one have allowed historians to reconstruct aspects of the sodomitical subculture of the capital. They provide information about what men sexually interested in other men said and did and about contemporary sexual assumptions, attitudes, and anxieties.
(Bibliothèque de l'Arsenal, Paris, Ms 10254, October 21, 1723. Translated by Jeffrey Merrick.)

LEONARD GOBERT
apprentice mason living at the quarries near Charenton
native of Paris, 45 years old, unmarried

Said Gobert has been known for many years as an infamous sod[omite] and as a corrupter of young folks, as well as for having in the past supplied such to Monsieur the duke de Brancas. For 5 or 6 years he had been living on the Montagne Sainte-Geneviève, where he did not have a good reputation, always having with him young folks from the neighborhood, whom he lured to his place and often made sleep with him, about which the neighbors as well as the late Michaud, a used clothes dealer, in whose house the said Gobert then lived, informed the late Monsieur d'Argenson, who ordered Monsieur Simmonet to bring him in to speak with him and that he should be reprimanded as he deserved and in case of recidivism that he would send him to the Hospital, said late Michaud having found the said Gobert going up with two young children from neighborhood families whom he wished to corrupt as they stated at the time. And since that time, this infamous man has continued in more or less the same way and in order to hide his cards better bought for life a little house at the quarries that he fixed up as he liked and where he has lived with a young man for four years, as he has stated and also said that he was a carpenter and that he put him up as a good friend. Said Gobert having always reserved a small room on the Montagne Sainte-Geneviève, in the house of a candlemaker named Gosset, in order to come there sometimes to amuse himself there with his friends, especially young folks. He has also been known to Monsieur Théru for a long time.

Being this day Monday 21 October in the Luxembourg gardens around six o'clock in the evening, I encountered the said Gobert, who was looking for a good time there in the places where all the infamous men go. Having seated myself on the grass, he placed himself next to me and showed me his p[enis] through his shirt, while telling me the story of his adventures on the subject of sod[omy], among others about a certain Cadeau who was arrested by order of the king by Monsieur Simonnet for the same reason, who went to the Mississippi, with whom he lived for a while as man and wife and that he missed him all the time, being one of the good-looking boys of Paris. He also told me that he had something to do with a priest whom he had met on the half-moon and that a month ago he had more-over found a young man there with whom he had had a good time, but that he had caught something bad out of it, and that a week ago he had also found a man in the Luxembourg with whom he had gone to la Roquette and had a good time together, which man the said Gobert invited to come see him in his house at the quarries. Said Gobert told me that he put it in and that he did not like women at all and that his whole pleasure was to have something to do with good-looking boys and you might say that he had been of this inclination all his life. Then said Gobert having suggested to me that we go drink a mug because he did not want to do anything in said garden, because they arrested people every day and that we would be safe in a tavern to amuse ourselves, having left said garden by the gate on the side of the rue de l'Enfer, said Gobert was arrested by order of the king by Monsieur Simmonet, who led him to prison in the Petit Châtelet around eight o'clock in the evening.

21 Trial record of a woman executed for sexual relations with women and cross-dressing, Germany 1477

Records of arrests or trials of women for sexual relations with other women are very rare in early modern Europe. There are almost none in southern Europe – at the same time there were thousands of accusations of sodomy involving men – and just a handful in the cities of northern Europe. The few that did come to trial are similar to the case reprinted here, in that one woman took on a male role – wore men's clothing, pretended she was a man, and often used a dildo – and she was more harshly treated than the woman who remained in the female sexual and social role. In this case, the accused confesses to having had a long-standing sexual relationship with one woman (who she originally called her 'sister' but later denied this and who apparently escaped trial) as well as making sexual advances to two other women, who are also punished. The actions are described in the records, but the crime is not given any name.
(Helmut Puff, 'Female Sodomy: The Trial of Katherina Hetzeldorfer (1477)', *The Journal of Medieval and Europe Modern Studies* 30 (Winter 2000), pp. 58–59. Reprinted by permission.)

[Stadtarchiv Speyer 1 A, 704/II, fols. 12r–14r] Else, wife of Wendel Muter, says, among many other things, that around four weeks ago she who stands in the dock [i.e., the accused] came to her at her house when her husband was not at home. She knocked on the door so long that in the end she [i.e., Else] let her in. Among other things, [she says] when they were together she put her up in a different bed. Then [however] she who stands in the dock lay down in bed with her and, during many quarrels, sat down on top of the above-mentioned Else, and tried to seduce her and to have her manly will with her. [*In the margin at this point:* As she in fact did it with her once just like a man. She (i.e., the accused) also says that if she is to be punished she did it once. She also says that her semen is so much that it is beyond measure, that one could grab it with a full hand.] She [i.e., Else] grabbed it [the penis] and felt that it was a huge thing, as big as half an arm. She thought it was like a horn and pointed in front and wide behind. She could hardly ward her off. Among other things, when she broke loose she who stands in the dock [i.e., the accused] jumped out of the window. She also says when she came to her she showed her the penis and tried to have her will with her and offered to give her eight florins. She [i.e., Else] also says that she [i.e., the accused] urinates through this thing. She also says that she who stands in the dock prohibited her [from telling others], and she promised not to mention it to anybody. She also says that she who is supposed to be her sister said in her brief that she who stands in the dock had deflowered her and had made love to her during two years. She also said that she did not know anything other than that men should be granted such roguery.

Else, wife of Henck [?] Michel [?], says that during carnival she saw that she who stands in the dock stood, whored like a man, and she grabbed her just like a man. She also says that with hugging and kissing she behaved exactly like a man with women, as she said.

Ennel Helmstetner says that once upon a time she asked the accused for information about her sister ... asked how it came ... that she ... her sister ... she was her husband.

Hannss Welcker says, among other things, that he had heard from Ennel Helmstat[ner] that she said that she who stands in the dock and who is supposed to be a man – that she abducted her, whom she calls a sister, from a noble and is not her sister.

Katherina Hetzeldorferin from Nuremberg [testifying]: She says that she did it at first with one finger, thereafter with two, and then with three, and at last with the piece of wood that she held between her legs to the extent she said and confessed before. (She also says that the woman who was with her is her sister and that she has nothing to do with her [i.e., has had no sex with her]. She was ready to die for that [i.e., it is really true].) She says that she who was with her is not her sister and says that she encountered her in Wefthelm and took her here [to Speyer] (she did not court her nor do anything

65

dishonest with her) and had her ways with her. And she also says thereafter that she made an instrument with a red piece of leather, at the front filled with cotton, and a wooden stick stuck into it, and made a hole through the wooden stick, put a string through, and tied it round; and therewith she had her roguery with the two women and her who is supposed to be her sister.

She was drowned – requiescat in pace – on Friday before the deposition of Saint Guido.

When the Schreckenspoenn said such about her, and when she insisted that she did not know anything other than that she was a man and committed an act of knavery with her three times, she remained arrested because of that until the aforementioned Katherina was executed, [in order to find out] whether Katherina wanted to absolve her for not knowing anything other than that she took her for a man, and [in that case] ban her ten miles' distance from the city. Similarly Else, wife of Wendel Muter, with whom she had to do once [i.e., had sex with her once], remained arrested. And on the following Saturday they both swore ten miles from the city [i.e., they were exiled ten miles from the city].

Friday after Judica, 1477.

IMAGES OF YOUTH

22 Popular story of a cross-dressing young woman, Portugal 1599

Though unmarried women and men were regarded as suspicious by religious and political authorities, and their behavior was restricted, people also told stories about young people who defied conventions and lived adventurous lives. Early modern literature is full of stories of young men who traveled widely and encountered many opportunities to show great skill and bravery. There are also a few stories of young women who followed the same path, although the only way that it was possible for them to do so was to dress in men's clothing. Many of these stories of both men and cross-dressing women are claimed to be true, and it is difficult to separate fact from fiction. The following is one of these accounts of a cross-dressing heroine, taken from Duarte Nunez do Leão's *Descripção do Reino de Portugal* written in 1599 and published posthumously by the author's nephew, Gil Nunez do Leão. The author describes in a very romantic, sentimental, and exaggerated fashion the wonders of Portugal, starting with its glorious history, natural resources, and some national heroes and heroines. The latter comprise mainly of members of the nobility and of saints, but the selection highlighted here is the story of a young girl of modest means who ran away from home and led a life of high adventure. The experience of Antonia Rodriguez was hardly typical of young women in early modern Portugal, and there is no way to know whether she actually had such a life, but her story was very popular. (Duarte Nunez do Leão, *Descripção do Reino de Portugal*, Second edition (Lisbon: Na Of. de Simão Thaddeo Ferreira, 1785 [1610]), pp. 346–350. Translated by Darlene Abreu-Ferreira.)

In the town of Aveiro of one Simão Rodriguez mariner and of his wife Lianor Diaz was born a daughter named Antonia. She whom her mother brought to this city of Lisbon to another of her daughters who is married here. This girl not able to suffer the severity of her sister and the ill treatment that she received, she determined to leave her house and go to foreign lands, as she did at the age of twelve years: for which she went to a street where ready-made clothes are sold, and from the small peculium that she had she bought an outfit according to what boys wear who serve at sea in merchant vessels. And having already cut her hair she went to the fields and in a hidden place she removed her woman's clothing that she wore and dressed as a boy: and walking along the beach she approached a master of a caravel that was loaded with wheat for Mazagan [Morocco] in which she sailed: and she served on that voyage as a cabin boy as skilfully as a man who had always done that work, mounting the mast to handle the sails and doing everything else as a skilful mariner, changing the name Antonia to Antonio. Arriving at Mazagan it was reported to the captain that the master of the caravel had stolen and falsified [the volume of] wheat that was shipped; and in obtaining witness reports on the situation it was the cabin boy Antonio among them who discovered the truth. For which the captain did not allow him to return to the caravel for fear that the master would harm him; and he placed him among the soldiers, and he began to call himself, Antonio Rodriguez. Who in a short period of time made himself so skillful in weaponry that when they went to target he challenged the others and he had so much advantage no one defeated him. And on the streets he fenced and did all the games of battle with such ease as if he had done them all his life. For these reasons and for his gentle temperament he was much loved by all the soldiers and each sought to be his comrade. He did his night vigils without ever missing them, and with the soldiers he ate and laid in bed and slept among them yet always dressed in jerkin and drawers with which he never parted so that he was never found out. And thus he served a little more than a year as a soldier. Because of his abilities he became known and the captain favoured him, putting him up on a horse and giving him a salary and upkeep as all the cavalrymen.

On horseback he outdid the others in dexterity, good bearing, and swiftness with which he mounted from the ground: and in attacks on the enemy in the biggest and important undertakings, the captain always nominated him to lead as the most skilful cavalryman he had. And so he found himself in many battles and encounters where many leading Moors and their horses were captured and killed, in which Antonio Rodriguez participated as the best cavalryman of his company. Never failing to keep vigil during his watch on the [fort] walls, he would go to the fields with his musket on horseback to gather wood and hay. And many times he helped kill pigs on the Moors' camp of which he would bring his portion.

The fame of this young woman in disguise as a valiant cavalryman was such that for that and for looking as a young gentleman and with many graces he was much regarded and favoured by the young ladies of Mazagan, particularly by one daughter of a top cavalryman in whose house the pretender Antonio Rodriguez had had much familiarity that all supposed that he would marry her. And with all the intimacies that the parents of the young lady saw in him not without tenderness and gallantry they did not mistrust him: because he was provided with many handkerchiefs and shirts, and everyone thought that he would marry there. Having served in that man's costume for five years, he was anxious of being discovered by someone who had caught sight of some signs of a woman he determined to do it himself, and going to the provisor he disclosed it to him and told him the reasons for which until then he had been in those clothes. The provisor disclosed him to the governor and made him put on women's clothing. And thus she sought shelter in the home of a married top cavalryman where the young ladies to whom she spoke of romance visited her, the ones who transformed their love they had had for her into friendship and paid her for the gallantries that she had said to them with gifts of distaff and spindles and other similar things. This woman wished to return to the Realm in company with other women that were found. But she was too well loved by the captain and by everyone in the town, men as well as women, that they would not allow her to speak of it. A few days later a young cavalryman from one of the leading families in town married her and with him she returned to the Realm with a certification of the services she did with weapons, and the King granted her with a reward of two hundred *cruzados* for expenses and a *fanega* [a dry measure] of wheat per month and ten thousand *réis* all as pension for the rest of her life. And now recently her son was given a post in court as a page for the services she rendered, his mother. Today she is a widow and is in this city and with another appeal: she is still a young woman under 35 years of age, of good appearance and who has many graces when she speaks and very lively spirits, which well justifies what is said of her.

What of this woman can be praised the most is her chastity and deportment with which she always conducted herself going about with so many soldiers dressed as a soldier eating and sleeping in bed with them triumphing thus that is the greatest of all victories. And thus among the women of Mazagan exists the name of one of great merit and of whom much is said and to all who know her is known as the *Cavalheira* [cavalrywoman] for the courage that in combat she showed.

23 Portrait of Anne Bonney dressed as a pirate, Netherlands 1725

Stories describing the exploits of adventurous young men and women were often printed in illustrated versions so that people whose reading skills were minimal could still gain something from them. This is a highly romanticized portrait of Anne Bonney, (born Anne Cormac) reputed to have been the illegitimate daughter of a prominent Irish lawyer and his wife's maid, born about 1700 in Cork. As the story goes, Cormac and his mistress and Anne fled to the Carolinas, where Anne later married a ne'er-do-well sailor named James Bonney, and later went with him to the Bahamas, a center of piracy in the Caribbean. Anne left her husband and joined up with the pirate captain Calico Jack Rackham, and they marauded around the Caribbean. There are a few historical records that refer to Anne – as well as another female pirate, Mary Read – and many more songs and stories detailing her fights, murders, pardons, pregnancies, and lovers. This is from a book titled *Historie der Engelsche zeerovers* (History of the English Pirates) published in Amsterdam in 1725.

Anne Bonney als Pirat

24 Portrait of a young standard-bearer with mercenaries, France 1497

Young men who served as soldiers were also idealized in stories, songs, and visual illustrations. Most armies in early modern Europe relied on hired mercenary soldiers whose lives were actually very grim, but who were often portrayed in striking costumes and heroic poses. The youngest and best-looking individual in many of these pictures is the standard-bearer who carried the flag of the unit. (Both he and his flag were also called an 'ensign', a rank that still exists in the military.) This is a woodcut by an anonymous artist, which illustrated Jakob Locher's play *Spectaculum de Thurcorum Rege et Sultano rege Babiloniae more Tragico effigiatum in Romani Regis honorem* (Strasbourg, 1497). The play advocated a campaign by the Holy Roman Emperor against the Turks, which would have required thousands of mercenaries.

Questions for discussion

1. What types of scholarly and religious activities occupied early modern university students? What types of 'extra-curricular' activities?
2. How would you compare the opportunities available to young men for advanced education with those available to young women?

70

3 What activities of unmarried young people do political authorities appear to be most worried about? What reasons do they give for their worries, and what appear to you to be unspoken reasons?

4 What are the primary issues of concern in lawsuits regarding pregnancy out of wedlock? How are these solved?

5 According to the Strasbourg ordinances, how do women end up in city brothels? How are they kept there?

6 What do the city authorities of Paris view as particularly objectionable when they arrest Pierre Goubert for sodomy?

7 How would you compare the idealized stories and illustrations of young people with the realities of their lives? Why do you think there is a discrepancy between them?

3

COURTSHIP, LOVE, AND WEDDINGS

The most important decision facing adolescents and young adults in early modern Europe was the choice of a spouse, for this could determine their social and financial situation, as well as their personal well-being and happiness. This decision was far too important to leave up to the young people themselves, and family, friends, and even neighbors played a role in finding an appropriate spouse and bringing the marriage to realization. Particularly among the upper classes, there were often complicated marriage strategies to cement family alliances and expand family holdings, and some young people were more or less forced to marry who their parents wished. Among the lower classes, neighbors and public authorities often helped determine whether a couple would marry, the neighbors through pressuring courting couples and public authorities by simply prohibiting marriage between individuals regarded as too poor. Among the middle classes, couples certainly received advice on marriage and perhaps even threats from their families about their choice of a spouse, but they were more free to marry who they wished than upper-class individuals were.

There are numerous examples of children and parents who fought bitterly over the choice of a spouse, but in the vast majority of marriages, the aims of the people involved and their parents, kin, and community were largely the same: the best husband was the one who could provide security, honor, and status; the best wife one who was capable of running a household and assisting her husband in his work. Therefore even people who were the most free to choose their own spouses, such as widows and widowers or people whose parents had died, were motivated more by what we would regard as pragmatic concerns than romantic love. This is not to say that their choice was unemotional, but that the need for economic security, the desire for social prestige, and the hope for children were emotions just as important as sexual passion. The love and attraction a person felt for a possible spouse could be based on any combination of these, with intense romantic desire often viewed as more likely to be disruptive than supportive of a marriage.

Opinions about marriage itself in this period were varied, but generally became more positive than they had been in the Middle Ages. During the fifteenth century, some writers began to argue that God had set up marriage and families as the best way to provide spiritual and moral discipline, and, after the Reformation, Protestants championed marriage with even greater vigor. They wrote large numbers of tracts trying to convince people – especially men – to marry and advising them how to choose the best spouse. Opinions about marriage were not contained simply in written works, but were reflected in woodcuts and engravings and were communicated orally through marriage sermons and homilies. Because people in many parts of Europe were required to attend church, there was no way they could escape hearing them. The Catholic response to the challenge of the Protestant reformers included a response to the elevation of marriage. As with so many other issues, Catholic thinkers reaffirmed traditional doctrine and agreed that the most worthy type of Christian life was one both celibate and chaste. Catholic authors also realized, however, that despite exhortations to celibacy, most people in Europe would marry, and so wrote marriage manuals to counteract those written by Protestants. The ideal wife they described was exactly the same as that proposed by Protestant authors – obedient, silent, pious – and the ideal husband also the same – responsible, firm, and honorable. In Jewish opinion, like Protestant, all people were expected to marry, and the ideal wife was described as thrifty, cheerful, obedient, never jealous, and always responsive to her husband's physical and emotional needs; the ideal husband was a scholar, which meant that Jewish women were expected to be more involved in economic matters than Christian women were.

Spouses did not live up to the ideals set for them all the time, of course, and people regarded it as important to stipulate many legal and financial arrangements with a marriage contract. Marriage contracts were not limited to the wealthy, but quite ordinary people, including servants and artisans, had marriage contracts drawn up before they wed. Contracts were especially important in second and third marriages, as they had to stipulate how any inheritance might be divided among all of the children. Only after all parties had signed the contract (often including the parents of both spouses, if they were still living) could the actual marriage ceremony proceed. Ceremonies varied throughout Europe, but they generally involved some sort of religious ceremony, followed by as expensive a feast as the family could afford.

Women of all classes were expected to bring a dowry to their marriage, which might consist of some clothing and household items (usually including the marriage bed and bedding) for poor women, or vast amounts of cash, goods, or property for wealthy ones; in eastern Europe the dowry might even include serfs or slaves. This dowry substituted in most parts of Europe for a daughter's share of the family inheritance, and increasingly did not include any land, which kept land within the patrilineal lineage. Laws regarding a woman's control of her dowry varied throughout Europe, but in general a husband had the use, but not the ownership, of it during his wife's lifetime, though of course if he invested it unwisely this distinction did not make much difference. Women could sue their own husbands if they thought they were wasting their dowries however, and courts in many areas sided with the women, taking control of the dowry out of the husbands' hands. During the late medieval period, women appear to have been able freely to bequeath their dowries to whomever they chose, but in many parts of Europe this right was restricted during the sixteenth century to prevent them from deeding property to persons other than the male heirs.

CHOOSING A SPOUSE

1 Advice on choosing a wife, Portugal 1540

Just as they do today, how-to books provided guidance on many issues for early modern Europeans. Among these were a large number of advice books on marriage, written by a wide range of (largely male) authors. These advice books often discuss whether one should marry or not, and also provide specific advice on choosing a spouse. The example provided here, written by a Portuguese scholar, is divided into four parts, each presenting a set of arguments on questions of matrimony, with the pro and anti sides narrated at great length. Part four contains twelve prerequisites for the start of a happy marriage, and some apply to both partners, including good health, no children from previous relationships, and [sexual] potency. Other suggestions are more specifically gendered; a man contemplating matrimony was supposed to be able to support a wife and household, and the future wife was supposed to be a virgin and of average good looks. In the excerpt below it is obvious that the intended audience for this book was men as they are advised on the advantages of courting within their own circles.
(Doctor João de Barros, *Espelho de Casados*, Second edition, edited by Tito de Noronha and António Cabral (Porto: Imprensa Portugueza, 1874 [1540]), f. LVIIIv–f. LIX. Translated by Darlene Abreu-Ferreira.)

The eleventh essence or quality that some say a good marriage must have is that it be with a known neighbor daughter of his native neighbor, because as the proverb goes: the woman and the cow are found out back. The neighbor is aware of and knows the defects of his neighbor, and knows the customs and faults of his daughter, and the [female] outsider he never saw at times is very different from what he wants or from what pleases him. What is more appropriate is for the man to marry with his native than with the [female] outsider, for with this he honors and adds to his land and the Republic where he lives, and his neighbor knows what are his qualities: of what sort and of which customs and if these suit hers: or are disagreeable.

He will also know if she is content with him or not for many [women] marry against their will to obey their parents who make them do it. Others marry men they never met who promise them oceans and mountains and after all there is nothing and [they] find themselves greatly deceived. When a man and a woman are neighbors they cannot deceive one another, and neighborliness is the cause of much love. The neighbor presumes that he knows the deeds of his neighbour, and of him Solomon says that he is better than a brother far away. The law has ordained many things in favor of neighbors that they cannot torment one another, and have to be friends with their neighbours: they cannot throw out something that hangs from the neighbour's house: nor do something that smells badly and they are obliged to repair the fountain between him and the house of the neighbor that was destroyed by the violence of the fire which did not spread from it to others. By the law of the Realm he cannot make a door in front of the neighbor's door, and if his house is falling apart he is obliged to repair it. This way I say that the marriage with a [female] known neighbor is good and Joam Fabro says that he who marries should see if he can test the customs of the woman with whom he will live, and therefore the marriage with the [female] native and neighbor is better and more certain.

2 Qualities of the ideal wife, England 1617

There were a large number of prose works and poems describing ideal wives and husbands or providing advice on domestic relations published in early modern Europe; some of these were reissued several times, which means that they found a good market of readers. The following is a very typical one, titled *The Bride*. (Published by Samuel Rowlands in London in 1617.)

You that intend the honourable life,
And would with joy live happily in the same,
Must note eight duties do concern a wife,
To which with all endeavour she must frame:
    And so in peace possess her husband's love,
    And all distaste from both their hearts remove.

The first is that she have domestic cares,
Of private business for the house within,
Leaving her husband unto his affairs,
Of things abroad that out of doors have been
    By him performed, as his charge to do,
    Not busy-body like inclined thereto.

Nor intermeddling as a number will,
Of foolish gossips such as do neglect,
The things which do concern them, and too ill,
Presume in matters unto no effect:
    Beyond their element when they should look,
    To what is done in kitchen by the cook.

Or unto children's virtuous education,
Or to their maids, that they good housewifes be,
And carefully contain a decent fashion,
That nothing pass the limits of degree:
    Knowing her husband's business from her own,
    And diligent do that, let his alone.

The second duty of the wife is this,
(Which she in mind ought very careful bear).
To entertain in house such friends as his
As she doth know have husband's welcome there:
    Not her acquaintance without his consent,
    For that way jealousy breeds discontent.

Third duty is, that of no proud pretence,
She move her husband to consume his means,
With urging him to needless vain expense,
Which toward the counter or to Ludgate leans,
    For many idle housewives (London knows)
    Have by their pride been husband's overthrows.

A modest woman will in compass keep,
And decently unto her calling go,
Not diving in the frugal purse too deep,
By making to the world a peacock show:
    Though they seem fools, so yield unto their wives,
    Some poor men do it to have quiet lives.

Fourth duty is, to love her own house best,
And be no gadding gossip up and down,
To hear and carry tales amongst the rest,
That are the news reporters of the town:
    A modest woman's home is her delight,
    Of business there, to have the oversight.

At public plays she never will be known,
And to be tavern guest she ever hates,
She scorns to be a street wife (idle one)
Or field wife ranging with her walking mates:
    She knows how wise men censure of such dames,
    And how with blots they blemish their good names. . . .

Fifth duty of a wife unto her head,
Is her obedience to reform his will,
And never with a self-conceit be led
That her advice proves good, his counsel ill:
    In judgement being singular alone,
    As having all the wit, her husband none . . .

When as the husband bargains hath to make,
In things that are depending on his trade,
Let not wife's boldness power unto her take,
As though no match were good but what she made:
    For she that thus hath oar in husband's boat,
    Let her take breech, and give him petticoat.

Sixth duty is to pacify his ire,
Although she finds that he impatient be,
For hasty words, like fuel add to fire,
And more, and more infenceth wrath's degree;
    When she perceives his choler in a fit
    Let her forbear, and that's a sign of wit.

Many occasions unto men do fall,
Of adverse crosses, women not conceive,
To find us honey, they do meet with gall,
Their toil for us do their own joys bereave:
    Great shame it were, that we should add their woe,
    That do maintain, and keep, and love us so.

If that a hasty word sometime be spoke,
Let us not censure therefore they are foes,
Say tis infirmity that doth provoke,
Their hearts are sorry for their tongues, God knows:
    Since we by proof each day and hour find,
    For one harsh word, they give ten thousand kind.

The seventh duty that she must endeavour,
Is to observe her husband's disposition,
And thereunto conform herself for ever;
In all obedient sort, with meek submission:
    Resolving that, as his conditions are,
    Her rules of life she must according square.

His virtues and good parts which she doth find,
She must endeavour for to imitate,
The vices whereunto he is enclin'd,
She must in patience bear in mild estate:
    So that the meekness of her loving carriage,
    May be peace-maker of all strife in marriage.

She must not do as foolish women use,
When they are met about the gossip's chat,
Their absent husbands with their tongues abuse,
But utterly abhor to offer that:
    Resolving that a husband's least disgrace,
    Should cause the wife to have a blushing face.

The eighth last duty she must take upon her,
To bind all t'other seven to be done,
Is love and chief regard to husband's honour,
Which if at true affection it begun,
    Then be he poor or sick, or in distress,
    She still remains most firm in faithfulness.

3 The perfect wife, Switzerland 1586

Visual illustrations as well as written texts depicted perfect wives in early modern Europe. This is a woodcut from the first book ever published in Europe devoted solely to women's dress, *Im Frauwenzimmer Wirt vermeldt von allerley schönen Kleidungen und Trachten der Weiber*, published in 1586. The woodcuts for the book were made by the Swiss artist Jost Amman, and the accompanying verse written by Konrad Lautenbach, a Protestant pastor, translator and poet.
(Translated by Merry Wiesner-Hanks.)

A woman of Basel

In Basel the wives
All have healthy and vigorous bodies,
And are naturally pretty and attractive.
They dress appropriately
Without unnecessary pomp,

But maintain honorable dress,
They are friendly, happy, and brave,
And let God care for them.

Ein Fraw von Basel.

ZV Basel haben die Wyber
Gesunde vnd starcke Lyber/
Sind auch von Natur hübsch vnd schon/
Mit Kleidern zimlich angethon/

Ohn allen vnnötigen Pracht/
Sonder halten ein erbar Tracht/
Sind freundlich/frölich vnd Mannlich/
Vnd lassen Gott sorgen für sich.

4 The perfect wife, Ottoman Empire late sixteenth century

Muslim women in eastern and southern Europe were generally expected to appear veiled when in public. This is an illustration of a Turkish woman, also found in a costume book, in this case Cesare Vecellio's *Habiti Antichi*, published in 1598. Vecellio's description accompanying the illustration read: 'All Turkish women wear long gowns like those of men, and without veils or head scarves. The humble women wear a small hat on their head made of velvet or some other fabric, to which they attach a little square of veil that reaches to their mouths and covers nearly the whole face, so that they can see but are not seen. [Their gown] is closed to the waist with buttons, and they never reveal themselves to anyone when they are outside their home. They wear little boots like those of men. Underneath they wear trousers made of delicate silk. When they go out, they are never bothered by [improper] words or deeds.'

380

5 Advice on choosing a wife for artisans, Germany 1745

Much advice on choosing a wife was very general, but occasionally authors recognized that husbands from different social classes needed different skills in the women they married. The following advice comes from the German economic and social reformer Georg Heinrich Zincke, and appeared in his general guide to crafts and manufacturing.
(Georg Heinrich Zincke, *Teutsches Real=Manufactur=und Handwercks=Lexicon* (Leipzig, 1745), p. 773. Translated by Merry Wiesner-Hanks.)

A wife is a married female person, also called a housewife. Artisans' wives have much in common with other wives from the lower and middle classes, but also much that is distinctive. In terms of the former, all housewives have certain distinct rights, duties, and functions in view of their husbands, children – especially their daughters – and their servants – especially the female ones – and also in terms of economic matters – especially the oversight and operation of the kitchen, cellar and the whole house in terms of the maintenance, cleaning, and preparation of clothing, linens, brewing, baking, washing, sewing, weaving, and other tasks with wool and flax, yes, everything in terms of the cleaning of the house and the maintenance of the household goods. Their functions are not primarily earning a livelihood, but preserving, maintaining, and paying attention to this income, and finally advantageous, thrifty, careful, and intelligent use and spending. A woman who is talented in this, and who has the required qualities of body and soul, along with various other feminine virtues such as fear of God, chastity, friendliness, docility, industriousness without stinginess, measuredness, patience, modesty, and cleanliness, is a major treasure for her husband – especially for an artisan or factory worker – even if she is not exactly pretty, rich, or elegant, as long as she does not have a loathsome face, an unhealthy body, or a social position that is too dissimilar. . . . The wives of artisans in particular must also help in the shop or craft of their husband, either by working alongside of him or learning how to sell his goods properly. They must therefore be quick learners, somewhat talkative, smart, and witty, have learned something about figuring and writing, be able to handle themselves with all types of people with modesty, honesty, and humility, and know how to accommodate themselves to others. Such a wife can help an artisan prosper, while another would destroy him.

6 Letter describing considerations in choosing a wife, Wales 1604

Along with advice in books, people received advice on marriage from their friends, family, and acquaintances. This included advice on specific marriage partners, or on marriage in general. The following is a letter from John Wynn, a member of the Welsh gentry, to his servant William Lloyd in London. Wynn is responding to Lloyd's report that his son John Wynn junior had begun courting a Miss Fletcher, and asks him to investigate her family. He begins with the qualities of the prospective wife's father (the 'he' in this selection) and only then suggests that Lloyd find out about the woman herself. Wynne shows an interesting awareness of heredity, too, in his desire to know about prospect's siblings.

(N.L.W., MS 9052E, f. 27, June 7, 1604. John Wynn at Gwydir to his servant William Lloyd in London. Excerpted by Katharine Swett.)

Many things are to be considered before I determine a match there, which you are to hearken out and to Resolve me of. first, a man of what life and conversation [i.e., the way one deals with others] he and his family are of, and of what birth and present living and what future hope there is of his preferment and how esteemed in his country [i.e., home area], what is his credit with the king and upon what friends and faction doth and hath depended. What you can learn of the young woman and of her nature and whether she have been bred cockney like or after the country manner, what children he hath besides and of what towardness [i.e., inclination] . . . in this dependeth the good happ [i.e., fortune] of my estate. especially in discerning and learning the nature and condition of the woman.

ENGAGEMENT NEGOTIATIONS

7 Letter from a young woman to her suitor, Wales 1605

Early modern matchmaking often began discreetly, with friends and relatives inquiring about possible partners and their families. Once it had reached a certain stage, however, it became more public, and the prospective spouses themselves might begin to participate. Most of the sources about engagement negotiations came from the men involved, and the young women usually appear to be silent and passive participants in the matchmaking process. This letter is thus unusual, in that it documents a young gentlewoman's actual response – well-educated and skeptical with a touch of wit – to a suitor. It was written by Bridget Grey, a young gentlewoman, to John Wynn, the young man whose romantic interest in another young woman was mentioned in Source 6. No marriage resulted in this case, for the Wynns heard through friends that Bridget's 'mind was not for Wales', that is, that she did not want to move to Wales. The following year John married Margaret Cave, but the spouses did not get along well. In 1612 he took off for a belated Grand Tour of the continent, which doubled as an unofficial separation from his wife, and he died of an illness in Lucca, Italy, in 1614.

(N.L.W., MS 9052E, f. 52, n.d., but probably January 1605. Bridget Grey, to John Wynn, a suitor. Transcribed by Katharine Swett.)

Sir, if women should value men's affections by their words then wooing and speeding might still go together. for mine own part as I have no cause to distrust the sincerity of your protestation so have I as little reason to be too credulous knowing that the children of wisdom are slow of belief. if I have been provident in propounding doubts it is because love is by nature blind and often times apprehendeth false objects especially when she meets with such as love with their eyes but not with their minds, in whose number though I cannot justly rank yourself yet may you err in your affections as well as other men. but because my pen is not powerful enough to discover such errors it shall give an end to these scribbled lines which may suffice to witness that the writer doth rest, a friend to her friends, Bridget Grey.

8 Letters from a son to his father regarding the son's marriage, Wales 1615

A variety of things needed to be balanced when choosing a spouse: family connections, the wealth of both partners, personal qualities. At times these decisions set parents against their children, but often all parties were motivated more by pragmatic concerns than romantic love. The following is a series of letters from young Sir Richard Wynn (the younger brother of the John Wynn of the last two sources, who had died in 1614 leaving Richard as his father's heir) to his father Sir John regarding the arrangement of Sir Richard's match during a crucial period in 1615. Richard is very articulate in negotiating, bargaining with his father for some autonomy in the choice and using every hint, every moral flourish, subtle reproach and threat ('if I do marry') possible to influence Sir John, while claiming total filial obedience. Richard makes it very clear, however, that all he absolutely must have is veto power, for his inheritance as heir is more important to him than the choice of a wife and he is not about to do anything that would threaten this. His father is apparently concerned most about the bride's dowry and grandsons. Sir John and Richard finally do agree on a good match, to Anne, daughter of Sir Francis Darcy, a fellow courtier. but not until 1618.

(N.L.W., 9055E, f. 118, May 13, 1615. Richard Wynn at Northampton House to Sir John Wynn at Gwydir. Excerpted by Katharine Swett.)

I pray god it may be my fortune (if I do marry) to light of one whose conditions (qualities) may so well please, as hers did. I pray you assure yourself I have a free man, and that there is no face nor no fortune can engage me (past recalling) without your consent, yet I must ingeniously confess that if I had free liberty to choose, I had rather take her with much less money than any other I know, and especially when I think of my brother's unfortunate match , , , there is nothing that may concern me but that I will deal freely with you in it, and I wish no longer to live, then to be directed by you in this or in anything that may be for my good.

(N.L.W., 9055E, f. 123, July 1, 1615. Richard to Sir John.)

I understood you by your first letters that it was not merely money that you stood upon, but such a one as had a convenient fortune and conditions that might best fit the country she was to live in, but now since I see it is otherwise, I pray you give me leave to find out such a one as shall both please you for portion and me for condition, for I find (by too late an example) the misery of not considering what the woman was, as well as her estate. give me time to please myself and upon my credit what I do shall likewise please your expectation.

(N.L.W., 9055E, f. 124, August 22, 1615. Richard to Sir John again.)

it is a common report here [London] (& especially amongst our country-men) & other great ones (who have questioned me about it) that you would sell me in the market, for who gave most, and have been in hand with divers chapmen [peddlers]. this I believe not (though I can hardly satisfy others) but there is nothing I can hear nor nothing that can be done to me that shall make me forget the duty I owe you . . . I have not as yet since the last motion [matchmaking attempt] broke off, seen any in that kind because I would not bring myself upon the stage for a common suitor, but the next business . . . that I will be seen in, shall have a great deal of probability, both of pleasing you and myself.

9 Letter from a son to his mother regarding his marriage, Wales 1654

Mothers as well as fathers were often involved in finding appropriate spouses for their children, or in negotiating between fathers and children who disagreed. In this letter to his mother, Richard Wynn (the nephew of the men in the previous sources and an only child) uses the ultimate threat – that he will not marry at all – in order to get his father to relent over the size of the dowry a prospective wife would have to bring. He was more forceful about the match he wanted than his uncles had been earlier in the century, and this marriage did take place. When his wife Sarah died in 1671, Richard did not remarry even though they had no son, which was unusual for wealthy heirs.
(N.L.W., 9064E, f. 96, April 25, 1654. Richard Wynn from Chirk, where he was courting Sarah Myddelton, to his mother Lady Wynn at Gwydir. Excerpted by Katharine Swett.)

Dear Mother, I have received your letter. I am worried to receive such a check [warning] from you for I am sure whatever the words of my letter might be the meaning of the writer was far different from what you con-ceived it to be. Truly Madam I need not be informed of my condition by any, for I am sensible enough of it; insomuch that if this match should break off (which is a thing I thank God I do not now at all fear) I am resolved to tie myself for my lifetime to a single life that my father need not put out any more great jointures for me. That you would be pleased to pardon the errors of this letter as well as of the last is the humble and earnest desire of your most dutiful son Richard Wynn.

10 Letter from a noblewoman regarding the marriage of a younger friend, Denmark 1572

Particularly for young people whose parents had died, friends often provided the most important matchmaking activities. The following letter is from Anna, Electress of Saxony (1532–1585) to Birgitte Gøje (1511–1574). Anna was the sister of the Danish King Frederik II (ruled 1559–1588), and after her marriage and move to Saxony in Germany she remained in close contact with a number of Danish noblewomen, among whom were Birgitte Gøje and Anne Hardenberg. The letter reveals the marriage plans for Anne Hardenberg that Electress Anna and Birgitte Gøje were engaged in. Their efforts can be interpreted as an expression of care for Anne Hardenberg as well as a desire to prevent contact between her and King Frederik II, who had been in love with Anne earlier, but only the day before this letter was written (20 July 1572), married Sophie, Princess of Mecklenburg (1557–1631). Regardless of the motives, the letter indicates that, apparently, the most efficient way of securing a new protector for Anne Hardenberg was through marriage. The plans succeeded and on 11 January 1573 Anne Hardenberg married the prominent and wealthy nobleman Oluf Mouritzen Krognos (1535–1573), who already in 1558 had asked for her hand. However, only six months later Krognos died and Anne Hardenberg inherited his vast estate, which she managed until her death in 1589.

(In 1893, a copy of the letter was in the Hauptstaatsarchiv, Dresden, which perished in World War II. It has been published in *Breve til og fra Herluf Trolle og Birgitte Gøje*, ed. G.L. Wad (Copenhagen, 1893). Translated by Grethe Jacobsen and Pernille Arenfeldt.)

To Birgitte Trolle, born Gøje.
Anna.

Our gracious will [with you] as always. Honorable, dear and distinguished [Birgitte]. We do not wish to hide from you that upon our arrival we confidentially discussed the marriage in question with George Rosenkrantz and [we] understood from him this much[:] not only would he himself like to see this marriage, but [we can] also rely on his trustful advice and further help. Even though the other friends are not quite inclined towards it, we have no doubt [it will be accepted] when you and George Rosenkrantz advise the person it concerns [i.e. Anna Hardenburg] and diligently persist. He will also continue to [pursue the matter with] other friends and thus it will be possible to realize this business. Therefore, we graciously wish that you politely inform the person concerned if it has not already happened and, according to our will, accompany this young lady here to Copenhagen next Thursday, and employ all your diligence so that this marriage can progress and be consummated as soon as possible. When this has been accomplished my wishes will be fulfilled and you and yours will with my grace remain unforgotten.

Given in Copenhagen 21 July Anno etc. 72.

11 Court decision breaking off an engagement, Ottoman Empire 1541

Getting from courtship to engagement to marriage was not always easy in early modern Europe. The following case from the local court records in sixteenth-century Aintab, a city in southeastern Anatolia near the Euphrates River, concerns an engagement that has gone awry among Armenian Christian residents of the city. Whether Vanis, the erstwhile groom-to-be, is really dragging his feet or whether the father of Harim, the intended bride, is looking for an excuse to end the engagement is not clear. In any event, Vanis is able to recover the gold objects he has given as preliminary dower, the groom's gift to the bride at a wedding. As with the Muslims of the community, it was customary for fathers to negotiate the marriage of their daughters, although the dower legally belonged to the bride herself.

(National Library, Ankara, Gaziantep Siciii 2, f. 9Ib. Translated by Leslie Peirce.)

The dispute between Bedir son of Ghazal and Vanis son of Yakub

The aforementioned [Bedir] came to the court and summoned Vanis. [Bedir] said, 'I gave my daughter Harim to be engaged to this Vanis. But now he makes no move to marry her. Let him get out of my daughter's way.' When the aforementioned Vanis was questioned, he said, '[Bedir] granted a three-month grace period. He agreed that if I did not come and marry his daughter during the three months, he would not bring a suit against me. He owes me a gold [ring] and a pair of bracelets and a gold florin, so let him return these items.' Bedir agreed to give back the said items. The foregoing was recorded at the request of both parties. Dated July 12, 1541.

12 Court case involving stalled engagement negotiations, Ottoman Empire 1540

Though the young women concerned rarely appear as active agents in most marriage negotiations, sometimes they are able to support or block arrangements. In the following double case concerning stalled engagement negotiations, also from the court of Aintab, Fatma, a young peasant woman, has been able to hold up marriage arrangements involving several members of her extended family. In so doing, she has repeatedly defied local and regional government authorities, whose motivation in trying to get the dispute resolved probably stems from fear that it might erupt into a local blood feud; this is suggested by the extraordinary number of witnesses, including distinguished local office-holders, who appended their names to the record of this case. At last, Fatma's paternal uncle Yakub agrees to her conditions, a family package deal that includes the betrothal of her brothers to Yakub's daughters. Why is it this young woman who appears to be the arbitor of the situation and not one of her brothers? Most likely because of the Islamic legal principle that a woman cannot be given or taken in marriage without her express consent (young men did not enjoy similar legal protection under Islamic law). Consent of both spouses was required, at least in theory, in Christian and Jewish marriages throughout Europe as well, and there are similar court cases – though not many – from other parts of Europe. Ottoman marriage patterns were distinctive in that first-cousin marriage was a common practice, in rural areas, primarily to property within the family; Christian marriage law forbade such consanguinous marriages, though the allowable level of consanguinity varied. The dowers awarded the women in the case below were twice the average amount for Aintab in these years.

(National Library, Ankara, Gaziantep Siciii 161, f. 153a, b. Translated by Leslie Peirce.)

The female named Fatma daughter of Yusuf, from the village of Arablar, has had severe dispute with her paternal uncle's son Hüseyin son of Yakub and with her maternal uncle's son Ömer. Many times [the court] has received orders and agents from the governor-general [ordering it to settle the affair]. At long last, Fatma has been summoned to the court with the cognizance of the agent Sinan. In the presence of the aforementioned girl's paternal uncle Yakub and her maternal uncle Ahmed, she made the following statement: 'If my paternal uncle Yakub will marry his two daughters to my two brothers, I for my part will give my consent to marry his son Hüseyin. Otherwise, I won't marry anyone from either side.' Her statement was recorded at the request of Yakub.

In the matter of the marriage of the girls mentioned in the previous record, Yakub gave his daughter Mihri to his brother's son Musa with an assigned dower of 1,600 silver coins and his daughter named Tursun to Musa's brother Mustafa, likewise with a dower of 1,600 silver coins. In order for Musa's sister Fatma to be married to Yakub's son Hüseyin, a dower of 1,600 silver coins was likewise assigned. The foregoing was recorded with the consent and request of both sides. Dated December 16, 1540.

13 Request to break off an engagement, Spain 1683

During the early modern period, engagements (promises to marry in the future) were seen as legal commitments to marry. Once such a promise had been made, a legal agreement was required to end the relationship and allow each person to marry another. In this document, the relationship between Gregorio and María had been damaged by unfounded rumors of sexual intercourse, and they decided to end their engagement.

(Carta de Apartamiento, Archivo Histórico Universitario de Santiago de Compostela, protocob, 1673, nf (1683). Translated by Allyson Poska.)

Gregorio Fernández and María do Seyja, unmarried . . . they said that in as much as the said María do Seyja has gotten a bad reputation as it has been said and supposed that she had had sexual intercourse with the said Gregorio Fernández the younger, and that being contrary to the truth because the aforementioned has always lived and lives honestly and reclusively as is known and notorious . . . she separated and separates herself from the said Gregorio . . . and asks the judge . . . not to pursue a case against the said Gregorio Fernández nor his goods as he is innocent and without fault for what is rumored and said vulgarly.

MARRIAGE CONTRACTS AND AGREEMENTS

14 Marriage contract, Iceland 1423

Once engagement negotiations had been finalized, people in many parts of Europe made formal contracts detailing the economic arrangements surrounding the marriage. This was particularly important for wealthy families, but even quite ordinary people regarded a marriage contract as a sound decision. The following is a marriage contract between two powerful Icelandic families of the fifteenth century, and, like many such contracts from all parts of Europe, is primarily concerned with property. Though Iceland was Christian, church concerns enter in only in the opening words 'In dei nomine amen', and in the fact that the marriage had been *lýst*, that is to say, proclaimed publicly in the Church. (This ceremony, called 'reading the banns', was conducted on the three Sundays before the wedding, and was common in much of Christian Europe; it was retained in Protestant areas after the Reformation.) Note the role played by the bride's mother in this arrangement, particularly in securing joint possession of property for the spouses; separate possession (in which each spouse retains ownership of his or her own goods and property) had earlier been common in Iceland and other parts of northern Europe.

(The actual document exists in a handwritten copy from the year 1486, and was to be found in the belongings of a woman called Gudrun Eggertsdóttir, who lived at the farm Bær in Rauðasandur; a printed version is in *DI: Diplomatarium Islandicum. Islenzkt fornbréfasafn*, vol. IV, p. 312. Translated from the Icelandic by Agnes S. Arnórsdóttir.)

In dei nomine amen.

On the wedding day on the farm Vatnsfjörður was this marriage settlement contract published, proclaimed [*lýstur*] and confirmed, by Guðmundur Arason and Helga Þorleifsdóttir. . . . Gudmundur gave twelve *hundruð hundraða* [a money of account, worth about six cows per *hundruð hundraða*] to the settlement with Helga. Her father Þorleifur Árnason gave against this his daughter the landed property of Bær á Rauðasandur to the settlements with Guðmundur for one *hundruð hundraða* as well as one *hundruð hundraða* in other landed property and one *hundruð hundraða* in moveables.

Guðmundur gave Helga a gift of one fourth *fjórðungsgjöf* [a gift that was one fourth of his property] from his twelfth *hundruð hundraða* that he had for doing this settlement with her. Kristín Björnsdóttir decided that her daughter Helga should have joint ownership of Guðmundur's property, considering their wealth and what wealth they would eventually gather in the future. Kristín did this with the consent of Guðmundur and Rafn Guðmundsson, his father's brothers that were his closest relatives on his side. Helga should also own in addition to this 40 *hundruð* other useful tools that Guðmundur had given her as *bekkjargjöf* [a gift from the husband to the wife].

Those were the witnesses of the wedding: Loptur Guttormsson, Rafn Guðmundsson, Audunn Salamonsson, Arni Einarsson, Gamli Marteinsson, Gunnar Andrésson and Helgi Guttormsson.

And to proof this did we those above mentioned men put our seals on this letter, written on the same place, on the same year, two nights later than this did happen.

15 Marriage agreement, Russia 1665

In pre-modern Russia, marriages among the landed elite were arranged by families to promote economic and political agendas. Well-dowered brides were in great demand, and bridegrooms and their families counted on the wealth brides brought with them. In contrast to marriage contracts which list what both spouses will bring to the marriage, Russian nuptial agreements listed in detail only what valuables the bride would bring with her into the marriage. In doing so, the document simultaneously guaranteed the groom's family against fraud, and enumerated the bride's possessions to be returned to her family in case of her death.

(Published original Istoricheskie i iuridicheskie akty XVII–XVIII stoletii in *Chteniia obshchestva istorii i drevnostei rossiiskikh pri Moskovskom universitete*, bk. 4 (Moscow, 1869) pp. 59–60. Translated by Eve Levin.)

I, the widow Uliana, Boris's daughter, wife of Boris Fedorovich Puzinov, along with my children Mikhailo and Mikita . . . give my daughter and our sister by birth, the maiden Fedora Borisovna, in marriage to Mikita Demidovich Kireevskii. By God's mercy, I, the widow Uliana grant my daughter, and we, Mikhailo and Mikita, grant our sister Fedora: an icon of the Most Merciful Savior; an icon of the Most Holy Mother of God of Kazan, with a silver cover; an icon of the Most Pure Mother of God of Tenderness [These are copies of famous miracle-working icons of the sixteenth and seventeenth centuries]; an icon of the blessing of Princess Anna [Princess Anna of Kashin was newly canonized and was especially popular among residents of the locality], with a silver cover; and a chain with a cross. Also the dowry clothes: a cap sewn with gold, a green silk cap, two pearl women's necklaces; earrings with pearls; a caftan of crimson; buttons oversewn with silver embroidery; a yellow summer robe; a coat of red brocade; an expensive green coat; two fur coats, one of warm fox and one warm stole of squirrel; a caftan of calico. The entire dowry is worth eighty rubles. Also the maiden Klavda, daughter of the Lithuanian captive Mark Tikhanov. Also our hereditary estate, the village of Shchepunova in Kashin district apportioned to our peasants: Kondrashko Sergeev with his wife and children, with his peasant property, and with his stepson Ganka and Ganka's wife and property. In addition to the dowry clothes, he, Mikita, will take from us according to this agreement eighty rubles in money. And if I, the widow Uliana for my daughter, or my children Mikhailo and Mikita for their sister, do not give to him, Mikita Kireevskii, the dowry and those estate peasants . . . he shall take from us, the widow Uliana and Mikhailo and Mikita, three hundred rubles in cash . . . March 11, 1665.

16 Marriage contract, France 1546

Marriage contracts in France, as in most of Europe, included both parties specifying their mutual commitments regarding possessions, often in front of witnesses. What makes French contracts, particularly those from northern France, unusual is the absence of dowry arrangements in many cases, and prevalence of arrangements for the widow's dower. The dowry consisted of the goods and money the bride brought to the marriage, and dowry was very common further to the south in Europe, especially in Italy. In Paris, while a contract might or might not mention goods or money that constituted a dowry, by legal custom and common practice the bride as a possible future widow received a promise of a dower, a pre-set or customary amount that would be hers if her husband died before she did. Such an arrangement was also common in parts of England and Germany. In this brief document, two people acting on their own behalf record their intentions to marry, and arrange for the future of the woman if her future husband should die before she does. Although the woman's father is alive, he lives in another part of France, and so she acts on her own, though with his consent. (Paris, Archives Nationales, Minutier central, Étude XI/26, May 16, 1546. Translated by Carol Loats.)

[Were present] the honorable Jehan de la Place, merchant butcher, *bourgeois* of Paris, living at the butchery Saint Geneviefve, in his own name, on the one hand, and Jehanne Picquevel, daughter of Michel Picquevel, farm worker, living in Chavline en Brye, also in her own name, on the other hand. [The parties] willingly, etc., in the presence of Jehan Brenant, merchant living at Saint Marcel in Paris, cousin by his wife of the said Jehanne Picquevel, and with the will and consent of the said Michel Picquevel, father of Jehanne, and other kin and friends of the said Jehanne Picquevel, they say, will affirm that they have made, will make, and make, together and one with the other, the contract of marriage, agreements, gifts, and arrangements which follow.

That is to say, the said de la Place has promised and promises by this [contract] to take the said Picquevel as his wife and spouse, and she on her part promises also to take him as her husband and spouse if God and our Mother Holy Church allow, as soon as this can simply be done and is decided between them, their kin, and friends, with the possessions, rights, and material interests that they have on one side or the other.

And therefore and in consideration of this the said de la Place has given and gives to the said Jehanne Picquevel, his said future wife, the sum of 40 *livres tournois* as pre-set dower, to be paid one time this dower to have and take as soon as dower takes place, without holding back, from all and each of the inheritances and possessions of the said de la Place, according to the customs of the city, *prévôté* [provost under the king] and *vicomté* [larger regional government] of Paris.

Because thus, etc., promising, obligating, each in his own right, etc., renouncing, etc. Done and passed in duplicate in the year 1546, Sunday, the 16th day of May.

17 Marriage contract, France 1555

Many marriage contracts recorded more complex arrangements than those in the previous source. In the following document, the future bride was present and consenting to the contract, but her father was there in her name and acting for her. The practice of a common trade linked the future husband and the father of the bride-to-be, a situation addressed in the contract. The younger man was not yet a master, at a time when it was often difficult to make the step from compagnon, or skilled wage worker, to master and shop owner. In theory a person became a master (*maître*) in a trade after serving several years of apprenticeship, working for several more years for wages as a skilled compagnon, and then meeting certain requirements of mastership, such as completing an expensive masterpiece which reflected competence in the trade, and paying certain fees. This document is also interesting in the list of possessions which the woman would bring to the marriage, in contrast to the previous one which lacked such a list.
(Paris, Archives Nationales, Minutier central, Étude XI/15, August 10, 1555. Translated by Carol Loats.)

Were present in person Jehan Thomyn, master cobbler [shoe-repairer], living in Paris at Mont Saint Yllaire, in the name of and stipulating for Claude Thomyn, his daughter, present and with her willingness and consent, on the one hand; and Jehan Carbonnyer, *compagnon* cobbler, living in Paris, present and in his own name, on the other hand.

The parties willingly, etc., they say, witness and affirm that they have made, will make, and make together, in good faith, the arrangements about

91

the contracts, agreements, dower, promises, obligations, and arrangements which follow.

[They do this] in the presence of Florant Carbonnier, brother of the said Jehan Carbonnier; Loys de Lespine, first cousin of the said Jehan Carbonnier; Jehan le Manot, also cousin of Jehan Carbonnier; and Laurence Thomyn, son of the said Jehan Thomyn.

That is to say, Jehan Carbonnier has promised to take as his wife and spouse the said Claude Thomyn, who on her part promises to take him as her husband and spouse, if God and our Mother Holy Church allow, as soon as they can and it is [decided] among them and their kin and friends.

[They each promise to marry] with all the reputations, possessions, rights, and material interests that they have and could have on either part, to bring together to be theirs jointly.

In consideration of this future marriage and to arrive at it the said Jehan Thomyn, [the] father, promises to the said Jehan Carbonnier, the future spouse, to have him pass into mastership in the said trade of cobbler in this city of Paris at the expense of the said Jehan Thomyn, as soon as [Thomyn] is able to do it.

And with this, to give and deliver a bed of oak wood stacked up, a bed bolster stuffed with feathers, a cover, a white canopy of hemp cloth trimmed with its paints and fringes, a table fitted with two trestles, a form, a chest with a lock, all of oak; six sheets of hemp cloth; two tablecloths, twelve table napkins, all of hemp cloth, a gown of new wool cloth . . . along with all the clothing the said Claude, as a daughter, has at present in use; and this to do on the day of their wedding and before it.

And therefore and in consideration of this, the said Jehan Carbonnier has given and gives the said Claude Thomyn, his future wife, the sum of twenty *livres tournois*, to be paid once, and she will be able to take by priority right all her clothing that she then has for her use, without it being part of the inventory, as soon as the dower takes place.

Thus promising, etc., obligating, each, etc.. Done the year 1555, Saturday, the 10th day of August.

18 Marriage contract made by a woman, France 1541

Even a woman whose father was alive and living near her might sometimes act on her own behalf in making a marriage contract in many parts of Europe. In the following document, though the father is present and assents to the arrangements, he is not a party to the contract. Instead, the bride-to-be, alleging that she is at least 25, contracts for herself.
(Paris, Archives Nationales, Minutier central, Étude XIX/160, May 9, 1541. Translated by Carol Loats.)

Were present in person Claude Dubray, merchant in furs living in Paris, for himself in his own name, on the one hand, and Magdelaine Roland, aged 25 years or so, she says, daughter of Jehan Roland, also living in Paris, on the other hand.

The parties willingly, etc., acknowledge and affirm that, with the will and consent of the said Jehan Raouland, father of the said Magdeleine, present here, they have promised and promise to each take the other according to the name and law of marriage, with all the appropriate rights that belong to them, as soon as they are able to do it simply and God and the Holy Church allow.

And therefore the said Claude Dubray has given and gives the said Magdeleine Roleand, his future spouse, the sum of 50 *livres tournois* for her dower right and to pay once, for her to have and take beyond her rights of joint property as soon as the dower takes place, from all his belongings and those that belong to his heirs due to his death. The dower will not in any way be subject to return, and will remain with and belongs to her and those of her own lineage.

And further, the said Dubray has wished and wishes that, if he departs from this life before his said future spouse without a surviving child or children of the two of them, she will have and take, by first right and before any division [of the estate] is done, all her clothing, rings, and jewels that she has in use.

Promising, etc., obligating each in his own right, etc., renouncing, etc. Done and passed in duplicate, in the year 1541, Monday, the 9th day of May.

19 Marriage contract for a second marriage, France 1540

Second and even third marriages were also formalized before notaries. Although widows could legally act on their own behalf, some widows were represented by their fathers as the marriage contract was formalized. The arrangements made in these cases sometimes reflect the previous marriage. In addition to these factors, the following marriage contract also brings the bride's future inheritance into the current marriage arrangements.
(Paris, Archives Nationales, Minutier central, Étude XIX/155, June 12, 1540. Translated by Carol Loats.)

Present in person were Blanchet Moreau, *hacquebutier* [maker of a particular sort of early firearm], living in Paris, in the name of and stipulating in this [matter] for Anne Moreau, his daughter, widow of the late Jehan Gibert, who while living was also a *hacquebutier*, on the one hand; and Alexandre Loiseau, similarly *hacquebutier*, living in Paris, for himself in his own name, on the other hand.

The parties, because of the marriage which, to the pleasure of God, will be made and solemnized in front of the Holy Church between the said

Loiseau and Anne Moreau, acknowledge and affirm that they have made and make between them the contracts, agreements, dower, promises, and arrangements which follow.

That is to say, the said Blanchet Moreau has promised and promises to give the said Anne, his daughter, according to the name and law of marriage, to the said Loiseau, who has promised and promises to take her as his wife and spouse tomorrow, if God and Holy Church allow, free and clear of all debts whatsoever.

In consideration of [this] marriage the said Blanchet has promised and promises in the said name to give and pay to the said future couple, without the least advance, the sum of 20 *livres tournois* in cash, with the personal property which follows.

That is to say, a bed [frame] of wood, a bed and bolster stuffed with feathers, a white canopy, a cover of red linen, six sheets of hemp cloth, six tablecloths, a dozen table napkins, a locking oak chest, a table, two trestles, a sideboard on a lockable counter, which property the parties estimate among themselves at a value of 15 *livres tournois*, which brings the value, including the cash, to the sum of 35 *livres tournois*.

[This sum] the said future couple will be obliged to postpone by half, as coming to them by inheritance from the said Blanchet Moreau and from Moudette Louprat, his wife, father and mother of the said Anne.

And the said Blanchet further pledges to give and pay to the said future couple the sum of 10 *livres tournois* payment and wages to their said daughter for serving her said father and mother since the death of her said dead husband up to now.

The said Loiseau affirms that he has received from the said Blanchet three *livres* 10 *sous tournois* toward the two sums in cash, with which he is satisfied and [which he] considers Blanchet to have paid, saying that he can release and releases the said Blanchet of obligation for the cash that [Blanchet] has received for [Blanchet's] daughter as her customary dower ... and has renounced and relieves the heirs of the said Gibert, her first husband, of obligation, and [releases Blanchet of obligation for] all other things which ... [have come to] his said daughter for whatever cause there might be, from the past up to today.

And therefore the said Alexander Loiseau has given and gives the said Anne Moreau, his future spouse, the sum of 30 *livres tournois* in cash, to pay once as pre-set dower and without return, for all right to dower, if there is a surviving child or children of theirs at the time of the dissolution of their said marriage, for her to have and take as soon as dower takes place, and beyond her rights of common property, from all the belongings which belong to the heirs of the said Loiseau at his death ...

And further the said Loiseau has willed and wills that if he dies before his future spouse without a surviving child or children of the two of them from legal marriage as is said, that she have and take by priority right and before any dividing up with the heirs, all her clothing, rings, and jewelry she has in use at that time.

Thus has the content above been received [by the notaries], passed and agreed between the said parties. Promising, etc., obligating, each in his own right, etc., renouncing. Done and passed in duplicate, in the year 1540, Saturday, the 12th day of June.

20 Marriage contract made by a widow, France 1555

In contrast to the above contract, in this next one a widow acts on her own behalf, as she was legally allowed to do. She brings goods and money to the marriage, and the document arranges the future responsibility for any debts of the two parties, contracted prior to the marriage.
(Paris, Archives Nationales, Minutier central, Étude III/236, October 13, 1555. Translated by Carol Loats.)

Present were Jehan Languais, merchant master carpenter in Paris, for himself on the one hand, and Claude Hucher, widow of the late Robin des Jobartz, who while living was a master embroiderer in Paris, also for herself, on the other hand.

[The] parties each willingly, etc., acknowledge and affirm that they have made and make the contract, agreements, dower, and other arrangements which follow, due to the marriage which, to the pleasure of God, will soon be made and solemnized between Languais and Claude Hucher.

That is to say, the said Languais and Claude have each promised and promise to take the other according to the name and law of marriage as soon as they can, if God and Holy church allow, to bring their possessions together according to the custom of the city of Paris.

On behalf of this marriage and to arrive at it, the said Hucher has promised and promises to bring to the said community of goods, by the day preceding their wedding, the sum of 300 *livres tournois* to be paid once in cash and in her clothing and jewelry at the value of 100 *livres tournois*, together with 13 *livres* 11 *sous* three *deniers tournois* of [regular] income that belongs to her from several sources, without the said Languais being obliged to pay any of her debts contracted before today. Also the said Hucher will not be obliged for debts of Languais contracted prior to the said future marriage.

Therefore the said Languais has given and gives the said Hucher, his future spouse, the sum of 60 *livres tournois* to be paid once as pre-set dower, which will not be subject to return, if she survives the said Languais without children of the said future marriage, on the day of the dissolution of the marriage, or customary dower, at the choice and selection of the said Hucher; whichever one of these forms of dower she chooses, she will have and take as soon as dower takes place. And she will have and take, as soon as dower takes place, and by priority right, before any dividing up [that is, before any other dividing of the inheritance], her clothing, rings, and jewelry that she then has in her use, up to the value of 60 *livres tournois*, to take once, if she survives the said Languais without children, as indicated.

Also it has been agreed that if she dies before the said Languais without children, as indicated, in that case he can take his clothing and jewelry by priority right and before any dividing up, up to the equal value of 60 *livres tournois*.

Thus, etc., promising, etc., obligating each in his own right, etc., re-nouncing, etc.. Done and passed in the year 1555, Sunday, the 13th day of October.

21 Marriage contract made for a servant, France 1554

Sometimes the marriage contract indicates how the bride-to-be was currently earning a living, and formalizes arrangements related to her employment. In the following contract, Jean Gobelin formally contracts for his servant. He acts for a woman whose father has died, and who has been a servant to his mother and himself, while the groom's father also acts on behalf of his son. Most notable is the provision that Gobelin makes for the woman – a large sum of money, essentially a dowry.
(Paris, Archives Nationales, Minutier central, Étude XXXIII/39, April 23, 1554. Translated by Carol Loats.)

Were present in person on the one hand the honorable lord Jehan Gobelin the elder, merchant dyer living at Saint Marcel in Paris, contracting in this matter for Marie Grillet, daughter of the late [blank] Grillet, who while living was *amballeur* [a person who made containers and packed goods for shipping] living in Paris, the said Marie servant and chambermaid of the said Gobelin; and on the other hand Jehan Barreau, *mégissier* [preparer of skins for gloves, parchment, and book bindings] living at the said Saint Marcel, rue de Lourcynes, acting for Guillaume Barreau, also *mégissier*, his son, present and consenting.

The parties willingly, etc., acknowledge and affirm that they had made, will make, and make together, in good faith, the arrangement of marriage, settlements, dower, promises, agreements, and obligations which follow.

That is to say, the said Gobelin has promised and promises to give, according to the law and name of marriage, the said Grillet, his servant, to the said Guillaume Bareau, who, with the will and consent of his father, has promised and promises to take her as his wife and spouse, tomorrow, if God and our Mother Holy Church allow it, and this with the possessions, rights, reputations, and claims whatsoever that the said parties have and might have on one part or the other.

And further, in favor of the said marriage and to arrive at it, the said Gobelin has given and paid to the said future married couple the sum of 138 *livres tournois* that the said Boureau affirms that he has received from the said Gobelin, given, etc., receipted, etc., and this both for the wages and compensation that the said Grillet is able to have earned and deserved in the household of the said Gobelin and the deceased Catherine Langlois, his mother, from previous times up to today, and for the considerable affection that the said Gobelin has for the said Marie Grillet.

And the said Jehan Bourreau on his part pledges to free and release his son of all debts and mortgages whatsoever up to today. And also he has paid to the said Guillaume Barreau, his son, in consideration of this marriage, the sum of 23 *livres tournois* that Guillaume affirms to have received from his said father, given, etc., receipted, etc.

And in consideration of this the said Guillaume Barreau has given and gives to the said Marie, his future spouse, the sum of 50 *livres tournois*, one time, as pre-set dower, that the said Marie may have and take as soon as [dower] takes place, and without hesitation, equally from all the possessions and property of the said Guillaume Barreau, his heirs, etc., or customary dower to have and take according to the customs of the city, *prévôté*, and *vicomté* of Paris, at the choice and selection of the said Marie. And the preset dower, if chosen, will be and remain the property of the said Marie for herself and her [lineage], without being subject to return.

And it has been agreed between the said parties that if the said Guillaume Barreau departs from this life before the said Marie, his future wife, without child or children born to the two of them in legal marriage, in that case she will have and take by priority right and in addition to her said dower, preset or customary, her clothing, rings, and jewels that she has at that time at her disposal, without having to submit them to inventory or division, if that seems advantageous to her.

Thus, etc., promising, obligating, each in his own right, etc., renouncing, etc. Done in duplicate, the year 1554, Monday, 23rd day of April, after Easter.

22 Marriage contract made for a servant, France 1543

Most servants in this time period in Europe lived in the households in which they worked. The marriage of a servant typically resulted in her departure from that job and household. As in the previous contract, in this one, the marrying woman is a

servant, and her current employer, Remy de Halle, acts in the marriage contract on her behalf. Also similar is that de Halle makes a generous gift to the couple, in this case a place for them to live. But the ownership of the residence by de Halle makes it possible that he will continue to employ the bride after her marriage.
(Paris, Archives Nationales, Minutier central, Étude VIII/476, May 29, 1543. Translated by Carol Loats.)

Were present Guillaume Gillebert, bread baker, living in the outskirts of Paris outside the Porte Saint Denis, for himself and in his own name, on the one hand; and the honorable man Remy de Halle, bourgeois of Paris, stipulating in this matter for Jehanne de Bresse, his servant, here present and with her consent, on the other hand.

Gillebert and Jehanne de Bresse, with the authority of her master, have promised and promise to each take the other with all their qualities and possessions whatsoever, according to the name and law of marriage, if God and our mother Holy Church allow, and as soon as they are able to do it and it is decided among them and their kin and friends, etc.

And in consideration of this marriage the said de Halle has given and gives, etc., to the said future couple their residence, for a period from the next feast day of Saint John the Baptist [June 24] for the following four years. [The residence is] in the building where the said Gillebert is at present living, situated in the outskirts of Paris outside the Porte Saint Denis, belonging to the said de Halle, adjoining on one side '*l'hostel de la vetelle*', and on the other side '*l'hostel de l'esper*'. [two buildings well-known to residents] And for their said residence [de Halle] has relinquished to them the room overlooking the rue Venge, the passage looking onto the courtyard, a storehouse, with their ease to come and go through the courtyard, and the stairway in the said courtyard, with the cellar, etc., and oven that are there. . . . [All of this] will be given to them as it pleases the said de Halle to use for the said time period without them having to pay any rent. The said future couple will be obliged to maintain the said living places during the said time . . .

And therefore the said Gillebert has given and gives the said Jehanne de Bresse, his future spouse, the sum of 20 *livres tournois*, to pay one time, as preset dower, or the customary dower, at her choice and selection, to have and take as soon as dower takes place, from all and each of the possessions of the said Gillebert and of his heirs. And the said pre-set dower, if it is chosen, will be and belong to the said Jehanne de Bresse and to [those] of her own lineage without being subject to return, provided that there are no children of this marriage that survive her.

Because thus promising, etc., obligating, each in his own right, etc., renouncing. Done Tuesday the 29th day of May, 1543.

LOVE

23 Love poem, Dalmatia, late fifteenth century

Engagement negotiations and marriage contracts make very little mention of the emotional content of personal relationships, but it is clear from other types of sources that people in early modern Europe developed strong emotional attachments and fell in love. As they are today, their ideas about love were shaped by songs, stories, and poetry, expressed both orally and in written texts. One of these ideas was that of courtly love, which developed in the Middle Ages and shaped romantic conventions for centuries. In the courtly love tradition, the lover (generally male) swears undying loyalty to his beloved (usually female) and vows to do great deeds on her behalf. Courtly love gained a following in eastern Europe, in the commercial cities of Dalmatia on the Adriatic Sea across from Italy. The poet Dzore Drzic (1461–1501) composed a number of love songs depicting the joys and sorrows of romantic liaisons. In this poem, the male speaker describes his female beloved as a 'vila'. The vila is a figure from Slavic folklore, a female spirit that inhabits streams and forests, ensnaring the affections of naive men. Although the folkloric vila ought to be feared as much as loved because of her power and willfulness, Drzic's vila is gentle and flighty. (Translated version published in *Monumenta Serbocroatica*, ed. Thomas Butler (Ann Arbor: Michigan Slavic Publications, 1980), p. 187. Reprinted by permission.)

The vila that rules me and my life
   has caused me great pain by her heavenly beauty.
By her heavenly beauty she has enchanted me so,
   That during this whole century, and later, everyone will pity me.
Everyone will pity me, because I have surrendered my soul,
   To that vila whom I chose to serve.
Whom I chose to serve, thinking I'd be blest,
   and not that I'd suffer, wounded and desolate.
Wounded and desolate, I wither in a sorrow,
   which will be assuaged only when I take my last breath.
Only when I take my last breath will they write above me:
   'I desired to rest, to accept dark death.
To accept dark death, for it was far better
   to depart this world and to have no more unhappiness.
To have no more the unhappiness I felt because of the vila,
   Like a stag in the field, wounded by an arrow.'

24 Merchant's love letter, Italy 1625

Non-literary sources that reveal emotions of love are relatively rare in early modern Europe. The following, a love letter written by an Italian merchant, only survives because in 1625 a working woman named Cristina Collari was brought before the

Venetian Inquisition on charges of heresy. Chief among them was the accusation that she had had carnal knowledge of a Jew, a charge for which the primary evidence was a collection of letters her Jewish lover, a merchant, had written her when he was away from Venice on business.

(Venice, Archivio di Stato di Venezia (ASV), Sant'Uffizio, B. 80, no. 2, document 7 (1625). Translation by Monica Chojnacka.)

My Dearest One,

I have already written to you, my soul, and I sent that letter in the same manner in which you will have this one, and you have not deigned to respond, which surprises me, though I fear that, as they say, far from the eyes means far from the heart; nonetheless I remain patient, and there remains the affection and the love that I have always had and have now, and will continue to have, clinging with heartfelt affection to the vivid memory of many precious embraces with sweet kisses. . . . In all of my good life I swear to you as fervently as I can that in writing you it seems that I am speaking to you, and that from day into night I am near tears, and sigh from my heart. . . . Above all I beg you to write to me and tell me how you are. . . . If it pleases you to give my greetings to your neighbor and her husband do so, but do not show this letter to anyone under any circumstances, and with heartfelt affection I kiss your hands and your sweet precious mouth and pure white breast and other things, O my God, how precious and sweet it is to be with you upstairs in the house, in bed, Thus I will wait for your response, begging you to remember who loves and desires you so greatly.

25 Woodcut of a young woman in love, Germany 1570

Young people in love were frequent subjects of woodcuts and engravings, which served either as illustrations for books and pamphlets or were printed as single sheets and sold by booksellers and peddlers. This is a German single-leaf woodcut by the artist Wolfgang Strauch, with an accompanying poem by the well-known playwright Hans Sachs. A corresponding wood-cut and poem about a young man in love has been lost. (Woodcut from Walter L. Strauss, *The German Single-leaf Woodcut, 1550–1600* (New York: Abaris Books, 1975). Reproduced by permission. Verse translated by Merry Wiesner-Hanks.)

The young woman speaks

My heart is wounded
To the ground
By Cupid
With his love-beam
Oh, I was his love

And was so constant
As he acknowledges
I was inclined to him,
But love's security
Often fails
And brings all kinds of danger
To morality and honor.
So – go away young man,
I won't answer you anymore.
   The young woman continues
In many places
Love often fails
It brings garbage with it
And has troubled me.
Love brings many dangers.
In the beginning love is hot
But it doesn't last long.
Many heroes steal away
After love becomes frozen
And cold
And leave in various ways.
For that reason I won't
Risk the game with you
Because love brings
Much unhappiness.
   The young woman speaks
At the beginning you declared
The power of firm love
And because you complained
I declared my love for you
But not any more.
Such is faithfulness, virtue and honor,
That now you have gone
'My loyal servant',
But you left.
Your uniting love has gone from here.
I will do the same.
I loved you alone
For all time.
In love there is sweetness
As long as God gives me life.

26 The fool and the naked maiden, Germany mid fifteenth century

In the same way that preachers and advisors recommended that people beware of the power of love when making choices about a spouse, illustrations often depicted the ways in which love made one appear foolish, particularly when they were showing young men. This is an engraving by the anonymous artist Master E.S., which was reprinted in many different books during the sixteenth century and so widely seen. Publishers frequently hired engravers to copy the work of others for their own books; they often did not attribute them to the original artist and certainly did not pay them for the permission to reprint their work.

(Original in Kupferstich Kabinett, Dresden. Reprinted by permission.)

WEDDINGS

27 Expenses for a noble wedding, Denmark 1503

Wedding customs varied widely throughout Europe, though in most places by the
sixteenth century they involved some sort of religious ceremony along with family
festivities. These were simple for poor families, but could be enormously elaborate
for the wealthy. Actual records of wedding expenses are quite rare. The following
comes from Oluf Stigsen Krognos, one of the wealthiest noblemen in Denmark, who

in October 1503 or 1504 celebrated the marriage of his oldest surviving daughter, Magdalena, to their neighbour and Magdalena's cousin, Tyge Brahe. The bride was about 15 years old and the groom in his early twenties. The marriage lasted only until 1510 when Magdalena died, leaving one daughter who survived infancy. In his second marriage Tyge became the grandfather of the famous siblings, the astronomer Tyge Brahe (1546–1601) and the scientist Sophie Brahe (1556/59–1643). Oluf Stigsen carefully noted down all the expenses he incurred, probably to make sure that his two other daughters, alive at that time, would in due time enjoy a wedding and dowry equivalent to Magdalena's, as the Danish inheritance laws demanded. The account falls in four parts: (1) Expenses for Magdalena's trousseau, which included the traditional gift of shirts for the groom and his friends as well as the wedding carriage. (2) Beer, wine and other expenses for the food for the 300 guests. (3) The food, prepared by Oluf's own servants. (4) The furnishings that Magdalena brought with her to her new home, as part of her dowry. Prices are given in Danish (mark, shillings) and German money (Rhenish gulden). The measure for cloth was an alen which was 20–23 inches. Only partially included in the accounts is the food (meat, game, fish, vegetables, fruit, and spices) that a wealthy and fully equipped household would ordinarily have supplies of. The editor of the wedding accounts has calculated that the bride's father bought 19,000 litres of beer (=5,016 gallons) and 1,400 litres (=370 gallons) of wine for her wedding guests. Judging from the amount of hay for horses (and assuming each horse brought one guest because the roads were few and very bumpy, so that horseback was the most common means of travel) there were 300 guests. Assuming also that the wedding lasted from Sunday to Thursday – stopping before the normal fast on Friday – that gives 63 litres of beer per guest for the 5 days, or 3.3 gallons of beer per day, along with about 1 litre of wine.

(Printed in *Nationalmuseets Arbejdsmark* (1980), pp. 35–37. Translated by Grethe Jacobsen and Pernille Arenfeldt.)

This following have I Oluff Stigssøn paid for my daughter Magdalena at her wedding

Primo: 8 *alen* golden brocade, 10 Rhenish gulden the yard and a shorter piece for 2½ gulden

Item, 10 *alen* red velvet, 6 mark the yard

Item, 16 *alen* black velvet, 6 mark the yard

Item, two bundles of ermine [about 80 skins] each bundle for 10 mark

Item, 8 *alen* yellow damask 3 mark the yard

Item, 7½ *alen* black velvet, 6 mark the yard that came upon the yellow damask

Item, 10 *alen* green English [cloth] of the best kind. 3 mark the yard less 4 shillings for a pair of clothes [cape and tunic]

Item, 16 mark for the lining that came underneath

Item, 10 *alen* red English [cloth] 3 mark the yard less 4 shillings for a pair of clothes [cape and tunic] 24 mark the lining under the tunic and the cape

Item, 5½ *alen* yellow damask, 3 mark the *alen* that came upon a blue tunic

Item, 6 *alen* for a green tunic, 4 mark less 4 shillings the *alen*

Item, another green tunic came 6 *alen* to, 4 mark less 4 shillings the *alen*

Item, 5 *alen* for a red tunic with ermine, 48 shillings the *alen*

Item, 4 *alen* green London [cloth] for an under tunic, 3 mark 4 shillings the *alen*

Item, 5 *alen* velvet, 4½ mark the *alen*

Item, a gold headband, a chain, a necklace, a brooch which price is obvious

Item, 16 *alen sindal* [a type of cloth], 6 shillings the *alen*

Item, 27 *alen* pearls, besides the pearls in her tunic, the 27 *alen* cost 60 mark, they came upon Magdalena's pearl bonnet and Tyge Brahe's shirt front

Item, [to] Tønnes the pearlstitcher for making the bonnet

Item, [to] Tønnes the Pearlstitcher for making the front of Tyge Brahe's skirt

Item, 32 ounces goldthread, each ounce 3 mark of the 18 ounces, of the 14 ounces each ounce 3 mark less 4 shillings

Item, [to] Tønnes Pearlstitcher 4 shillings for each shirt front of the 15 shirts

Item, 6 ounces pearl thread for her pearl tunic each ounce 30 mark of the 4 ounces. Item of the other 26 mark

Item, 36 mark for the work

Item, 6 *lod* [= 84grams] gilded silver, 3 mark the *lod*

Item, 6 *alen* cloth for the tunic, that the pearls were sewn on, the *alen* 26 shilling

Item, 2 ounces pearl thread for her head-dress, the one ounce 28 mark the other was her mothers

Item, 9 mark for the work

Item, 10 *alen* linen, 2 mark the *alen* for two wedding shirts

Item, 8 shirts, 5 *alen* in each shirt, 18 shillings the *alen*

Item, 6 shirts, 5 *alen* in each shirt, 5 shillings the *alen*

Item, 1½ pound silk for 15 mark

Item, a piece of Leiden cloth for her carriage and for the boy and girl, for 30 mark

Item, 4 *alen* red Leiden cloth, 24 shillings the *alen* for her boy who ran along

Item, 20 mark for her carriage and two sides of pork

Item, the painter 16 mark and 2 sides of pork

Item, the smith 26 mark and 2 sides of pork

Item, the cordwainer [harness maker] 20 mark

Item, the journeymen cordwainers 4 shillings

Item, the journeymen smiths 6 shillings

Item, one mark for bringing the carriage

Item, 9 mark for the buttoms on the carriage

Item, two grey horses for the carriage, they are not appraised

The food for the wedding

Primo, 6 lasts [each 12–18 barrels] of German beer, the last 10 Rhenish gulden

Item, 4 casks of Rhine wine, 20 mark each cask, the fourth Tyge Brahe got

Item, 5 casks French wine, each cask 17 mark

Item, 2 barrels of beer from Einbeck, each barrel 17½ mark

Item, 3 barrels, each barrel 13 mark [presumably beer]

Item, 3 barrels Prussian beer, each barrel 8 mark from Mats Tailor of Falsterbo

Item, 2 barrels Hamborg beer, 6 mark the barrel

Item, 12 barrels mead to the meals and to the kitchen, 8 mark the barrel

Item, 16 barrels of flour for small breads [rolls]. 4 barrels of wheat

Item, the master cook 20 mark

Item, the other cooks 10 mark

Item, the trumpeters 20 mark

Item, the drummers 6 mark

Item, Hans Wost 10 mark for he mixed the Ippocras [a type of wine punch]

Item, Tønnes Pearlstitcher 10 mark for the [decorative wax] dishes he made, and for the torches, and for other small items he made, and for the window he made [i.e., decorated] in the Great Hall

Item, 10 mark for wheat bread and for the peppercake and onion from Oluf Lauferberg

Item, 2 barrels dried fish from Oluf Lauferberg

Item, 2 barrels drinking cups from Morten Mercer in Malmoe, 5 mark the barrel

Item, 4 barrels of vinegar, 3 mark the barrel

Item, ½ barrel pure honey for 5 mark

Item, 5 pound wax, 6 mark the pound

The brewing and the baking

Primo, one half last malt in the week of the Birth of our Lady [September 8]

Item, the following week ½ last malt and 4 barrels of flour

Item, the following week ½ last malt and 4 barrels of flour

Item, the following week ½ last malt and 8 barrels of flour

Item, 2 barrels of eel

Item, 2 barrels of herring

Item, 4 barrels of cod

Item, 3 barrels butter for the table

Item, 3 barrels butter for the kitchen and the meals outside the banquet hall

Item, 40 sides of pork

Item, 6 pound flour for small breads and cakes

Item, 4 pound malt was sent to Ystad, which was brewed for the household

Item, 4 cow carcasses smoked

Item, 40 smoked sheep

Item, 10 oxen for fresh meat and green [i.e., lightly] salted meat of which 5 were salted 10 days before the wedding as green salted meat

Item, 60 lambs, the lamb 4 shillings
Item, 8 *worder* [10 pieces each] of large cod each *worde* 14 shillings
Item, 5 *worder* ling [a type of fish], the *worde* 2 mark
Item, 12 *worder* hake [a type of fish], the *worde* 12 shillings
Item, 12 mark for flounder
Item, 2000 dried fish, each hundred 4 shillings
Item, 1 barrel of salmon 10 mark
Item, the fodder came to 900 bushels of oats
This furnishing my daughter Magdalena brought with her to her home
Primo, 3 masterbeds
Item, 3 pair of Dutch linen sheets
Item, 2 Flemish bedclothes
Item, 1 English bedclothing
Item, leather sheet
Item, 3 big mattresses
Item, 3 head bolsters [pillows]
Item, 1 pair of silk canopies
Item, one red damask pillow stitched with gold
Item, a pair of silk sheets for a bed
Item, 2 red pillows of Damask stitched with gold
Item, 2 red and blue draperies for her solar [sitting room] stitched with gold thread
Item, one sown curtain for the Hall
Item, 4 cushions for the benches
Item, 12 new Flemish cushions and draperies for the benches in her solar
Item, draperies for the benches in the Hall
Item, a tablecloth sewn in silk
Item, 2 towels sewn in silk
Item, one blue sewn towel
Item, 3 big master bedcovers
Item, 11 pair of servants' sheets
Item, 17 new mattresses for the servants' beds
Item, 3 long white tablecloths
Item, 10 pots
Item, one large mortar
Item, 2 big candlesticks
Item, 1 big washbasin
The headband 200 gulden
The gold chain 60 gulden
Item, the necklace 30 gulden
Item the brooch 60 gulden

28 A Turkish bride, Ottoman Empire, late sixteenth century

Weddings in many parts of Europe involved processions of the wedding party through the streets, with the bride often veiled in Christian, Jewish, and Muslim traditions. In Muslim areas, the bride might also be carried through the streets on a veiled cart, or, as in this case, veiled while she rode through the streets on a horse; wealthy women might continue this mode of travel after they were married. This illustration appeared in Cesare Vecellio, *Habiti antichi*, a book of costumes published in 1598, and Vecellio adds the comment: 'Turkish men can have several wives, but one of these is the principal wife, with whom [the man] sleeps on Friday nights, which is a holiday for them. When this wife goes about the city, she rides on a decorated horse, under a canopy carried by four servants with curtains round that cover her to the knee, so that she can see passers-by but they cannot see her . . . and even though these wives go about in such an enclosed manner, they still wear their most costly and beautiful clothes of brocade and silk, decorated with jewels and pearls. The other wives go about with less formality.'

29 Village wedding, Switzerland 1580s

Scenes of village life were popular with many artists and engravers. In these, the
Swiss artist and playwright Christoph Murer shows the dancing and music at a village
wedding. The musicians are playing a bagpipe and a long brass instrument, and one
has a lute or other stringed instrument over his shoulder in a bag.
(Walter L. Strauss, *The German Single-Leaf Woodcut, 1550–1600* (New York: Abaris
Books, 1975). Reprinted by permission.)

30 A bride's memoir of her wedding day, Germany 1777

Though weddings could go on for days, most did not, and the reality of a young person's wedding day could be very different than anticipated, as revealed in this memoir from a young German woman, Ernestine Voss.
(Heinrich Voss, *Briefe nebst erläuternden Beilage*. Hrsg. v. Abraham Voss, vol. II (Halberstadt, 1829–1833), pp. 14–15. Translated by Merry Wiesner-Hanks.)

After breakfast [Johann Friedrich] Voss [her husband-to-be] went for a walk, so that he could be out of the way for the cleaning up. I was not allowed to lend a hand to anything, so I was the only one left. In my solitude I braided a pretty bridal wreath out of the branches of a myrtle that a poor gardener's wife had brought . . . I had my hair done and thoroughly powdered. Because Voss made up his mind to do the same with his hair, I arranged it myself with the help of a relative . . . Voss himself put the bridal wreath, which also gave him joy, in my hair, and it pleased me greatly that he secured it with a kiss and said he had a very pretty bride. We were barely finished when his mother came to fetch us for the ceremony. I was not ashamed of my tears, for the firmness with which he held my hand told me that he was very moved as well. The pastor, who was distinguished but practically unknown to us, discussed in a long sermon how the heathens had already had a high opinion of marital happiness, and continued on through the Christian religion, and then some practical advice for the bridegroom . . . and for the bride . . . he blessed us and wished us a happy marriage. Voss took me in his arms with these words: Now only death will part us. A dreadful afternoon in a crowded room followed, with, in our opinion, much too strait-laced company. The sun shone so hot, and there was no way to get out. In front of the window there were steps that led to the large church-yard that was surrounded by trees. The whole afternoon curious lower-class people stood there watching us. As the lamps were lit, young people who were my close relatives also gathered [on the steps] but it would not have been appropriate to go out to them. How often in the last few years has Voss said that this was the most boring day of his life.

31 A wedding disaster, France c. 1400

As they sometimes do today, weddings occasionally got out of hand in the early modern period and led to tragedy. This is the report of events at a wedding, recorded by the French royal chronicler Jean Froissart; given the amount of alcohol consumed at wealthy weddings as noted above, these events are probably not too surprising.
(Jean Froissart, *Chroniques*, translated and quoted in Thomas Johnes, *Chronicles of England, France, Spain, and Adjoining Countries*, vol. II (London, 1839), pp. 532–533.)

There was in the king's household a Norman squire . . . who thought of the following piece of pleasantry to amuse the king and the ladies. . . . For the ball that night, he had six cloth coats made and then had them covered with flax that looked like hair in shape and color. He dressed the king in one [four young nobles in others] . . . and the sixth one he wore himself. When they were all dressed up by having the coats sewed around them, they appeared to be wild men *(hommes sauvages)*, for they were covered with fur from head to foot. This masquerade pleased the king greatly, and he expressed his pleasure to his squire. It was so secretly contrived that no one knew anything about it but the servants who attended on them.

Sir Evan de Foix [one of the masqueraders] . . . said to the king: 'Sire, I advise you to give strict orders that no one come near us with torches, for if but a spark falls on the coats we are disguised in, the flaxen fur will catch fire, and we will burn up before anyone can do anything about it.' 'In God's name', the king said, 'you speak wisely and well, and it shall be done.'

Then he sent for one of the sergeants at arms who was on duty at the door and told him: 'Go to the ballroom and in the king's name command that all the torches be placed on the far side of the room and that none of them come near the six wild men who are about to enter.' . . . it was done, but] soon after this, the duke of Orleans entered, attended by four knights and six torches. He knew nothing of the king's orders or the six wild men who were about to make their appearance. First he watched the dancing and the women, then he began dancing vigorously himself.

At this point the king of France made his appearance with the five others, all dressed like wild men and covered from head to foot with flaxen fur as fine as human hair. No one present could recognize them. Five of them were attached to one another and the king came in first and led the others into the dance. When they entered the hall, everyone was so intent on watching them that the order about torches was forgotten. Fortunately the king left his companions and, impelled by his youth, went to show himself off to the ladies; passing first in front of the queen, he went along next to the duchess of Berry, who was his aunt and younger than he was. For fun the duchess took hold of him and wanted to know who he was, but the king stood there and would not give his name. 'You won't ever escape me', the duchess said, 'unless I know your name first.'

Just then the other five wild men met a great accident caused by the duke of Orleans . . . who was too eager to know who they were. As the five were dancing, he lowered the torch that one of his servants held in front of him, bringing it so close that the flame ignited the flax. And flax, as you know, cannot be put out once it is afire. Moreover, the flames heated the pitch with which the flax was attached to the cloth. The costumes themselves soon burst into flame, for they were covered with pitch and flax, were dry and delicate, and were all yoked together.

Those who wore them were in agony and began to cry out horribly. The situation was so dangerous that no one dared to get near them, although several knights did come up and try to strip the burning costumes off them, but the pitch burned their hands and disabled them for days thereafter. One of the five, Nantouillet, figured that the bar must be nearby, so he broke away and threw himself into a washtub full of water for rinsing out cups and plates. This saved him; otherwise he would have been burned to death like the others, and he still was badly injured.

Questions for discussion

1   What qualities do all the authors agree are important in an ideal wife? What differences do you see among them? Why do you think there is no similar body of literature on choosing a husband?

2   What were the major sources of conflict between parents and children regarding the choice of a spouse? Major sources of agreement?

3   What were some of the things that could go wrong during an engagement to block a marriage?

4   Marriage contracts address a variety of concerns. Which seem to be most important in the contracts included here? How does the social class and ages of the spouses influence this?

5   How is love portrayed in the Dalmatian poem and the two illustrations? Does love enter into any of the other documents of this chapter?

6   How do the reports of wedding festivities fit with the process of choosing a spouse and arranging a marriage?

7   The differences between the process of choosing a spouse in this period and in the contemporary western world are quite obvious. What similarities do you see?

4

MARRIED LIFE

Marriage was supposed to be the bedrock of both the family and society, upon which the stability of both rested, in a number of different ways. First, the marital household was the basic economic unit of early modern society. Moreover, the household served as the basic administrative unit for the neighborhood and parish communities. Thus, the Christian Church and the state had a deep investment in marriage as an institution, and both worked to insure its stability. Jewish and Muslim authorities also regulated marital life, for the adherents of these religions, though in practice they tolerated a range of interpretations of legal principles.

The majority of early modern people, apart from those who took religious vows, expected to marry. Age at first marriage varied according to region and social class. For example, people in the north tended to marry later than people in the south. Women from the upper classes were generally quite young (sometimes as young as fourteen or fifteen) when they wed, while peasant or urban working women often waited until their early or mid twenties to marry.

Region and class also affected living patterns of married couples. In rural and southern areas, young couples often settled into the home of the husband's family, thus entering an extended kinship household. In the north, and in cities, marriage usually meant independence for newlyweds, as they moved into their own home.

Many women and men married more than once. These second or third unions brought with them a series of complications, including property disbursement and ownership, inheritance and, to use a modern term, 'blended' families. While widows often felt pressure to remarry (see chapter 8), the first husband's family and heirs reasonably feared for their rights to her wealth, which could range from possession of extensive tracts of land to certain guild privileges. Whereas a first marriage theoretically bonded a woman unequivocally to her husband and his family's interests, a second marriage could place her in a maelstrom of competing strategies and agendas, between her natal family, her new husband, and her children from the first union.

There was little ambiguity in this period about the economic basis for marriage. The marriage contract was a crucially important one. When a couple wed, both husband and wife brought an agreed-upon portion of money or goods to the union. The contract stipulated who was to contribute what, and in addition had to cover every possible development, including what would happen to the couple's property when one or both of them died. This became especially complicated when the bride or groom was marrying for the second (or third) time, and had several potentially competing interests, usually in the form of children.

In addition to its role as familial and economic foundation, marriage was also the central social institution of early modern Europe (as indeed it remains in most of the modern world). The union was truly a partnership, even if made up of unequal partners. A woman needed a husband to provide for her and her children. A man in turn needed a wife to run the household and raise a family. Running the household often included working alongside the husband in his business, keeping the account books, and educating the children. When a man lost his wife, he usually remarried quickly or brought in a sister or other unmarried female relative to run the household and raise his children.

No matter what the social or economic level of the couple involved, virtually every marriage involved a contract to ensure the transmission of property to the next generation, thereby securing familial interests. Marriage and inheritance went together. Thus, it is not surprising that in most marriages the parents of the couple were closely involved in the selection of a spouse. To ignore a parent's wishes meant risking disinheritance and in some cases legal penalties.

Once married, the couple formed a partnership in the interests of the family and household they hoped to build. But the partnership was not an equal one. Legally, women across Europe were largely subordinate to their husband in all matters financial, legal, religious, and social. The husband frequently exerted control over his wife's property. But he was bound by certain expectations that he manage the property responsibly. If he did not, his wife could seek redress, and sometimes obtain justice.

The definition and nature of marriage changed over the course of the early modern period. One historian, Georges Duby, has suggested that a new type of family model appeared in the medieval period. Up to that point, Duby has identified, in France at least, two conflicting models of marriage. The first was the priestly form, whose characteristics included exogamy (marrying outside of clan or bloodline), the indissolubility of marriage, and the free choice of spouses. The second was the knightly or aristocratic form, which included endogamy, strong parental control over the choice of spouse, and the possibility of divorce and remarriage. By the thirteenth century, a basic agreement had been reached, whereby a valid marriage consisted of freely given consent by a man and woman who had reached the age of reason. Men were agreed to have authority over their wives, just as clergy had dominion over the laity in spiritual matters.

Another important moment of change in the marital relationship came with the Protestant Reformation. With their emphasis on the role of the head of the household – the husband – as a spiritual guide for his family, Reformation institutions largely removed the role of the Church from the household. By investing the husband with such authority the Protestant churches further solidified the traditional patriarchal system.

In some ways, the Protestant faith strengthened the marital union. Protestants exalted the married state and denied the moral superiority of celibacy. In Protestant lands, the possibility of divorce and remarriage was introduced. But Protestants eliminated the confessional with priests – a traditional source of emotional support for women – and abolished the career option of the convent. Finally, did the option of divorce help early modern women? The answer is by no means obvious. Women in Protestant lands could leave bad marriages, but now it was also easier for men to leave their wives, which often left women poorer and with children to support on their own.

As the documents below show, the relationship between a wife and a husband could be just as complex in early modern Europe as it is today, with intersecting bonds of sentiment, obligation, and financial interest. The marital union was a bond colored by economic interest, religious conviction, and affection, the degrees of which shifted according to period, region, and class.

DEFINITIONS OF MARITAL STATUS

1 Men, marriage, and service to the King, Portugal early seventeenth century

Marriage was an important institution for both women and men in early modern Europe. Although women are often referred to by their marital status more so than men, the pressure for men to marry was real enough, especially if they hoped to enter certain professions. In this ordinance, the King of Portugal made clear the importance of marriage to men who hoped for government careers.
(José Justino de Andrade e Silva, ed., *Collecção Chronologica da Legislação Portugueza (1603–1612)* (Lisbon: Imprensa de J.J.A. Silva, 1854), p. 189. Translated by Darlene Abreu-Ferreira with thanks to Frank Dutra for his assistance.)

I the King make it known to those to whom this charter reaches that, further to the ordinance in Liv.1, Tit. 94, it is prohibited and ordered that Ministers and Justice Officials of the Realm and Dominion cannot serve their offices without being married for more than a year during which time they shall marry, for it serves me and Justice to have it so. Even though the

Court Chief Justices have made an order that another year be granted, besides the concessions made to the said offices by the said Ordinance, to enable them to serve their offices without being married, I demand that no more time whatsoever be given them than the said year by the Ordinance, the said Order notwithstanding, which in this part be annulled; and I demand that it not be used, nor the said Court Chief Justices grant further said licenses to said Justice Officials to serve unmarried; and so it pleases me that from this day forward the duties of Chief Justices, Corregidors, Purveyors, Magistrates, Judges, and Lawyers not be served by unmarried [men]; but this does not apply to our Chief Justices who presently serve me and who prior to starting their service, and taking up their duties, were already 40 years of age; and in the residencies, to which they are obliged, the Corregidors, Purveyors, Magistrates, External Judges and other Officials, the Arbitrors will ask if they are married; and in the acts of said residencies there will be special mention of this; and those found to be unmarried will not be able to return to service and promoted in said offices without first marrying. And I order the Administrator of the *Casa da Supplicação* [the High Court] and the Governor of the *Casa do Porto*, and the chief justices of said *Casas*, and the Corregidors, Magistrates and Judges to carry out and comply with this Charter, according to its content etc.; that which will be registered in the *Livro da Casa do despacho do Desembargo to Paço*, and in the books of the said *Casa de Supplicação e Porto*. And so it be that it be valid, have the force and vigor of the Law, as it were a Letter done in my name, and signed by me, notwithstanding the Ordinance that determines the contrary in Liv. 2, Tit. 44, that states that no Ordinance or Law shall be altered by me unless explicit mention is made.

2 A marriage law, Austria 1526

Local, territorial, and national law codes all regulated aspects of married life, including financial matters and spousal relations. This is a section from the Law Code of the territory of Salzburg, Austria from 1526.
(Franz V. Spechtler and Rudolf Uminsky, eds., *Die Salzburger Landesordnung von 1526*, Göppinger Arbeiten zur Germanistik, Nr. 305 (Göppingen: Kimmerle, 1981), pp. 119, 154, 197. Translated by Merry Wiesner-Hanks.)

It is to be accepted that both spouses have married themselves together from the time of the consummation of their marriage, body to body and goods to goods . . .

The husband shall not spend away the dowry or other goods of his wife unnecessarily with gambling or other useless frivolous pastimes, wasting and squandering it. Whoever does this is guilty of sending his wife into poverty. His wife, in order to secure her legacy and other goods she has brought to the marriage, may get an order requiring him to pledge and hold in trust for her some of his property. In the same way he is to act in a suitable manner in other things that pertain to their living together and act appropriately toward her. If there is no cause or she is not guilty of anything, he is not to hit her too hard, push her, throw her or carry out any other abuse. For her part, the wife should obey her husband in modesty and honorable fear, and be true and obedient to him. She should not provoke him with word or deed to disagreement or displeasure, through which he might be moved to strike her or punish her in unseemly ways. Also, without his knowledge and agreement she is not to do business [with any household goods] except those which she has brought to the marriage; if she does it will not be legally binding . . .

The first and foremost heirs are the children who inherit from their parents. If a father and mother leave behind legitimate children out of their bodies, one or more sons or daughters, then these children inherit all paternal and maternal goods, landed property and movables, equally with each other . . .

Women who do not have husbands, whether they are young or old, shall have a guardian and advisor in all matters of consequence and property, such as the selling of or other legal matters regarding landed property. Otherwise these transactions are not binding. In matters which do not involve court actions and in other matters of little account they are not to be burdened with guardians against their will.

3 A definition of divorce, Ottoman Empire sixteenth century

This fatwa (a religious ruling based on Islamic law) points to the vulnerability of the institution of marriage under Islamic law. The ease with which a Muslim male could obtain a divorce, by simply uttering a verbal formula, meant that a marriage could be ended instantaneously. On the other hand, it was difficult for women to obtain divorce. Some men in this period apparently had the habit of using the divorce formula when they swore. For example, a man might say, 'if I ever do such-and-such again, let my wife be divorced'. They could then find themselves in the position of having to arrange a formal remarriage with their now former wives. The fatwa suggests that women wanting out of their marriage took advantage of this situation by refusing to remarry. Women's refusal must have been a widespread practice since the mufti's opinion that women could be forced back into marriage is in tension with the legal principle that a Muslim woman must give her explicit consent before being married. (Süleymaniye Library, Istanbul: Şemseddin Ahmed Kemalpasazade, Fetava, MS. Dar ul-Mesnevi 118, fs. 16a, 42b. Translated by Leslie Peirce.)

Query: If a man pronounces something by way of swearing and must later remarry his wife, and she will not agree to the marriage and will not accept it and says, 'I'm divorced, I won't ever return to my husband', what must be done according to the law?

Response: Force can be used [to compel her to remarry].

4 Court record validating a marriage, Ottoman Empire 1541

The following case from the court of Aintab involves the dilemma of a man who has unintentionally placed his marriage in jeopardy by divorcing his wife by proxy while he was suffering from delirium. Relying on a locally issued fatwa, the Aintab judge rules that the marriage has not been invalidated, which goes against the fatwa in Source 3. (National Library, Ankara, Gaziantep Sicili 161, f. 350. Translated by Leslie Peirce.)

Dervish Ali son of Alijan came to court and declared, 'Some time ago, when I was ill and confined to bed, I apparently made Mehmed son of Hizir my proxy to divorce the woman Nigar daughter of Yusuf the painter, who is my wife. Now I don't have any knowledge or any memory of this, I don't know what I said when I was ill, and I wasn't thinking about getting divorced, and [I didn't mean to turn us into divorced people].' A fatwa on this matter issued by Mevlana Hasan Efendi, foremost among learned scholars, was presented; it was declared according to the intent of the fatwa that divorce had not been accomplished, and in accordance with the fatwa, permission was given for his wife to be returned to him. The foregoing was recorded upon request.

5 Letter ending an ambiguous marriage, Spain 1690

Despite the decrees of the Council of Trent that reasserted the confinement of sexual activity to the marriage bed, many Catholics continued to live together outside of wedlock; this was also true in Protestant Europe, especially among the poor. Many of those relationships were formulated on some promise to marry in the future. When those relationships ended, the jilted partner was required to formally release the other from his or her promise to marry before a new marriage could take place. In this Letter of Separation from 1690, Pedro Vàsquez's longtime girlfriend, Constança de Bal, had to release him from any obligations to her or their child before he could marry another woman.
(Carta de Apartamiento, Archivo Histórico Provincial de Ourense, caja protocolos 3420, f. 109 (1690). Translated by Allyson Poska.)

Constança de Bal, an unmarried woman making a letter of separation on behalf of Pedro Vàsquez

Pedro Vàsquez, also single, the son of Bartolomé Vàsquez and Margarita González, residents of the parish of San Martín de Cornoces, until now had sexual intercourse and carnal copulation with the plaintiff which resulted in making her pregnant and giving birth to a child named Pedro that she continues to raise. The said Pedro Vàsquez intends to prepare himself to enter the married state which has moved the plaintiff to put forward an impediment until he might give her satisfaction for the discredit that she has suffered . . . he insists that he has given the plaintiff some little things to aid in her reparation and he wants to give her two aprons and one cloth bodice. As it is evident that he has given the plaintiff satisfaction for whatever claim, action, and recourse that she might have or has against the aforesaid . . . now and for always, she allows . . . the said Pedro Vàsquez to dispose of himself however he wishes . . . she swears to God our Lord by the sign of the cross that she does not do it out of fear that Justice would not be done, but only for the reasons referred to and by virtue of them she does it voluntarily of her free and gracious will without the force or violence of any person.

LOVE AND COMPANIONSHIP

6 A tale of love and devotion, Russia fifteenth-century

A model marriage is depicted in the fictional tale of the Russian saints Peter and Fevronia. In style, it draws from the traditions both of hagiography and of folklore. Although the princely couple Peter and Fevronia allegedly ruled the provincial city of Murom in the twelfth century, this tale was composed in the late fifteenth century, and circulated widely after that. The first section of the tale describes how Prince Peter contracted a skin disease from the workings of black magic, and how Fevronia, the daughter of a humble woodsman, healed him through her saintly abilities. As the price of the cure, she demanded that Peter take her as his wife. He ultimately agreed, albeit after some resistance. Together they confronted danger and hardship, ruled a kingdom, and died as true companions, as described below.
(*Khrestomatiia po drevnei russkoi literatury XI–XVII vekov*, ed. N.K. Gudzii (Moscow: Uchebnopedagogicheskoe izd., 1962), pp. 233–241. Translated by Eve Levin.)

In that manner, Fevronia became the princess. They returned to their patrimony, the city of Murom, and there they lived in complete piety, not omitting anything from God's commandments. . . .

The boyars did not like Princess Fevronia for their wives' sake. For she had become princess not because of her ancestry, but because God glorified her because of her good life . . . After some time, the boyars approached [Peter] in anger, saying, 'Prince, we all want to serve you justly and keep you as our ruler. But we do not want Princess Fevronia, who ruled over our wives. If you want to be a ruler, you must have another princess. Fevronia can take sufficient wealth for herself, and go where she wants.' The blessed Prince Peter, as was his custom, did not get angry over this, but replied calmly, 'Go speak to Fevronia, and we will hear what she says.'

Those perfidious men, filled with stupidity, thought to arrange a feast. And so they did. And when they were cheerful, they began to raise their stupid voices, like dogs barking . . . 'Lady Princess Fevronia! The whole city and boyars say to you, "Give us what we ask of you . . . Lady, we all want Prince Peter to rule over us. Our wives do not want you to rule over them. Take sufficient wealth for yourself, and depart, going where you want." She said, "I promise you, whatever you ask for you will get." I say to you, "Give me what I ask of you." ' These evil ones were happy, not knowing the future, and they gave their oath that, 'as you said, you may take one thing without any restrictions'. She said, 'I ask nothing else of you except my husband, Prince Peter.' They said, 'If he wants the same, we cannot tell you otherwise.' The Devil inspired their thoughts, for if Prince Peter left, they would establish another ruler for themselves, and each of the boyars took into his head that he himself would become ruler.

The blessed Prince Peter did not value temporal rulership more than God's commandments, but instead he followed the commandment which the Evangelist Matthew instructed in his Gospel, 'If anyone divorces his wife, except for reason of adultery, and marries another, he commits adultery.'

. . . These evil-minded boyars gave [Peter and Fevronia] boats . . . for there was a river, called the Oka, by the city . . . There was a person in the boat with the blessed Princess Fevronia, and his wife was in the same boat with him. This man received a thought from an evil demon, and looked upon the saintly woman with desire. She perceived this evil thought, and soon revealed it. She said to him, 'Ladle up some water from the river on this side of the boat.' He ladled up the water, and she instructed him to taste it. He drank. Then she said to him, 'Ladle up some water from the other side of the boat.' He ladled up water again, and she told him to taste it. He drank again. She said, 'Is the water the same, or is one sweeter?' He said, 'It is the same water, Lady.' Then she said, 'And so all women have the same nature. So why would you think to leave your wife for another?' This man then recognized that she had the gift of clairvoyance, and feared to desire such a person.

Evening neared, and they camped on shore. The blessed Prince Peter began to think, 'How will it be, having relinquished my rulership?' The wondrous Fevronia said to him, 'Do not afflict yourself, Prince; the merciful God, the creator and sustainer of everything, will not leave us in poverty.'

. . . [Next morning] when the people had already placed the cargo in the boats from shore, the nobles of the city of Murom arrived. They said, 'Lord Prince, of all the nobles and from the entire city of Murom we have come to you, asking that you not leave us orphaned, but instead return to your patrimony. Many of the nobles of the city have perished by the sword.

120

Each wanted to rule, and they have killed each other. All who are left with all the people beg you, saying, "Lord Prince, if we have been angry with you and irritated you by not wanting Princess Fevronia to rule our wives, now we are all your slaves along with our households, and we want you, and love you, and beg you not to leave us, your slaves." '

So the blessed Prince Peter and the blessed Princess Fevronia returned to their city. . . .

When their honorable decease approached, they prayed to God that their deaths would come in the same hour. They recommended that they be laid in a single grave and ordered two tombs carved for themselves in a single stone, with only a lattice between them. They took monastic vows at the same time. [In pre-modern Russia, it was common for elderly or ill men and women to take monastic vows, and so live their last days in higher devotion to God.] The blessed Prince Peter was called David in monastic rank, and the revered Fevronia was called Evfrosinia.

At that time the revered and blessed Fevronia, called Evfrosinia, was sewing with her own hands a chalice-cover for the cathedral, decorated with depictions of the saints. The revered and blessed Prince Peter, called David, sent to her, saying, 'O Sister Evfrosinia. I am ready to depart from my body, but I am waiting for you, so we can go together.' She replied, 'Wait, lord, until I finish sewing the chalice-cover for the holy church.' He sent to her a second time, saying, 'I can wait only a little for you.' And when he sent to her a third time, saying, 'I am ready to pass away and I cannot wait for you', she stitched the last work on the holy chalice-cover, having embroidered the last saint's face but leaving the robe unsewn. She inserted her needle into the chalice-cover and wrapped up the thread, and she sent to the blessed Peter, called David, that they could pass away together. And so, having prayed, they gave their souls into God's hands on the 25th day of June.

After their death, the people wanted the blessed Prince Peter to be buried inside the city in the cathedral church of the Mother of God, and Fevronia outside the city in the church of the Translation of the Cross in the women's monastery. They said that 'it is improper to place two saints who had taken monastic vows together in a single tomb' . . . The next morning, when the people arose, they found the separate tombs in which they had laid them empty. They found the two holy bodies in the cathedral church of the Mother of God in the city in the single tomb that they themselves had had prepared. The people did not understand that just as they were intertwined in life, so it was to be in their honorable decease, and again they laid them in separate tombs and took them out. The next morning they again found the saints together in one tomb. After that, they did not dare to touch the saintly bodies, and they buried them in a single grave, the one they had ordered, in the cathedral church of the Nativity of the Mother of God inside the city . . .

7 A letter from a nobleman to his wife, Denmark 1502

Real marriages, as well as idealized fictional ones, provide evidence of companionship and affection. Royal service provided an opportunity for marital partnership. The following letter was written in 1502 by a high-ranking nobleman in charge of one of the border fiefs between Norway and Sweden. During a Swedish uprising against the Danish king, he had to leave the castle as well as the administration of the fief in his wife's care while he was raising an army and campaigning for the king. Although his father-in-law, himself a high-ranking noble and experienced royal administrator, was staying at the castle, the letter reveals that the wife was in charge during her husband's absence, dealing with taxes paid either in kind or in money as well as hiring staff.

(*Missiver fra kongerne Christiern I.s og Hans's Tid. I–II*, ed. William Christensen, vol. II (Copenhagen: Selskabet for Udgivelse af Kilder til dansk Historie, Gad, 1912–14), pp. 180–181. Translated by Grethe Jacobsen and Pernille Arenfeldt.)

Honest and wellborn woman, Anne Rudsdatter, his dear wife is lovingly sent this letter.

Friendly and loving greeting sent with God. You must know, dear Anne, that I just received your letter. You write to me about our Lord, the King, and about the fief, well, you must do what you think best with the business, until God wills it that I return, as you know our mind. You write about the butter, and you decide what to do and dispose of it so we can make the most of it and so that we receive money and cloth as soon as possible. And if you receive additional butter and more than we need at the castle, then sell it.

And if some of the men have not received their money then let them get what they should have, of the money that comes in from the fief.

And if any good men arrive, who will serve for money and clothing, and who are suitable for the job, I have to do, then hire them.

And I ask you, dear Anne, that you guard the castle together with your father against fire and treason, as you know we are very concerned about that.

And let the oxen be returned from the peasants who have fattened them.

And may you know, dear Anne, that so far, the commoners we have dealt with have agreed to join our Lord, the King, for as long as we want and today we are negotiating with the commoners around Oslo and will then proceed to Oslo castle and do our best and prove us worthy of our Lord, the King's confidence in us.

Dear Anne. If you hear from our Lord, the King, then let me know and also of other business and take good care of Sophie [their daughter].

Hereby you are commended to God and Saint Oluf.

Written in Oslo Our Lady's Eve (August 14th) anno domini md2° under my seal.

Henrik Krummedige, Knight.

8 Two letters between a gentry landholder and his wife, Wales 1661

These excerpts from two letters between a husband and wife, both members of the Welsh gentry, offer a glimpse into a later seventeenth-century marriage that appears to have been very successful, in part because both parties accepted the ground rules, such as that Richard was the more important partner but cared a great deal for Sarah. She accepted her subordination without much difficulty, in part because of his affection. The letters suggest that love, consideration, and male dominance could all go smoothly together if both spouses cooperated! The first excerpt **(a)** comes from a letter from Sir Richard Wynn at Gwydir to his wife Sarah at her parents' home, Chirk, after her father's very recent death there. The second excerpt **(b)** is from a letter from Lady Sarah Wynn at Gwydir to Sir Richard Wynn at the King's Head tavern against Temple Gate in Fleet Street, London.

(N.L.W., Add. MS 469E, f. 52, December 20, 1666. Excerpted by Katharine Swett.)

(a) My Dearest . . . for Gods sake have a care of thyself. remember me and thy little girl . . . I would feign be satisfied when certainly the funeral will be that I may come to you sometime afore: little Mally was well this afternoon and begs your blessing and joins with me in desiring you to make much of yourself for her sake and mine . . . I pray let me hear once every three days from you . . . once more think of me and make much of thyself for my sake and poor Mallys . . . God bless my Dearest . . .

(N.L.W., Add. MS 469E, f. 9, June 13, 1661. Excerpted by Katharine Swett.)

(b) My only Joy, it having pleased my good god to join me to thee as upon this day seven years I could not omit giving thee the trouble of these lines, that thou mayest know that I am in health, and rejoyce this day that I have served apprenticeship to so good a master, beseeching the almighty to bless thee, granting thee health and life many a seven years for to come, and the short time he shall allot me, make it a comfort to thee, is the prayer of her who presents thee with the endeared loves of thy most faithful wife Sarah Wynn.

9 Excerpt from a will, Spain 1658

Disease and warfare wreaked havoc on many early modern marriages. As a result, many men and women married two, three, and even four times during their lifetimes.

Such misfortune befell Costanza Forneyra, who was widowed three times while still a young woman. Her last marriage, however, was much longer and happier. In her last will and testament, Costanza expressed her love for her fourth husband, Antonio González, with both kind words and a significant inheritance.
(Testament of Costanza Forneyra, Archivo Histórico Procincial de Ourense, caja protocolos, 3669, f. 134 (1658). Translated by Allyson Poska.)

For the love and affection and obligation that I have for him, and for having had more than twenty-two years of marriage, one with the other, during which he has esteemed me and treated me like an honorable man should with much kindness and goodwill . . . I leave him a vineyard . . . a piece of land . . . half of the territory with the chestnut trees . . . and the fifth part of all of my possessions. . . .

10 A loving letter from husband to wife, Wales 1612

This letter was penned 35 years into a long and successful marriage, and illustrates the comfort such a union might offer. Sir John is confident of his wife's interest in the small details of his doings and health, and though scarcely a day's journey from home, wishes to communicate with her; she benefits from his affection too. But notice that she needs her husband's permission to leave home to go visit their daughter for the Whitsun holiday.
(N.L.W., MS 9054E, f. 35. April 9, 1612. Sir John Wynn at Wrexham, Flintshire, to Lady Sydney Wynn at Gwydir. Excerpted by Katharine Swett.)

To my dearest the lady Sydney Wynn at Gwydir.

Good Sydney, I am come hither in health I thank god and feel myself the better by travel and I hope will be better and better for I take but small journeys nor will not over labor myself . . . I have sent thee a token [small gift] by my son Bodvel having no time to write unto thee. pray for me and I will for thee and thy brats [young children]. to god's holy protection I commend us all god send us a merry and joyful meeting. I will not break promise with thee. thou shall [go] to Kylken against Whitsontyde and from thence I mean to have thee to London if my Return be deferred as I fear me it shall. Wrexham 9 April, my birth day. thine own John Wynn of Gwydir.

11 A husband's provisions for his widow, England 1580

Spousal affection sometimes emerges in wills. Though some of the language of wills is formulaic, personal emotions do show through occasionally, and in some parts of Europe, such as England, spouses could also show their love and concern by the economic provisions made in the will. In this will, William Gerard gives his wife a third of his moveable property to use during her lifetime in addition to the income of one third of his freehold lands that was his wife's dower by law. His wife had had bouts

of mental illness, and he makes special provisions for her because of this. Gerard's heir is his elder son Gilbert, and his children are all adults.
(Prerogative Court of Canterbury. 26 Darcy. February 16, 1580. Sir William Gerard. Excerpted by Katharine Swett.)

Where god has pleased heretofore to visit my wife divers times with such sickness as bereaveth her from all sense & understanding, I foresee that if care be not had to the preservation of those things I have, if god shall please to visit her in that time, the same would be purloined from her & my children. & if she's not looked to carefully in her time of sickness, there is doubt of her perfect recovery . . . [for this reason] my will and request to her is to live with her son and they not separate house . . . if my wife would please I wish Gilbert took charge of the house . . . [they] are to receive all incomes from land jointly and share jointly in all household goods during her lifetime, and Lady Gerard is to have at least four personal servants. Gilbert will inherit the residual goods [when his mother dies] for his better maintenance & ability to welcome his brothers & sisters & others his friends . . . if my wife mislikes living with her son & wants to live alone . . . [provides for half of a house in Chester, with quarterly income] . . . not less than one third of all my livings farms etc. to use. . . . And I charge Gilbert, as he shall answer before God to the contrary, that he serve obey & lovingly treat his mother, & if god please ever to visit her with her accustomed sickness, to see her so kept & used (as though I lived) . . .

MARRIAGE AS PARTNERSHIP

12 A wife's will, Spain 1628

As many early modern married couples struggled to survive, a woman's financial contribution could mean the difference between comfort and misery. This was particularly true in the parts of Europe where women received significant portions of inheritance through partible inheritance, in which the inheritance was divided equally among all of the heirs, male and female. For instance, in early modern Spain, women often brought significant financial resources to the marriage and actively participated in the investment of those resources. The last will and testament of María Fernández, the wife of a carpenter from Santiago de Compostela in Spain, reveals how she and her husband were not only man and wife, but partners in a number of land holdings. (Testament of María Fernández, Archivo Histórico Universitario de Santiago de Commpostela, caja protocolo 1530, f. 112 (1628). Translated by Allyson Poska.)

Item, I say that my husband and I lease out the benefice of Santiago de Numide next to the middle bridge. . . . I leave to the said Jacome de Mata, my husband, the said quarto and a half of produce from this year that we have collected for him entirely, and the other quarto and a half from next year, I leave to my son-in-law, Alonso da Silva, that he have it and collect it entirely, with neither of them putting an impediment on the other.

Item, I say that I and my husband have some cows in San Esteban de Trasmontes and San Julian dos Cabaleiros. . . . I order that my husband and my son-in-law divide these in half. . . . Item, I say that I and my husband, Jacome da Mata, between us two, bought and rent the house where we live at present in La Algaria de Arriva. I want and it is my will that I leave the usufruct of the entire house and the part that is mine to the said Jacome da Mata for all the days of his life and after his death my heirs may have it. . . .

13 On the compensation of a wife's labor, Ottoman Empire sixteenth century

The following fatwa addresses a question about the apportionment of recompense for labor – in this case the making of cloth – within the marital household. Textile production, both within the household and in more factory-like settings, was a central feature of local economies throughout the Middle East.
(Süleymaniye Library, Istanbul, Şemseddin Ahmed Kemalpasazade, Fetava, MS. Dar ul-Mesnevi 118, f. 23a. Translated by Leslie Peirce.)

Query: If [a man] buys cotton and his wife spins it and weaves cloth from it, whom does [the cloth] belong to?
Answer: If the wife's labor is voluntary, it belongs to the husband. Otherwise, she receives fair recompense for her labor [i.e. the going wage rate].

14 A wife learns a trade, France 1543

Married life for a woman certainly did not mean the end of her life as a skilled worker in early modern France. Among many couples, husbands and wives each had their own distinct trades. Furthermore, marriage did not mean the end of possibilities for formally acquiring skills in a trade. In the following document, two men have reached an agreement whereby the wife of one will teach her own trade to the wife of the other. While the two wives would, in the end, have a trade in common, their husbands' trades were distinct from each other's and from those of their wives.
(Paris, Archives Nationales, Minutier central, Étude VIII/474, February 15, 1543 n.s. Translated by Carol Loats.)

Pierre Moisson, merchant of eyeglasses, living in Paris, rue Saint Denis, for himself and in his own name and as agent for Adrienne Benard, his wife, linen-maker of Paris, by whom he has promised and promises to have this contents confirmed and found agreeable, and whom he has authorized and authorizes for this, affirms that he has reached an agreement and contract with master Guillaume de Saint Loup, illuminator and copyist of Paris, present here.

[The agreement is] that he will have the said Adrienne Benard well and duly show and teach the profession of *lingère* [a maker and seller of linen] and the related work in which she is involved, to Germayne Feye, wife of the said master Guillaume de Saint Loup.

To do this, Germainne Feye will be expected to go before the said Adrienne always and whenever [Adrienne] views it as desirable, and Adrienne will be expected to show [Germaine] the said profession as above.

In consideration [of this] the said master Guillaume de Saint Loup, in doing this, will be expected, promises, and guarantees to deliver and pay to Moisson, or someone on his behalf, the sum of 40 *sous tournois* [20 *sous tournois* = 1 *livre tournois*] by the coming Easter.

Promising, etc., obligating, each in his own right, in the said names and each of them renouncing to the other, etc. Done in the year 1542, Thursday, the 15th day of February.

15 A couple, a medical practice, and an accusation, Denmark 1553

In early modern Denmark, ordinances and other legal records made a distinction between doctors of medicine, barber-surgeons, and the men and women who were connected with the public baths. Doctors usually had a monopoly on medical cures and were most often men. However, in the following testimony from 1553 we find a couple who apparently shared a medical practice. He is called 'doctor' and she a 'doctoress' implying that they were medical practitioners. However, the heading and the testimonies imply that they, and especially she, needed to clear themselves of charges of wrongdoing.

(*Malmø stadsbog 1549–1559. Rådstuerettens, bytingets og toldbodrettens protokol*, ed. Einar Bager (Copenhagen: Selskabet for Udgivelse af Kilder til dansk Historie, 1972), p. 132. Translated by Grethe Jacobsen and Pernille Arenfeldt.)

After Christmas 1553

Testimony, which the doctoress received in court in the presence of the proper jury. We, the Mayors and the City Council in Malmø and Valentin Køler, Reeve ibidem, hereby make public and acknowledge with this our open letter, that year etc. 1553 on Friday the 19th of February were summoned in front of us at our city hall, Johan Krumpis, called doctor, of Malmø and his wife, Magdalena, and brought with them these aftersaid our burghers and burgheresses, whom they had summoned to our court and asked and urged each and all of them to step forward and admit for God's and justice's sake, how they have dealt with them with medical skill and other things. Which people came forward and with raised fingers and stretched arms swore a holy oath as follows.

First Jesper Maler and Niels Erlandsson said that the doctor had helped them, so that they thanked him and wished him well. Morten Herløv, Mikkel Pramkarl, Hans Knudsen testified that he and she had helped their wives honest and well, so that they thanked them and wished them all well.

Marine Pibils recounted how the doctoress had helped her in childbed so that she thanked God and her for her health.

Marine Bartolemæus', wife of Jacob Rebslager, Bente Hans Knudsens, Gertke in the Cellar testified and swore that the doctoress had helped them in one way and the other with herbs, water and other things, so that they thanked her a lot, because she had helped them.

Adrian Nettelmager's wife and Anne Lydekone testified that she had helped their daughters in childbed and in other ways so that they thanked her greatly.

Jep Kedelsmed testified that she had helped him, next to God, during his illness with something to drink and other honest (cures) so that he thanked her highly and said he would be in the ground, had she not been around.

Hans Mortensen Skinder that they had helped him and that he had nothing to accuse them of.

Hans Nielsen Skomagere testified that the doctor gave him a drink, which neither harmed him nor did him any good and therefore he had neither thanks nor accusations to offer him.

Morten Østen testified that he knew that the doctor had helped a peasant and a girl, who were not present, so well that they thanked him and wished him very well.

Adrian Nettlere and Anders Jyde testified that they had been sent to Hans Roskom's house to inquire what they said about the doctor and the doctoress. Then they had said that they knew of nothing to accuse them of.

Jørgen Isenkræmmer and Peder Sittil recounted how they had been sent to Mikkel Overskærers' house about the testimony they could give, concerning the doctor and doctoress. Then they had answered that they had been in the house and left again so that they knew of nothing to accuse them of.

As further evidence that thus was sworn, testified and recounted in front of us, we have sealed this our open letter with the seal of our city.

16 Bellmaking husband and wife, Germany 1568

Husbands and wives often worked side by side in craft workshops, though only the husband was formally a member of the craft guild. This is a woodcut illustration from Jost Ammann's *Beschreibung Aller Staende*, a survey of crafts published in 1568. The picture shows the husband and wife working as a team making bells, though the accompanying poem only mentions the husband's labor.

Der Schellenmacher.

Ich aber bin ein Schellenmachr/
Zu Preng vnd Narrnweiß ein vrsacht/
Mach Zinnbel Schellen/groß vnd klein/
Zum Schlittenzeug / sauber vnd rein/
Auch wol gestimbt auff die Stech Bahn/
Darzu Schelln für den Prittschenmann/
Auch Schellen an die Narren Kappn/
Darmits zu Faßnacht vmbher sappn.

CONFLICT

17 Disappearance and remarriage, Spain 1591 and 1594

In many areas of Europe, men left regularly to do seasonal labor in other regions or to fish in faraway seas. During times of warfare, husbands were conscripted into the military. The long absences often left the abandoned wives unsure whether their husbands were alive or dead and whether they should remarry. In document **(a)**, a case brought before the Spanish Inquisition in 1591, Marina de Castro was charged with bigamy when her long absent first husband suddenly returned home. In document **(b)**, we see that women who checked into the exact circumstances of their husbands' deaths fared much better with the Inquisition, as is evident in the trial of Margarida López from 1594. (Relaciones de Causas, Archivo Histórico Nacional, Sección Inquisición, legajo 2042, no. 26, f. 13 (1591). Translated by Allyson Poska.)

(a) Marina de Castro, inhabitant of Verin (Ourense), accused of having been married two times, said that her first husband had left her alone and that she was notified that he was dead and having information that it was so, she married for a second time . . . she was absolved, but because we [the judges] are suspicious that the said information was false, she was reprimanded . . . and she was mandated not to live with either of the husbands until the ecclesiastical ordinary might determine with which of them she might make her life.

(Relaciones de Causas, Archivo Histórico Nacional, Sección Inquisición, legajo 2042, no. 34 folio 6 (1594). Translated by Allyson Poska.)

(b) Margarida López, the wife of Sebastián López of Pongin (Ourense), forty-three years old, accused of having been married two times . . . said that it had been more than twenty-eight years ago that she had married the said Sebastián López in the eyes of the church and had made a married life with him for five years. At the end of that time, the said Sebastián López had left the land and was absent from the land for twenty years at the end of which, understanding that he was dead, she had married a second time. Certain witnesses testified that it had been four years that they had said that her first husband had been dead and that they had found his burial place in the monastery of Valparaiso . . . she was absolved.

18 Reconciling an unhappy couple, Spain 1669

According to Catholic doctrine, marriage was a sacrament that could only be administered once and lasted throughout this lifetime and into the next. As a result, divorce was unthinkable and the Church worked hard to keep unhappy couples together. However, from time to time, couples just split up and went their separate ways without ecclesiastical intervention. In this excerpt from an episcopal visitation to a parish in northwestern Spain, the Visitor attempted to reunite and reconcile a broken relationship.

(Libro de Visitas, San Pedro Maus, Archivo Histórico Diocesano de Ourense, 45.2.6,
f. 43 (1669). Translated by Allyson Poska.)

NOTICE: In the parish of San Pedro Maus on the ninth of April (1669) his
Honor Cardinal Don Antonio Pando, Visitor General of this bishopric, was
notified that Juan Nieto Blanco and Feliciana Arias de Montenegro, husband and wife, inhabitants of this parish, do not live together nor cohabitate
as ordained by Our Holy Mother Church resulting in scandal and great
criticism in the parish . . . he demanded that the aforementioned appear
before his Holiness, and only the aforementioned Juan Nieto came as the
aforementioned Feliciana Arias could not be found because she had left.
They looked for her and, before the parish priest and other men of the
parish, His Honor found out that the aforementioned Feliciana Arias was at
fault for them not living together and making a married life, in as much as
for the past four years that they were married she did not want to live with
the said Juan Nieto . . . His Honor mandates that the parish priest, Licenciado
Pedro de Losada or his assistant curate, notify the said Feliciana Arias that
within four days she should go back with the said Juan Nieto and make a
married life with him. And the Holy Mother Church mandates this under
the penalty of *excomunión maior latae sentencia* and 20 ducats for repair of
the Episcopal palaces. This occurring, the priest should publicly declare her
excommunicated and, having found her, give an account to the ecclesiastical court in order that it might proceed towards the most appropriate solution and punishment.

19 Reconciling an unhappy couple, Denmark 1540

In Malmø, the City Council became a marital court for a brief period after the Reforma-
tion, granting divorces, but trying primarily to reconcile partners in troubled marriages.
(*Malmø rådstueprotokol (Stadsbok) 1503–1548*, ed. Erik Kroman, along with Leif
Ljungberg and Einar Bager (Copenhagen, Selskabet for Udgivelse af Kilder til dansk
Historie, 1965), pp. 174 and 217–218. Translated by Grethe Jacobsen and Pernille
Arenfeldt.)

Henrik Brabander skindere

Anno ut supra [1540] after Mathie apostoli [February 27] here at the City
Hall in front of the Mayors and the Council and the Royal Reeve was summoned Henrik Brabander, burgher of this town, who announced and made
public that he had been friendly and well reconciled with his wife and her
mother and friends, and because he had dealt with her improperly with
strokes and beatings, he promised here today by his honour, neck and life,
that here-after he shall behave as a Christian and just person toward her, as

an honest man ought to do, and if she be found deserving of punishment, then he shall punish her decently and properly as an honest man would in any way. If he behaves otherwise, then this case shall remain open together with the next one and he be punished accordingly, thus has he hereby committed himself.

Apparently he did behave, as a later notice shows:
Anno 1545 on Friday the 6th day of March here at the City Hall in front of the Mayors and the Council and the Royal Reeve was summoned modest man, Henrik Brabander Skinder, burgher of this town, accompanied by the honest man, Hans Nielsen, burgher of Copenhagen, and Hans Severinsen Skrædder, burgher of Malmø, his dear brothers-in-law who publicly revealed and announced that they were most friendly and well reconciled with aforesaid Henrik Brabander about the entire inheritance left behind in property, gold, silver, money, landed property and other property, household contents, movables and immovables, whatever there was or could be mentioned, nothing excepted, which has been probated between them as the inheritance of aforesaid Henrik Brabander's wife Eline, now blessed in God, sister of aforesaid Hans Nielsen and of Anne, Hans Skrædders wife, in such a way that aforesaid Henrik Brabander shall keep all property, gold, silver, money and household contents, without any deductions and waive any rights he may have obtained in landed property and other property, which shall remain with Hans Nielsen and his sister Anne, wife of aforesaid Hans Skrædder, and their heirs and aforesaid Henrik acknowledges to have no other rights in any way after this day. And upon this agreement they gave each other today a complete and firm waiver with hand and mouth on both sides and agreed to let each other's heirs, born and unborn, be free and unencumbered for all further claims and demands concerning this inheritance in any way after this day.

20 Petition for separation, Spain 1627

Although officially divorce was not an option for Catholics, the Church did allow some parishioners to petition for a permanent separation. Although such a separation ended the misery of living in an unhappy marriage, neither of the parties could remarry as the sacrament of marriage extended beyond this life and into the next. In this petition, Marcos Franco lays out many of the doctrinally accepted reasons for separation, including the forced nature of the marriage and Marina's inability to bear children. (Archivo Histórico Provincial de Ourense, caja protocolos 3231, f. 17 (1627). Translated by Allyson Poska.)

Marcos Franco, inhabitant of Xinzo . . . I am married to Marina Feijóo, a woman of 60 years of age, with whom there is no hope of having children, a troublesome, foul-mouthed woman of very harsh disposition, who provokes quarrels and misfortunes . . . And although at the time of the contraction of the marriage, I said some words in which I might have taken her for my wife or she might have consented to me as her husband (or something similar) let it be understood from this point on that I said them against my will and consent and only to avoid scandal and pain . . . and I insist on not living with her . . . as I have affirmed in other protests and testimonies.

21 Impotence and divorce, Denmark 1635

After the Reformation in Denmark, it was possible to get a divorce on account of impotence. In the following case, the husband was clearly impotent in more than the physical meaning of the word.
(*Sokkelunds Herreds tingbøger 1634–36*, ed. Karen Marie Olsen (Copenhagen: Landbohistorisk Selskab 1974), pp. 150–151. Translated by Grethe Jacobsen and Pernille Arenfeldt.)

Court session Thursday April 9th, 1635

. . .

Rasmus Madsen in Holte appeared on behalf of his stepdaughter Karen Hansdatter and recounted how, seven years ago, she entered into marriage with a man by the name of Oluf Lauridsen Jyde then living in Skovshoved, and [who] now on account of his old age and fragile health has been granted food and shelter in the hospital [poor house] in Copenhagen, and that as soon as they had entered into holy matrimony, she had found him completely unfit for marital love, for which reason they immediately separated, each in order to seek his or her own living, and as his weakness and fragile health have increased over the years so that he cannot provide her with clothes, food, shelter or in other ways as is mentioned above, and no improvement is to be expected, she can no longer support herself on her own. Thus testified aforesaid Oluf Lauridsen and said this to be the truth as written down, and [he] required witness by jury.

22 Ending a bad marriage, Denmark 1540

In early modern Denmark, marriage was primarily a practical matter dealt with by the parents of the bride-to-be, regardless of her own wishes, and the potential husband. This was even more pronounced among the nobility than in other levels of society. However, as the following verdict from 1540 shows, the woman did have the possibility of resisting if she possessed a strong will and was well connected. The noblewoman Birgitte Gøje (c. 1511–1574) did not intend to fulfill the engagement contract her parents had forced her to sign in her childhood, but it was not until her royal protector, Queen Dorothea (1511–1571), intervened that a formal case was initiated and the engagement finally was dissolved. It must be added that until 1582, the binding contract for

133

a marriage in Denmark was the signed engagement contract rather than the religious blessing of the union. Four years after this verdict was issued Birgitte Gøje did marry (at the age of 33) and supposedly out of her heart's desire. Her marriage to Herluf Trolle (1516–1565) is often referred to as an unusually happy marriage at the time, as the sentence he wrote on the back of the document also reveals (see below). (Original in the Danish National Archives, Copenhagen. The verdict has been published in *Danske Magazin*, ser. III, vol. 1 (Copenhagen, 1842). Translated by Grethe Jacobsen and Pernille Arenfeldt.)

High-born Prince, mighty gracious King and Lord, as Your Grace, His Royal Majesty, has commanded us, your subservient and humble servants, Rectors and Professors at Your Grace's University here in Copenhagen, to examine and consider this case regarding the marriage between honest and wellborn noble persons Jesper Daa of Enggaard and Lady Birgitte Gøje in order that we provide Your Grace with a Christian answer to the questions put forth as follows[:] whether or not the aforementioned persons' betrothal, which took place 15 years ago, was a rightful marriage, and whether or not the same persons, according to their statements and the circumstances of the case, may now be free and released from each other, both with a good conscience or not. Firstly, we meticulously considered and scrutinized the two written accounts that the two aforementioned persons each had entrusted us in this their marriage case according to Your Grace's command[;] in addition we listened to their statements and replies secretly and openly and properly instructed and admonished them according to the Holy Scriptures that they would confess to us or tell us nothing but the proper truth, which they both promised under sworn oath. When we had listened to and understood both their hearts' true confessions, followed by much mutual deliberation and discussion with each other and consulting the Holy Scriptures, we were asked what each of us would answer Your Royal Majesty with a good conscience to the questions put forward by Your Grace in this case. In the end, we unanimously agreed with the mind God has granted us that we could not but say, after considering statements and replies and the circumstances of the case, that there has not been a proper marriage in the eyes of God between the aforementioned honest and noble persons Jesper Daa and Lady Birgitte Gøje, because to proper marriage belongs true heartfelt and honest free will and consent from both parts, which in truth is not found to have existed at any time between the aforementioned persons[.] Firstly, because the aforementioned Lady Birgitte has sworn the salvation of her soul and the fate of the Kingdom of Heaven that she never consented with mind and heart [to take] the same Jesper Daa as her husband. But for what she said and did in this matter 15 years ago, she highly begs the pardon of God and people[;] not only was she, with

134

slyness and wiliness, seduced and coaxed in her foolish childhood, but also obviously urged and forced by her father and friends and particularly by her stepmother. Regarding the letter she gave the aforementioned Jesper Daa, she called God the Almighty to be her witness and explained that a nun in the Convent of Ring by the name of Mette Ovesdaughter, under whose discipline, subjection and punishment by birch she explained to have been around the time, both coaxed and threatened her to sign the letter after another letter she [Mette Ovesdaughter] presented to her, so with tears [and] against the will and consent of her heart because of intimidation and threat and some out of fear and danger, she wrote [her letter, and] this [she] demonstrably [did] with the letter of the aforementioned Mette Ovesdaughter. Regarding the 'yes' that she was to have answered to the questions she was asked when they were joined together, [she told us that] she prayed to God to truly relieve her from her distress and that she truly did not answer from her heart but solely out of the terror, fear and danger that she had of her father, stepmother and her other friends, who said that they were not willing to lose their honour for her sake. In the same way risking the loss of salvation of her soul, she said of the betrothal gift that the aforementioned Jesper Daa gave her, that her stepmother accepted it and hung it around her neck against her will and consent, neither at that time nor as long as her stepmother remained alive did she dare to denounce it. She said that at the time she was an inexperienced child not older than her eleventh year, at which age she dared not openly resist her parents and friends and [she] did not fully understand what is involved in marriage. During the time her stepmother lived she dared not speak out against her or anger her, but shortly after the stepmother's death, she did overtly make her heart's will and reasons known summoning the aforementioned Jesper Daa to Kolding [to tell him] that he should not place his trust in her, which he also confirmed [both] in writing and orally. Furthermore, she returned her betrothal gift to him. Thus, when she had reached her fourteenth year she announced that it was not with her will and consent that they had been joined together [in marriage]. Prior to the death of her stepmother she continuously [but] secretly lamented the fact that she was forced and coaxed to have this man whom her heart never held or would come to hold to her friends and to the ones she dared moan to, [and] that she truly did so was witnessed under his sworn oath and to his salvation by the honest and much learned man Mr. Peder Thomsen, Superintendent of Vendsyssel Diocese, who at the same time was in the service of her father. Similarly, during these 15 years, she never expressed any act of love or affection towards the aforementioned Jesper Daa neither with pleasing words, present[s] or in other ways, as usually happens between a properly betrothed man and woman[.] She never wished to see him or to hear his name mentioned without deep grief in her heart and bitter tears, which is not usual where there is good will and consent on both sides. Similarly we have also asked Lady Birgitte's father the honest and wellborn man and upright knight Lord Mogens Gøje and her three brothers, Albrecht Gøje, Eskild Gøje and Christoffer Gøje, and also her sister Lady Eline, if they at any time sensed that Lady Birgitte possessed will and love and of her heart consented to accept the aforementioned Jesper Daa[.] Everyone unanimously answered under sworn oath [and] according to their conscience's truth that they never sensed that from her, but it was known to them that she always cried and fell ill whenever she either saw him or heard his name mentioned. The same was confirmed and confessed under sworn oaths by the following honest and freeborn [people]: Lord Mourits Olsen, Claus Daa, Lady Sophie [wife of] Lord Axel Brahe, and Lady Sophie [wife of] Erik Madsen, who frequently associated with Lady Birgitte at the time when this matter was negotiated. The aforementioned Jesper Daa similarly confessed and confirmed that he, after Lady Birgitte had told him of the 'no' in her heart, which before had remained unknown [to him] and only at that time was he clearly told, never during these many years complained neither to her parents nor friends nor with any legal proceedings that he had been deserted by her or and that she had done him injustice, but he was fully willing to accept it and left it as such. Lastly, we clearly asked the aforementioned Jesper Daa if he would or could with several statements renounce and dispute any of the statements which the aforementioned Lady Birgitte had revealed and confessed to us[;] to this the aforementioned Jesper Daa replied that he neither could nor would ask more from her, except that she stands by her oath and obligation under God's wrath and eternal condemnation. After [considering] these recounted statements and replies and the circumstances of the case and Lady Birgitte's sworn oaths and obligations which stands written, we cannot but otherwise state and understand from the Holy Scriptures that there has been no proper marriage in the eyes of God between the aforementioned persons Jesper Daa and Lady Birgitte. In the same manner we have, according to the permission and command by Your Royal Majesty, summoned all Superintendents here in Your Grace's Realm, Denmark, and provided them with the particulars of this case and its circumstances that have been written here, which they also have closely examined and considered and unanimously decided and consented with us. This, our answer, which we have given and written in this account, is truly Christian [and] according to the laws of God and nature[.] Therefore we humbly and submissively beg Your Royal Majesty that Your Grace will accept this, our unanimous answer, in the best way, because we have rendered it to the best of our ability [and] with a good conscience

136

according to Your Grace's command[.] Written in Copenhagen Saint Lawrence day, Anno etc. M.D.XL under the seal of Your Grace's University.

(On the back:) The verdict of the University in Copenhagen between Jesper Daa and my dear wife Birgitte Gøje, and at the time of the verdict it was unknown to her and me that we by God's Providence would be joined. H. Trolle in his own hand.

23 Ordinance about marital separation, Portugal early sixteenth century

During the reign of King D. Manuel I (1495–1521), ordinances were compiled, organized and consolidated. Although these laws were not necessarily written during his reign, they are an indication of what was in effect at that time. The ordinance below suggests that marital separation was allowed, at least on the books, and that in such a case a child's upkeep was primarily the responsibility of the father, whether it was born in or out of wedlock.
(*Ordenações do Senhor Rey D. Manuel, vol. IV* (Coimbra: Na Real Imprensa da Universidade, 1797), pp. 175–176. Translated by Darlene Abreu-Ferreira.)

Titulo LXVIII. Upon the birth of any child of a legitimate marriage, and while the said marriage lasts between the husband and the wife both have to care for it at their own expense, and give it what it needs according to its station and rank; and upon the separation of the marriage for whatever reason without the death of either [parent], the mother shall maintain the upkeep of the child until it reaches three years of age, and this in milk only, and the father shall cover all other expenses that are necessary for its upbringing; but if the mother is of such station and rank, that she could not reasonably nurse her child, the father shall maintain at his expense the wetnurse, for the said period of three years, for the milk, as well as whatever other expense, that is necessary for its rearing.

1. And if the child is not born out of a legitimate marriage, be it natural or spurious, and of whatever other manner, the mother shall maintain the upkeep of the child in milk for the said three years, and all other expenses, in the said period, as well as after, shall be done at the expense of the father, as has been said of the legitimate child. And if in those said three years the mother has any expenses concerning this child, that is the obligation of the father, she can in all cases recover it, and have it from the said father, for she did it, when she was responsible for it.

2. And in all cases where a father is responsible to pay the upkeep of his child, if he does not have the means to do it, it [the expenses] shall be paid out of the child's inheritance; and if the child has no inheritance its upkeep will be at the expense of the mother, in as much as she can do, according to what we stipulate.

137

24 Wife's legal deposition against an abusive husband, Russia 1659

The following legal deposition was submitted in 1659 to the ecclesiastical court of the bishop of Ustiug, a prosperous provincial town in northern Russia. It consists of a complaint filed by Annitsa Osokina against her husband, who abused her, stole her personal property, and abandoned her. Women in pre-modern Russia were empowered to represent themselves in legal action, as Annitsa did here, but often they sought the assistance of their natal relatives. To gain the sympathy of the court, petitioners portrayed themselves in helpless, deferential terms and often exaggerated their dire straits. Even so, the wealth of detail attests to the reality of Annitsa's plight. The outcome of this suit is not recorded.

(*Akty kholmogorskoi i ustiuzhkoi eparkhii*, bk. 3 [Russkaia istoricheskaia biblioteka, vol. 25] (St. Petersburg, 1908), pp. 305–306. Translated by Eve Levin.)

Annitsa daughter of Semen, a resident of Ustiug, petitions the Lord Archpriest Vladimir and the monks of the Cathedral Church of Dormition . . . of Ustiug, against her husband, Kliment son of Isak Osokin, a resident of Ustiug.

Lord, last year, in 7166 [according to the Byzantine calendar; this year corresponds to the Western year 1658], during Lent, my husband Kliment got drunk and caroused. In that state, he came home, and beat poor me and injured me to [the point of] death many times. After that, my husband bragged that he would commit murder and all sorts of awful things against me. He took clothing from me, an orphan, linens, a hat, dresses, and shirts, and my trunk, and all the brass and iron and tin and woven housewares [he took] it is unknown where. He sold his house, where he and I lived together on Nikolskaia street in Ustiug. And now I, poor me, have gone into a final decline: I weep all the time; I go naked and barefoot; I am dying of hunger; and I can no longer go to pray to God in the church at all; and my husband took away from poor me my little bit of clothing and property. And when he sold the house, he gave a donation to the Archangel monastery in Ustiug, and now he lives there, in the Archangel monastery, and he does not provide for poor me to eat and drink, and he does not provide me with clothing and footwear. And I, poor me, pawned my gold-washed silver bracelets, and with that money I bought myself grain: five measures of rye and two measures of oats and half a measure of wheat, but my husband Kliment took that grain that I purchased out of the house and it is unknown where, and he left poor me to perish in the end.

Lord Archpriest Vladimir of Christ and monks, have mercy upon me, poor Annitsa. Order, Lord, that this my deposition be accepted and that my petition be recorded, and that this case by investigated immediately. Lord, be generous, have mercy.

This deposition was given on March 6, 7167

25 Cover of Hans Sachs' satirical poem, *The Nine Skins of a Bad Wife*, Germany 1554

The German poet and playwright Hans Sachs frequently wrote literary works based on popular stories and moral tales, which were performed and sold widely. One of these was the story of the nine skins of a bad wife, which holds that a wife has nine layers of skin, eight of which have the properties of certain animals, such as a bear, cat, fish, pig, and dog. These must be beaten off before her human skin can be reached, which the husband is doing with a chair in this picture. Husbands in all parts of Europe had the legal right to beat their wives, though in some areas there were limitations on this. In Germany a husband could beat a wife only 'until the blood flowed', and in England only with a stick that was smaller around than his thumb, which is the origin of the term 'rule of thumb'.

(Hans Sachs, *Die Neunerley heudt einer bösen Frawen, sambt ihren Neun Eygeenschafften* (Nuremberg: Georg Merckel, 1554.)

Die Neunerley heudt
einer bösen Frawen / sambt
jren Neun Eygenschafften.

Mehr das Bitter Süeß Ehlich
Leben.

Hans Sachs.

26 Israhel van Meckenem, *Battle for the Pants*, Germany late fifteenth century

Another common literary and artistic motif that both reflected and shaped real behavior was the 'battle of the pants', in which a husband and wife fight over his pants, which, then as now, stood for control over the household. In this engraving, the wife has her distaff, on which she spun thread, raised against her husband; the distaff was the most common symbol for women and the female side of the family, which is still occasionally called the 'distaff' side. Men in the sixteenth century wore pants over their hose, and tied both on with long strings.

(Original in Berlin Kupferstichkabinett. Reproduced by permission.)

27 Letter regarding marital conflict, Wales 1615

Woman with abusive husbands might turn to their own parents for help, though there were limits on what they could or would do, in this letter, Sir John Wynn writes to his son-in-law and good friend Sir Roger Mostyn. Wynn had just had an argument with John Bodvel, his other son-in-law, who was married to Wynn's daughter Elizabeth and had come early to fetch his wife home from visiting her parents. The Wynns don't think it is safe to travel because the roads are flooded and Elizabeth is pregnant. Sir John was disturbed by Bodvel's hostility toward his daughter, which had led to physical violence, though he accepted his husbandly power over her. Elizabeth did not die at her husband's hand, as her father worried, but out-lived him by thirty years.
(N.L.W., 9055E, f. 110, March 16, 1615. Sir John Wynn at Gwydir to Sir Roger Mostyn. Excerpted by Katharine Swett.)

I concluded with him that I was glad to understand his mind so fully and seeing he hated me and my daughter I said I would be advised by my friends whether it were convenient for me to adventure my child to cohabit with him, in that I had a late example of an aunt of mine killed . . . in the like manner. I told him he could no way so much hurt me as by killing of my daughter who he had made lose 2 children already and almost her life & now being by the goodness of God in way of recovery & with child again he meant to end her outright, which if he effected, he was to have a new wife & I the loss of my child and the inheritance which her child should have, therefore I assured him I would in despite of him . . . do my endeavor to keep my child, being in the case she is, out of tyrannous hands and possession. On Tuesday at night he struck her with his foot in the ham being in bed and asleep, that she shrieked. Such a toad, so false, proud and humorless I never knew. I pray you advise me what course to take in this business for I rely more on you then upon any other man. You know her nature to be Choleric and he will not cease to vex and abuse her until he kill her . . .

28 Criticism of marriage, Spain 1613

In a world where marital separations were doctrinally difficult and financially out of the reaches of most ordinary Catholics, marriage could feel like a curse rather than a blessing. Unhappy couples had few options other than stay together. According to the Spanish Inquisition, however, even making statements against the sacrament of marriage was heresy. In this case, a young María Afonso, the nineteen-year old wife of a tailor in Santiago de Compostela, faced punishment by the Inquisition after she publicly complained about her marital state.
(Relaciones de Causas, Archivo Histórico Nacional, Sección Inquisición, legajo 2042, no. 54, f. 1 (1613). Translated by Allyson Poska.)

... witnesses said that she said that she had been a concubine for a year and a half and that then it was in the service of God and at present she was married, and that was in the service of the devil. [She was sentenced to] hear mass wearing the tunic of the penitent, abjure de levi, and she was reprimanded and exiled from this city for one year.

29 A petition to reclaim a dowry, Germany 1539

Men and women frequently petitioned rulers and city councils with various requests. Such petitions were drafted by notaries or lawyers, so they are written in formal legal language and in a way that will best help the supplicant achieve his or her aims. It is thus difficult to say if everything in them is exactly accurate, but they are certainly based on the real circumstances of the case. This is a petition from Ursula Kolhauffer to the city council of Munich.

(Munich Stadtarchiv, Urgichten, Nr. 87 (1539). Translated by Merry Wiesner-Hanks.)

Honorable, wise, just, and careful sirs, I, Ursula Kolhauffen, Adam Wagner's wife, would like your wisdoms to know about the case involving me and my husband Adam Wagner, which your wisdoms certainly already know about in part. That is, that he is supposed to have another wife [besides me]. The situation that your wisdoms put to me, is that I was supposed to bring proof that she is still living, and I ventured to do this. But God called to me in the meantime, and I delivered the child with which I was pregnant. I was ill because of the child, and I had nothing other than what pious people shared with me. When the child was two weeks old, I got up and went with the child to Gaissing in the duchy of Fürstenberg, and I found her [the other wife] myself. I wanted to vindicate the case myself, but I did not have the power or right to do so. The authorities in Gaissing told me that if my husband Adam Wagner himself were there, they would handle the case quickly and help me gain what I sought, determine whether she was his wife or not, and whether I could set myself against both of them, as I had requested. He [Wagner] was seeking [to keep] my dowry, which I will swear on my life. For he heaped shame and insults with no justification on me, which threatened my body and life. That is, in the mayor's house in Gaissing, a man whose wife was standing next to him said that my husband publicly said in Zell and elsewhere that I had dishonored myself twice, and was a murderous piece of goods. He also said this to me when we were home – that I dishonored him twice and also sought to dishonor the children – so he used violence against me. After that he said further that I had moved away from him for whorish reasons and was now moving from place to place like a whore. But I can prove that when I moved out of Munich, I lived with pious honorable people, and supported myself and my child with hard work. Further, he said that the child that I had was not his, but I can prove to the day and hour [that it is]. I have already testified to all of this in writing, and sent it by messenger to the judge in Freising. The judge said to the messenger that he would not order him [Wagner] to appear because he did not have jurisdiction over the case because it had been started elsewhere. I asked not for his life or bodily punishment, but that he be compelled to give me my dowry back and to declare me free of him. He then offered, in the presence of two men, namely Jorgen Dylger and Franntz Federmacher, both citizens of Munich, to pay it back to me year by year and declare me free of him. That is exactly what I am now petitioning and requesting. If you will not agree to this, I will protest, and prove to your wisdoms that I made my request properly according to the law in the proper place, and the law itself is at fault here. I have done everything according to the law, and have revealed everything to you about his [Wagner's] actions. It is now my request and supplication to your wisdoms, that you prevail upon him to do what he himself agreed to do in front of Jorgen Dylger and Franntz Federmacher. I place myself under the care and protection of your wisdoms. Dated the eleventh of April, 1539. Your wisdom's obedient subject, Ursula Kolhauffen.

Questions for discussion

1 How were notions of marriage in this period different from our own?
2 What regional differences do you find here regarding relationships between husband and wife? What similarities?
3 Why did couples marry in this period? What was the point of marriage?
4 How do the wives and husbands who appear in these documents seem to consider their marriages? What is important for them in a marriage?
5 What was a legitimate reason for divorce or separation? What were the procedures for leaving one's spouse?

5

ECONOMIC LIFE

Economic life in early modern Europe, as today, consisted of a variety of types of activities. Land ownership remained a significant source of wealth – in some parts of Europe, *the* most significant – so that men and women who held property sought to retain or expand their holdings and pass them on to their heirs. Land owners included everyone from members of royal families down the social scale to free peasant property holders, which made their experiences quite diverse. Most inheritance systems favored sons over daughters, especially in terms of landed property, and in some places women were forbidden to own land at all; in other areas daughters could inherit, and women, especially widows, played a very active role in managing their estates.

Along with land, trade offered increasing economic opportunities, with the wealthiest families and individuals, such as the Medici of Florence or the Fuggers of Augsburg, making their fortunes through banking, international trade, and money lending on a grand scale. The Fuggers, for example, regularly loaned money to the rulers of Spain and Germany, and at one point owned Venezuela because it had been given as collateral on a loan and the rulers had subsequently defaulted. Most of the people involved in this level of commerce were male, for women had difficulty travelling to engage in commerce, and, if they were married, could generally only conduct business with their husband's approval. They did invest in overseas and regional trading ventures however, and a few made great fortunes. Many more women engaged in local trade, and along with men sold foodstuffs, clothing, and other goods at the public marketplace, found at the center of any town, or engaged in small-scale pawn broking and money lending. After 1500 the trade goods they handled often included merchandise from Europe's overseas colonies, such as sugar, chocolate, tea and coffee, new types of fabrics, for example calico, and new types of household goods, for example lacquerware and the porcelain that came to be known as 'china'. The amount of consumer goods in many households began to grow, though it was still tiny in comparison to modern households.

Production was organized in a variety of ways. In most urban areas, craft guilds had grown up in the twelfth and thirteenth centuries, which were generally male organizations and followed the male life cycle. One became an apprentice at puberty, became a journeyman four to ten years later, traveled around learning from a number of masters, then settled down, married, opened one's own shop, and worked at the same craft full time until one died or got too old to work any longer. Transitions between these stages were marked by ceremonies, and master craftsmen were formally inscribed in guild registers and took part in governing the guild. Women fit into guilds much more informally; the master's wife, daughters, and servants often worked alongside him and the journeymen and apprentices or sold the goods made in the shop, and masters' widows ran shops after the death of their husbands, though they could not participate in running the guild. By the fifteenth century many guilds began to restrict women's work, however, arguing that women took jobs away from men and destroyed the 'honor' of the guild. Women – and many men – continued to be employed in production that was not organized into guilds, making products that required little skill, such as soap or sauerkraut. Urban investors also began to hire rural individuals or households to produce wool, linen, silk, and, later, cotton thread, or cloth (or cloth that was a mixture of these), paying the household or individual only for the labor and retaining ownership of the raw materials and in some cases the tools and machinery used. This is often termed domestic or cottage industry, because production went on in a household rather than a factory. It was the earliest form of mass production, and would also provide cheaper consumer goods for European households.

Industrial production would later dramatically change the work and home lives of much of Europe's population, but its impact in the early modern period was more limited, and the total number of people employed in domestic industry remained relatively small. Domestic service was a much more common type of work, especially for young people of both sexes; many rural households hired servants, and between 15 and 30 percent of the population of most cities was made up of domestic servants. Some servants in Europe were, in fact, slaves, purchased from Eastern Europe in Italian and Ottoman households or from northern and western Africa in Spanish and Portuguese ones. Both servants and slaves often engaged in productive tasks in artisanal households, and generally ate and slept with the family, for there was rarely enough space for them to have separate quarters.

OWNERSHIP AND MANAGEMENT OF PROPERTY AND GOODS

1 Inventories of household goods, Germany 1530–1550

Inventories taken at the time of death or remarriage provide extensive information about the property, household goods, and work-related equipment found in early modern households. Cities often required such inventories, which were done by professional appraisers who noted everything in great detail. Inventories of wealthy

households went on for many pages, while those of poorer individuals were very brief. The following three inventories come from the German city of Nuremberg, the first two taken at the time of death and the third at a remarriage. The values placed on goods are expressed in a variety of monetary terms, with the most common being the silver pfennig (abbreviated d for 'denarius', the Latin word for penny), the pound (abbreviated £) and the golden gulden or florin, abbreviated fl. The values of these coins relative to each other changed depending on the relative value of gold and silver, but a pound was generally figured at 30 d and the gulden at £8 1s.
(Nuremberg, Stadtarchiv, Inventarbuecher, **(a)**, f. 101 (1530), **(b)**, fs. 83–84 (1537), **(c)**, f. 89 (1550). Translated by Merry Wiesner-Hanks.)

(a) I, Kunigunde, the late Fritz Trayfels wife and also a citizen of Nuremberg, list publicly with this inventory all of my goods and debts that were on hand at the death of my husband. I had them appraised in the presence of Albrecht Liner, pansmith, and Lorentz Osterreich as guardians of my daughter Fridl that I raised with my husband. I had all my goods appraised immediately by Margareth Pesolt, sworn appraiser, as follows here:

Tin dishes – 62 pounds, worth 20 pfennig (d) to the pound, total 4 gulden (fl), £6 1s 10d.
A silver beaker weighing 13 lot, 2 pounds, total 6 fl, 3d. 10 1/2 pounds of brass, the pound worth 15d. total £4 1s 11d.
30 1/2 pounds old copper, the pound at 10d – 1 fl £1 1s 11d. Three leather pillows – 1 fl.
A strawsack and a canopy [for a bed] – £5.
A table – 5s 10d.
A candleholder – 4d.
5 glasses and one curved glass – 1s.
A bench – 2s 1d.
A reel and spindle – 3s 4d.
A bird cage – 1s 10d.
A mirror and spoonholder – 3d.
A dress – £5.
2 pair of stockings – 4s 2d.
A camisole and two jerseys – £6. A green skirt – £2. An old hat – 4d.
A black smock – 3s 4d.
An old iron bucket – 3d.
One pound of feathers – 1s 8d. Two small baskets – 6d. A black bucket – 8d. A harness – 4s 2d.
A sofa, straw sack, underbed, 2 pillows, 2 linen sheets and a bed cover, all taken together – 7 fl.
Old rags in a small box – 10d.
Two cushions – 1s 8d.

One and a half *els* of linen cloth – 3s 4d.

A linen sheet – 2s 6d. Six tablecloths – £9. 7 handtowels – £2.

A small chest – 1s 10d. A sieve and a spit – 3s 4d. A meat fork – 4d.

Bowls and baskets – 8d.

Yeast and flour – 5d.

A red woman's dress – £4. A black coat – 3 fl. A cloak – £5.

Three hammers – 10d. Three lights – 10d. A belt – 5d.

The sum of all listed equals 31 fl £5 2s 1d. Now follows my debts on the death of my husband: To my brother-in-law Albrecht 4 1/2 fl; my sister-in-law Frennkin £8; for taxes £6; Mr. Ebersbass £3; Mrs. Frennkin £2; my brother-in-law Endress Frennkin 2 fl; the baker's wife 1/2 fl.

The sum of all debts equals 8 fl £2 0s 6d. Therefore when 8 fl £2 0s 6d debts are subtracted from the total of all goods 31 fl £5 2s 1d, 23 fl £3 1s 7d remain. Given with the protestation and oath that if I find any more, over a short or long time, that I haven't listed here and that was on hand, I'll report it as well and will keep nothing back.

The aforementioned widow has sworn to this inventory in the presence of the guardians as is legally proper.

(b) After Katherine Deunin, a sworn appraiser, died about six weeks ago, she left various movable goods at the house of Hans Soldnet, a tailor here. This tailor, on the recommendation of the honorable and wise Board of Widows and Orphans, had the following inventory and appraisal taken by Anna Mayrin, a sworn appraiser, as follows here point by point:

In cash – £2 1s 3d.

An underbed – £6.

A small straw mattress – 1s 9d.

A canopy – £1 0s 10d.

An old leather-colored cloak with a white lining – £5. An old slip – 2s 4d.

An old fur – 1s 3d.

Two old sheets – 1s 9d.

An old neckcloth – 8d.

Two old small trunks – 2s 4d. Two cups for brandy – 4d. Two old neckerchiefs – 5d. Old rags – 11s. Two bags – 5d.

Total sum of all goods listed here equals 2 fl £2 0s 5d. Now follow the debts of the aforementioned Deunin, known at her death. To Hans Soldner, tailor, her landlord, for rent and money for the funeral, and also for his trouble and time, one and a half gulden. To Barbara, Sebastian Pecken the mail-maker's wife at Spizenberg for a veil and 6 pounds of spun yarn, one and a half gulden. To Christina, a maid here, for a coat that she bought but did not pay for, one gulden. When the debts are taken from the goods remaining, the debts are greater by 1 fl £6 0s 6d. Further than this, I, Hans Soldner, have no information.

(c) I, Hanns Weykopf, citizen and cabinetmaker in Nuremberg, publicly attest that my present second wife, Barbara, brought the following to our residence after our first legitimate cohabitation. She placed into my hands, in the presence of the honorable Lucas Gryder and Jacob Ulherz, both citizens and the assigned guardians for the children of my first marriage, diverse money and movable goods to me. The movable goods and clothes were listed, estimated and appraised by the sworn appraiser Barbara Weyssin and are piece by piece described in order as follows:

In cash – received in good coinage in the normal currencies used in this area and pure gold – 50 fl. In clothing – a black Arles cloth cloak – 9 fl. A red satin underdress with a green border – 5 fl. A black coat with a white lining – 7 fl. A fur – £10.
A black jersey apron – 2 fl.
A black patched petticoat – £2.
A black camel-hair breastcloth – 3 1/2 fl. A red waistcoat – 1 1/2 fl. An el of black damask – 2 fl. A black veil – £5.
A jacketed apron – 1/2 fl.
A cotton pinafore – 2d.
A green pair of stockings – £3.
A bag lined with satin – 1/2 fl.
A white headcovering – £3. A gold ring – £5. A hat – 3 oft.
Six neckcloths – 1 1/2 fl. Three undershirts – 1/2 fl. Four bodices – 12d.

The total sum of all recorded property and goods is 94 fl £5 0s 9d. That I hold to with complete confidence. If I do not publish this [i.e., bring the inventory to the city council] it will be up to the guardians for my children from my first marriage.

Both partners have sworn to this with their oaths in the presence of the guardians.

2 Peasants report dishonest officials, Russia fifteenth century

It was sometimes advantageous for those conducting property inventories to make false reports. In this document, peasants of the village of Izboishcha petition their landlords and landlady living in the city of Novgorod about incorrect property reports.

This wealthy family owned large tracts of land outside the city, controlled a substantial portion of the international trade, and were entitled to claim one of the mayoral seats on the city council. Among the duties of landlords in fifteenth-century Russia was interceding for their dependents in judicial suits and protecting them from dishonest officials; by protecting them, landowners protected their source of revenue. The following document consists of a scrap of a note written on birchbark, which was used as a cheap substitute for paper, from fifteenth-century Novgorod, medieval Russia's primary commercial city. Most birchbark notes were brief, akin to the modern e-mail, and were discarded in the trash after being read. Archeologists have been unearthing them from excavation sites, where the waterlogged soil at the lower strata (dating before the mid fifteenth century) preserved them. Many of the documents survive only in fragmentary form.

(*Novgorodskie gramoty na bereste* (*iz raskopok 1956–1957gg.*) (Moscow: AN SSSR, 1963), pp. 137–140. Translated by Eve Levin.)

To lord Andreian Mikhailovich, lord Mikita Mikhailovich and our lady Nastasia, Mikhail's wife, the peasants of Izboishcha petition. Here, lords, in your district, court officials are from Gorotnia, and they are false officials. And here, lords, there are false documents. And they enumerated your property incorrectly. And the court scribe wrote out a false document, and placed a seal on it. [The placing of a seal marked the document as officially authorized.] And in Parfa they are writing. And your peasants petition you, their lords.

3 Sale of land, Russia 1620

Land was the primary source of wealth in most parts of Europe. In some areas, women could not inherit or own land, but in Russia women could legally own property, including land, and manage it themselves. Often they collaborated with kinsfolk, both men and women, in commercial dealings. Because business was usually based in families rather than in individuals, women appear as primary actors most often when they are widows, and thus the senior family member. In this document, dating to 1610, one widow, Fedosia, is selling a homestead that her deceased husband had received from another widow, Anna, as the result of a mortgage. The purchaser, Bogdan, shares the same profession as Fedosia's late husband – cannoneer. Fedosia avers that she owns the homestead free and clear, and promises to assume any costs of litigation, if claims to the property surface later and Bogdan's title to the homestead was challenged. Although the multiple recent transfers of this property make such claims more likely, in fact this language was standard in deeds of this sort.

(Published original in *Real Estate Transfer Deeds in Novgorod, 1609–1616*, ed. Ingegerd Nordlander (Stockholm: Almqvist & Wiksell, 1987), pp. 153–154. Translated by Eve Levin.)

I, the widow Fedosia Ivan's daughter, wife of the cannoneer Potafei Sidorov, have sold the mortgaged homestead of my husband to the cannoneer

Bogdan, Ovdokim's son, the master tailor. This, the cannoneer's, homestead, had belonged to the nun Anna, widow of Ulian, the scribe of St. Sofia Cathedral, and had previously belonged to the baker Vasilii, and is located on St. Vlasii Street. The homestead stands between the Monastery of the Savior and my, Fedosia's, house, on the other side, going from the Volkhov River to the Church of St. Vlasii. On the homestead there are the house, low cottage, hayrick, loft, and fence surrounding the garden. I, Fedosia, received from Bogdan Ovdokim's son the price of thirty altyny minus one grivna. [The altyn and the grivna were small silver coins; the total price here was the equivalent of a little more than one and a half rubles.] That homestead is untaxed, being in a tax-free area. I, Fedosia, do not have any debt on my husband's homestead, and there is no debt or mortgage on my husband's homestead [recorded] in writs or in wills. If anyone shall sue me, Fedosia, or Bogdan concerning my husband's mortgaged or encumbered house, and if [that person] shall cause Bogdan loss and bureaucratic involvement [The Russian term, *volokita*, means 'bureaucratic delay' or, as we might call it, 'red tape'.] because of that house because of my, Fedosia's, neglect to clear it, I, Fedosia, will assume that loss and bureaucratic involvement, according to this bill of sale. Witnesses to this are Tretiak Ivan's son Ruskii and the notice was written by the merchant Mikhailets Peter's son Ilkin in the year 7118 (= 1610), July 28.

4 Court case involving confiscation of property, Denmark 1553

In early modern Denmark, it was common practice that the wife and children inherited property (especially land) collectively from the husband/father, and this was clearly the case in this instance as the woman refers to the land as both her and her children's property. She clearly felt responsible for protecting not only her own but also her children's interests. As she was a noblewoman, the case was tried at the King's Bench.
(Original in the Danish National Archives. Additional copies in manuscript collections in the Royal Library, Copenhagen, Denmark. Most recent edition in *Danske Domme 13 75-1662, De private Domssamlinger, I: 13 75-1553*, Det danske Sprog- og Litteraturselskab (Copenhagen: Reitzel, 1978), pp. 361–362. Translated by Grethe Jacobsen and Pernille Arenfeldt.)

Was presented to us at our King's Bench our dear Byrge Trolle of Lillo, our faithful Lord and Councillor and had summoned our dear Lady Anne, widow of Axel Ugerup of Ugerup, and charged her for some axes, horses and carts that she had ordered to be seized from some burghers in our town of Væ in their own forest, which they have been granted by us and for which they render us and the Crown tax and manorial rent, and Byrge Trolle was of the opinion that she had done them injustice thereby.

To this the aforementioned Lady Anne answered that the axes, horses and carts she had ordered to be seized from the burghers of Væ had been taken from them in her own forest and property which belongs to her and her children, because they [the burghers] had entered and chopped trees in her forest without her permission and she had not let anything be taken from them on their own property and forest, which they have [been granted] by us. Lady Anne further explained that [some] noblemen have been ordered to examine the circumstances regarding the forest and forest boundaries over which they dispute and that the same forest which they dispute shall therefore remain physically and legally inviolate until a decision has been reached.

Then upon address and reply and the circumstances of the case, the court declared that if Lady Anne, [widow of] Axel Ugerup has taken any axes, horses or carts from the aforementioned burghers of Væ on the field belonging to their own town, of which they pay taxes and render us services, and this can be proven with satisfaction, then she has done them injustice, but because [some] noble men have been ordered to decide on the property and forest, which they dispute and [which] is declared inviolable, and no conclusion has been reached regarding it, then the land shall remain inviolate until it is decided who has the right to the land and that person shall have whatever is confiscated on the land.

Given in Copenhagen, on the Monday on the Feast of Saint Boniface [June 5], in the presence of our dear Lord Mogens Gyldenstjerne, Knight, Tage Thott, Verner Parsbjerg, Christoffer Hvidtfeldt and Lord Lauge Brahe, Knight, our faithful men and Councillors. 1553.

SALES AND TRADE

5 Petition requesting the prohibition of grain exports, The Azores (Portugal) 1591

Merchandise of all types, from basic commodities, such as grain and timber, to luxury goods, such as spices and silks, were traded widely in early modern Europe, with the merchants ranging from extremely wealthy international wholesale brokers to poor local shopkeepers and peddlers. Merchants at all levels sought a profit, which often meant they shipped goods to places where prices were higher. In the case of grain, this could lead to shortages, and political authorities were often faced with competing demands of two groups of citizens, those who wished to seek greater profits by exporting their products and the local populace who needed affordable food. In 1591 the town council of Velas, on the Portuguese Azorean island of São Jorge, dealt with a petition from some concerned citizens about the impending departure of locally grown grains.

(António dos Santos Pereira, *A Ilha de São Jorge, Séculos XV–XVII* (Ponta Delgada: Universidade dos Açores, 1987), f. 74–f. 75v [326–327]. Translated by Darlene Abreu-Ferreira.)

Year of the birth of our lord Jesus Christ of one thousand five hundred and ninety-one in this town of Velas of this island of São Jorge, having gathered together in the town council the distinguished officials João Teixeira and Pero Gomez d'Avila, ordinary judges, and Amtonio Gonçalvez Tagalas and Francisco Breves, councillors, and the procurators Amtonio Gonçalvez, procurator of the council, and Mateus Lopez and Mellchior Garcia, shoe-makers, and Amtonio Gonçalvez, weaver, procurators of the masters, by the said procurators of the council as well as the ones for the masters, it was said and requested to the said officials that it had come to their attention that in this region some provisions had arrived for some local individuals to freight wheat from their rents and harvest that they have on this island. They requested them in the name of God and of the King our lord that their Graces as fathers that they were of the people look after the necessity that so urgently exists in this region for the said wheat. All the Labourers in wheat complained that there was a third less wheat than they had last year and this from the best land that there was on this island. Last year with much more wheat ninety or one hundred *moios* [1 moio = 828 liters] of wheat from outside entered this town and all was used. Every year what this region has from the outside always comes to eighty or one hundred *moios* of wheat and all is used due to the little cultivation that there is of it [here]. They were informed that in the districts of this island where every year they were supplied there was also a shortage for which reason they were ready to collapse with great distress for not having a source of it. For this they requested of their Graces that they have a hand on what is gotten from the land, even if little, and with much vigilance not allow it [to be] loaded nor taken for any [other] part, and that guards be placed on the ports and on land and seal the ports. If their Graces do not do this they protested thus, that if any persons perish for lack of the said wheat their Graces account for it with God Our Lord, João Dias. The said officials, seeing the plea from the procurators and outcry from the people from the lack of the said wheat, had the ports sealed and ordered that it be announced that no boatman nor carter be so insolent as to freight out any wheat or barley or rye or any victuals without first showing the dispatch and judicial licence at the risk of a fine of fifty *cruzados* and the owners shall lose the wheat or barley or rye or victuals as already ordered another time. It was announced by Amtonio Mateos and by Bras Afonso town criers. Mateus Dias wrote it.

6 Account books of a retail dealer, Denmark 1559

Major merchants belonged to the upper levels of urban society and economy, while retail dealers were considered middle or even lower class. The following is an account book of one of them, Keluf Jens Nielsen (d. 1559), covering the years 1555–1559. The excerpt cited below relates to her dealings with a couple, Per and Johanne Klemitsen, and reveals the many activities a retail dealer, sometimes called a huckster, could engage in, in order to make a living. In this selection the monetary values are: 1 mark = 16 shillings, 1 shilling = 3 albi (witten).
(*Malmøskifter 2: Købmandsregnskaber 153 7–1559*, ed. Einar Bager (Copenhagen: Selskabet for Udgivelse af Kilder til dansk Historie, 1978), pp. 99–134: 'Keluf Jens Nielsens Räkenskaper'. Translated by Grethe Jacobsen and Pernille Arenfeldt.)

P. 94:

Item I, Keluf Jens Nielsen, and Per Klemmentsen settled our accounts one month before Christmas and he owes me 9 mark and 1 barrel of beer
Item for 2 mark 60 pots of German beer, each pot 2 albi
2 green socks of 'gottingsk' cloth [cloth from Göttingen] for 4 shillings
4 quarts of hemp, each quart 5 shillings
1 herring net 8 shillings
1 quart of peas for 4 shillings, at that time that was the price
Item last summer Johanne Per Klemmentsen gave me as surety 1 bedcloth for 13½ shilling
Item I redeemed Johanne Per Klemmentsen's tunic for 3½ marks
Item Johanne Per Klemmentsen lay here for seven weeks, food and beer for 6 shillings a week as much as she wanted
Item I pledged surety for Per Klemmentsen to Hans Dobelsten for planks for 12 shilling
Item I pledged surety for Per Klemmentsen for one barrel of German beer for his wedding beer for 3½ marks
Item the wife of Per Klemmentsen one pair of shoes, one pair for himself and one pair of soles Item in return I have received one cow for 6 mark and 3 geese for 1 mark
Item supplied Per Klemmentsen his wife with 10 shillings for 11 weeks, which he gave me. I bought ointment and rubbed her with Peter's oil [a plant oil] as much as I knew of
Item Johanne Per Klemmentsen 3 marks and 4 shillings, 6 shillings for 1 quart hemp, 4 albi and 4 shillings for 1 quart of peas, 3 shillings for wheat bread, 14 shillings for German beer the day Per Klemmentsen's child died, 14 pots of German beer, each pot 2 albi

[P. 111]

Per Klemmentsen one cupboard for 1 mark, 1 rapier 12 shillings, 1 hammer 2 shillings, pound of butter for 8 albi, 1 pound candle (wax) 8 albi

[P. 122. After Keluf's death in the fall of 1559 a list of her debtors was written, among them was:]
Peder Klemmentsen Tømmermand [carpenter]

1 cupboard	1 mark
1 rapier	12 shilling
1 hammer	2 shilling
1 pound of butter	7 1/2 albi
1 pound candle (wax)	8 albi

7 Women selling sardines, Portugal 1658

Along Portugal's Atlantic coast many communities depended on imported goods brought in by ships from other parts of Portugal or beyond. Everything that entered Portuguese harbors was subject to some form of taxation, and this record shows two entries involving the same woman dealing with the fodder of the poor, the lowly sardine. (Arquivo Distrital do Porto, Livro do Rendimento da Redízima . . . , No. 142, f. 143v (1658). Translated by Darlene Abreu-Ferreira.)

[24 May 1658] Arrived the master Fernão Alvres resident of Sesimbra [near Lisbon] with his caravel by the name of *Nossa Senhora da Peadade* with salted sardines that was evaluated at three hundred *milheiros* [thousands] of which the tithe comes to thirty, that was auctioned to Isabel Antonia da Ribeira at five hundred and fifty *réis* [per] *milheiro* amounting to sixteen thousand and eight hundred *réis*.

Arrived the master João Pinto resident of Sesimbra with his caravel by the name of *Nossa Senhora do Rosajro* with salt and sardines that was evaluated at four hundred *milheiros* of which the tithe comes to forty *milheiros* that was auctioned to the aforesaid [Isabel] at the said price amounting to twenty-two thousand and four hundred *réis* and it was left for her per João Antunes Barreto.

8 Selling wine, Portugal 1645–1646

Municipal governments had wide-ranging powers to regulate the local economy, and this document shows the extent to which this control had an impact on people's lives. Caterina, whose last name is not provided, perhaps because she was a mere servant of Francisco Pinto, has been given licence to sell a determined amount of wine, and, if she fails to stay within the set parameters, she will lose the right to use the cutello, the pruning knife – that is, she will not be able to practice her trade.

(Arquivo Histórico Municipal do Porto, Livro de Vereaçõens, No. 50 f. 19 (1645–1646). Translated by Darlene Abreu-Ferreira.)

And later on the same day behind month and year [January 21, 1645] came to this council Caterina servant of Francisco Pinto and she took an oath to sell sixty barrels of wine warranted by Francisco Pinto that it was from his cultivation. It cannot be sold but by the said Caterina and if sold somewhere else it shall be by her and she cannot sell more than the said sixty barrels [or receive the] penalty of being disallowed to use the pruning knife and that in case that another woman be sent to sell the said wine this council must be informed. Manoel Ferreira wrote it.

9 Ordinance for used-goods dealers, Germany 1488

Until the eighteenth century, most people in early modern Europe had very few consumer goods, such as clothing and household items, and often could not afford new merchandise. The trade in used items was therefore very brisk, and used-goods dealers could be found in every town. Such individuals handled merchandise that people gave them to sell – thus acting as pawnbrokers – and also goods that came on the market after a bankruptcy or a death if there were no heirs. City authorities were concerned that used-goods dealers did not sell stolen merchandise, and so wanted all their transactions to occur at public areas, such as the marketplaces that were near churches in most cities. Some cities required used-goods dealers to swear oaths with various stipulations; the following is from Munich in 1488, where city authorities were also concerned that Christian used-goods dealers should not be intermediaries in transactions between Jews. Because Jews were prohibited from owning land or joining guilds in many parts of Europe, they often engaged in selling used goods themselves, and in some places there are specific regulations for Jewish used-goods dealers, pawnbrokers, and moneylenders. Jews had been banished from Munich earlier in the fifteenth century, and a Christian church had been erected on the site of the Jewish synagogue in 1440.

(Munich Stadtarchiv, Zimilien 41, Eidbuch 1488. Translated by Merry Wiesner-Hanks.)

All used-goods dealers, male and female, shall swear that whatever is given to them to sell, they shall store, sell, and transfer at the highest price offered, and they themselves shall say who has offered the most money. When the transaction is over, they shall deliver the goods, and shall not buy or pay for any goods themselves. They shall also offer everything for sale publicly, and after the transaction shall bring the goods to no one other than the person who has offered the most for them. And they shall take or demand no commission from anyone higher than four pennies per pound's worth of goods. They shall also tell everyone what the goods are and who has sold them. All of them shall [swear] that they will always personally tell what everything is, whether it is inherited, owned, or possessed, and will sell their merchandise by the church of Our Lady and not by St. Peter's [church]. When they receive merchandise because of a bankruptcy, they should announce the goods publicly once a day for two days before they sell them, and on the third day announce them publicly every hour after noon. All goods that they receive because of bankruptcy they should lay out on a bench or table if the weather allows this, and if the weather does not allow it they should list the goods on a sheet and present the sheet [for people to see], and keep everything secure and safe. Whatever merchandise they receive from Jews, whether male or female, they are not to store it with Jews, male or female, nor trade it to Jews.

10 Warning about shady business practices, Russia fifteenth century

Merchants at all levels tried to get the most advantageous deals, and sometimes this led to questionable business practices. The following is another birchbark document from Novgorod, which hints tantalizingly at a conflict between two male businessmen, the brothers Esif and Foma, and their suppliers, two women named Tania and Iublia. Because it is not completely preserved, the details of the women's business cannot be fully discerned, but it is clear Esif is warning his brother. (Published originals in A.V. Artsikhovskii and V.I. Borkovskii, *Novgorodskie gramoty na bereste (iz raskopok 1953–1954gg.)* (Moscow: AN SSSR, 1958), pp. 64–66. Translated by Eve Levin.)

A petition from Esif to my brother Foma, that you send wax and honey, and a well-sewn sheepskin. For a sewn coat . . . And watch Tania, so she doesn't do anything wrong, and only sells to you according to the price. And what you buy from her and Iublia . . . is guilty. And otherwise everything is well here.

11 Country woman selling eggs, Italy late sixteenth century

People from rural areas, especially peasant women, often came into cities every day to sell their products they had raised, gathered, or made, including butter, eggs, nuts, mushrooms, firewood, and vegetables. They sold these at the city marketplace, went from house to house, or made arrangements with regular customers. This is a rural woman from Italy with farm produce, carried over her shoulder in baskets. From Cesare Vecellio, *Habiti Antichi* (1598). Vecellio's accompanying description reads: 'This outfit is typical of certain peasants who come to Venice to the market on Saturdays. When they enter the city, they remove a large wide-brimmed hat, made of thick straw which they wear in the countryside. Their dress is of heavy cloth, usually light blue, with a tight bodice laced with thick silk . . . Since they come from the countryside, which is often muddy, they wear their overskirt tied up with a leather belt at the waist . . . On their shoulders they carry two baskets, one holding fowl, the other holding cheese, eggs, or fruit.'

150

F

12 Couple selling merchandise at the public market, Germany sixteenth century

The center of economic life in early modern cities was the marketplace, where vendors often had permanent stalls. In this stall, a husband and wife sell a variety of merchandise, including armor, cloth, belts, and swords.
(From Cicero, *De Officiis* (Augsburg 1531).)

PRODUCTION

13 Ordinance of the Spurriers' [Spurmakers'] Guild of London, England 1345

Production of most commodities was handled by craft guilds, which had grown up in most European cities beginning in the twelfth century to regulate production and forbid non-members to work at the craft. The following is a very typical guild ordinance, setting out many aspects of training and limiting the length of the work day.
(James Harvey Robinson, editor and translator, *Readings in European History*, vol. I (Boston: Ginn, 1904) pp. 409–411.)

Be it remembered, that on Tuesday, the morrow of St. Peter's bonds, in the nineteenth year of the reign of King Edward III, the articles underwritten were read before John Hammond, mayor, Roger de Depham, recorder, and the other aldermen; and seeing that the same were deemed befitting, they were accepted and enrolled in these words.

In the first place, that no one of the trade of spurriers shall work longer than from the beginning of the day until curfew rings out at the church of St. Sepulcher, without [that is, outside of the city gate called] Newgate; by reason that no man can work so neatly by night as by day. And many persons of the said trade, who compass [know] how to practice deception in their work, desire to work by night rather than by day; and then they introduce false iron, and iron that has been cracked, for tin, and also they put gilt on false copper, and cracked.

And further, many of the said trade are wandering about all day, without working at all at their trade; and then, when they have become drunk and frantic, they take to their work, to the annoyance of the sick and all their neighborhood as well, by reason of the broils [fights] that arise between them and the strange folk who are dwelling among them. And then they blow up their fires so vigorously, that their forges begin all at once to blaze, to the great peril of themselves and of all the neighborhood around. And then, too, all the neighbors are much in dread of the sparks, which so vigorously issue forth in all directions from the mouths of the chimneys in their forges.

By reason thereof it seems unto them that working by night should be put an end to, in order to avoid such false work and such perils; and therefore the mayor and the aldermen do will, by the assent of the good folk of the said trade and for the common profit, that from henceforth such time for working, and such false work made in the trade, shall be forbidden. And if any person shall be found in the said trade to do the contrary hereof, let him be amerced [fined], the first time in forty pence, one half to go to the use of the Chamber of the Guildhall of London, and the other half to the use of the said trade; the second time, in half a mark [80 pence] and the third time, in ten shillings [120 pence], to the use of the same Chamber and trade; and the fourth time, let him forswear the trade forever.

Also, that no one of the said trade shall hang his spurs out on Sundays, or on any other days that are double feasts; but only a sign indicating his business; and such spurs as they shall so sell, they are to show and sell within their shops, without exposing them without or opening the doors or windows of their shops, on the pain aforesaid.

Also, that no one of the said trade shall keep a house or shop to carry on his business, unless he is free of the city [a citizen]; and that no one shall cause to be sold, or exposed for sale, any manner of old spurs for new ones, or shall garnish them or change them for new ones.

Also, that no one of the said trade shall take an apprentice for a less term than seven years, and such apprentice shall be enrolled according to the usages of the said city.

Also, that if any one of the said trade, who is not a freeman, shall take an apprentice for a term of years, he shall be amerced as aforesaid.

Also, that no one of the said trade shall receive the apprentice, serving man, or journeyman of another in the same trade, during the term agreed upon between his master and him, on the pain aforesaid.

Also, that no alien of another country, or foreigner of this country, shall follow or use the said trade, unless he is enfranchised before the mayor, aldermen, and chamberlain; and that, by witness and surety [guarantee] of the good folk of the said trade, who will go surety for him, as to his loyalty and his good behavior.

Also, that no one of the said trade shall work on Saturdays, after *nones* [about 3 pm] has been rung out in the city; and not from that hour until the Monday morning following.

14 Ordinances regarding women in gold production, Germany sixteenth century

Most guilds in Europe limited full membership to men, but widows were often allowed to continue operating a workshop in a limited form. The first of the following ordinances concerns widows in goldsmithing, and sets out very standard types of limitations. The second and third ordinances concern goldspinners, women who spun gold thread for luxury embroidery and usually worked in the shops of gold-smiths or gold-beaters (individuals who pounded gold into very thin sheets for gold-leaf work). Like the restrictions on single people included in chapter 2, these ordinances attempt to prohibit unmarried gold-spinners from living and working on their own.
(Nuremberg, Stadtarchiv, QNG, Nr. 68 I, 135 (15350, Nr. 68 III, 1097 (1560), Nr. 68 III, 1307 (1597). Translated by Merry Wiesner-Hanks.)

[From Goldsmiths' Ordinance, 1535]
If a goldsmith dies and leaves no son behind him that will use or work in his craft, or is not gifted in this or old enough to assume the *Meisterrecht*, then the goldsmith's widow may (if she wants) work in the craft for three years after the death of her husband, and no longer. Then this same widow will have to marry someone else from the goldsmith's craft who has already

been a master or wants to make his masterpiece, after these three years. Every widow that wants to work in the craft is obliged to carry out the usual duties, such as allowing her work to be inspected or any other things called for in the regulations of the craft the same as any other, and is liable for punishments for infractions according to the same regulations and ordinances.

[From Goldbeaters' Ordinance, 1560]

First, from now on no goldspinner is to be tolerated here unless she has first learned from an honorable master of the gold-beating craft. Those who are unmarried and want to live with the master are to be maintained by that master for a reasonable yearly salary.

Second, from now on no goldspinner is to have the power to spin gold for herself unless she has learned from a goldbeater. However, those spinners who have already learned before this ordinance will be allowed to continue. Whoever breaks this ordinance on one or more points and cannot behave or conduct herself properly will be liable to pay a fine of five pounds for every infraction.

From now on every master of the gold-beating craft shall pay every spinner and maid that he has living in his house seven gulden as a yearly salary if they spin him six strands each week. Also, those spinners and maids who can stretch out 100 *Ramm* [a measure of length] every day or sew together four books shall be given eight gulden as a yearly salary. If a spinner or maid spins, stretches or sews less in the year, then her salary will be deducted accordingly. Whatever she makes above this daily allotment should also be figured in to her benefit in the same way and also paid by the master. No master of the craft shall pay any spinner or maid who completes the daily work noted above any more or less, nor use any of his other servants for this work, all with a fine of five pounds. This applies only to the spinners and maids who serve the masters in their houses and absolutely not to those who work for themselves.

[From Goldspinners' Ordinance, 1597]

From now on no maid is to be taken on and taught for less than four years. Each maid is to be registered when taken on and let go as is normally required. Third, every spin-maid is to contract herself at the least for one year to a master and during that time not leave him without justifiable cause (which has to be proven to the authorities). Whenever a trained maid wants to contract herself to another master, she should report this to the sworn masters beforehand, so that they can see that this master does not already have too many maids. Fourth, every master should house and feed all his maids in his house. No unmarried maid should be given work to do for herself [i.e., if she didn't live with the master].

161

15 Shoemakers' shop, Germany 1568

This woodcut shows a very typical craft guild shop. The master shoemaker is standing on the right preparing leather, the journeymen are seated in the middle sewing
the shoes with a young apprentice behind them, and the master shoemaker's wife is
on the left selling the shoes. A very young child is playing with a boot in the
foreground; because the residence of the shoemaker was most likely behind or
above the shop, his children often simply played in the shop where their parents
worked until they were old enough to begin work themselves.
(Jost Ammann, *Beschreibung aller Staende* (Frankfurt 1568).)

16 Account book on taxes from sugar making, Portugal 1530s

Tax records can provide valuable insights into the local economy. The excerpt below
is from account books kept by officials on the island of Madeira in the early sixteenth
century, a time when sugar was clearly the island's main export. It was a great
source of income for merchant factories established as far away as Venice, and for
the crown; the local monastery enjoyed an annual royal gift of sugar of approximately
750 kilos, and the industry employed the majority of local peasants, including women
who made preserves for the royal kitchen.
(Fernando Jasmins Pereira and José Pereira da Costa, eds., *Livros de Contas da Ilha
da Madeira, 1504–1537* (Coimbra: Universidade de Coimbra, 1985), pp. 36–38, 44.
Translated by Darlene Abreu-Ferreira.)

Ytem first the said tax collector paid or handed over with me scrivener
[scribe] to Diogo Fernamdez scrivener of the factory in Venice per charter
of the king our lord – be it known – ordered by the tax collector seven
thousand *arrobas* [measures of weight] of sugar that were loaded on the
vessel *Bernalldez* to Venice.

Ytem the said tax collector paid and disbursed with me scrivener to
Miguel Samchez procurator of the friars of *Nosa Senhora de Guadelupe* fifty
arrobas of sugar per *padram* [a larger unit of weight] that they have of the said
lord who gives them alms each year.

Ytem the said tax collector paid to Ruj Mendez per commission to the queen dona Lianor our lady one hundred and twelve and a half *arrobas* of white sugar – be it known – one hundred that the said lady has in benevolence each year and twelve and a half that were rebated for her per weight in the past year of 1504 for whom the said lord ordered be paid per charter that was shown.

Ytem the said tax collector paid for the expense of victuals of the bookkeeper and his and mine scrivener to the wife of Louremço Vaaz packer per order of the bookkeeper in my presence scrivener three hundred and ninety *réis* [a type of coinage].

Ytem the said tax collector paid with me scrivener to Margarida Ousel for twenty-eight *arrobas* and nine *arratees* [a measure of weight, about one pound] of preserves for the pastry kitchen of the said lord at five hundred *réis* [per] *arroba* – be it known – twenty-five *arrobas* and twenty-six *arratees* from her at five hundred *réis* and two and a half *arrobas* at five hundred and fifty *réis* that make a total of fourteen thousand two hundred and sixty-seven *réis*.

17 Women as potters, Spain late sixteenth century

Women often became expert in certain trades, a fact about which some villages took great pride. In response to Phillip II of Spain's survey of his kingdom, the town of Alcorcon boasted of the pottery made by the women of the town.
(*Relaciones histórico-geográfico-estadísticas de los pueblos de España hecho por iniciativa de Felipe II: Provincia de Madrid*, eds. Carmelo Viñas y Mey and Ramón Paz (Madrid: CSIC, 1949), p. 43. Translated by Allyson Poska.)

. . . of the majority of the inhabitants of the said place, two-thirds are poor men and the other third have middling estates, the richest of which is worth four thousand ducats. As for the rest, the livelihood that they have is pitchers, pots, jugs, and little jugs that are made better in the said place than in other parts. These are made so well and the clay so fit for the ministry that they are taken to many faraway places and they have them in much of the kingdom. The women do this. It is a livelihood of much work and little profit, because the firewood and brushwood that is brought for the ovens is very expensive. . . .

18 Silk-making, Italy 1590

Italy dominated the market in silk production in early modern Europe, and women were the main workers in the initial stages of production, including raising the silkworm cocoons and reeling the silk. This is an engraving of some of their tasks; the

163

older woman (wearing glasses) on the left sorts silk-worm eggs, the women in the middle are putting the cocoons in a wine-bath to keep them moist, and the young women on the right are putting the cocoons in their dress bodices to keep them warm. The elegance of the interior was not realistic, as most of the women who worked in silk production were very poorly paid and worked in their own tiny houses or in rough workshops. This was also true of men in silk production, who did the later stages, such as weaving.

(Johannes Stradanus, *Vermis sericus* (Antwerp, ca. 1590).)

Afperfa vino terfag̃ oua vermium   Papillulis folent fouere virgines.

MEDICAL CARE

19 Woman's petition to be allowed to practice medicine, Germany sixteenth century

Medical treatment was handled by a hierarchy of individuals in most of Europe, ranging from university-trained doctors (who were all male), to barber-surgeons, apothecaries, and midwives, trained through apprenticeship, to a variety of medical practitioners who gained their training less formally. At times those groups which had received formal training protested to civic authorities when individuals were practicing medicine without being a member of their guild or organization. In this undated sixteenth-century petition to the city council of Munich, a female medical practitioner answers the charges against her.

(Munich Stadtarchiv, Gewerbeamt, No. 1020, Medizinalia Pfuscher. Translated by Merry Wiesner-Hanks.)

Modest answer and obedient report from Katherina Plumanerin Carberinerin

Honorable, just, careful, highly educated, and wise mayors and council of this electoral capital city of Munich, gracious and serving sirs:

Because of my humble modesty, I cannot let your honorable and gracious sirs go without an answer: A few days ago your city secretary (with somewhat harsh words) brought me an extract from a council meeting held on December 17 of last year, which included the following: that Plumanerin Carberinerin is to be earnestly forbidden to treat or look at patients. This decision, arrived at because of malice and not through any fault of my own, appears to me not only strange, but also totally deplorable. On one hand I use my feminine skills, given by the grace of God, only when someone entreats me earnestly and never advertise myself, but only when someone has been left for lost, and they ask me many times. I do whatever I can possibly do out of Christian love and charity, using only simple and allowable means that should not be forbidden or proscribed in the least. Not one person who has come under my care has a complaint or grievance against me. If the doctors, apothecaries, or barber-surgeons have claimed this, it is solely out of spite and jealousy.

At all times, as is natural, women have more trust in other women to discover their secrets, problems, and illnesses than they have in men (as long as no un-Christian means are used) – but perhaps this jealousy came from that. Undoubtedly as well, honorable husbands who love and cherish their wives will seek any help and assistance they can, even that from women, if the wives have been given up (by the doctors) or otherwise come into great danger.

Because I know that I can help in my own small way, I will do all I can, just as, according to the Gospel, we should help pull an ox out of a well it has fallen into on Sunday.

So that your honorable and gracious sirs can see that I am trying to follow your directions from now on as I have generally done in the past, I will not promote or advertise my healing. But if someone comes to me in an emergency and pleads with me, I cannot deny them my time or my troubles or the skill that God has given me out of friendship or out of Christian sympathy. Thus I humbly hope that you will not listen to any spite and envy any further but will allow me this out of your grace and wisdom. This is my answer given to you out of my duty of obedience.

20 Oaths of staff members in city hospitals, Germany sixteenth century

Hospitals in early modern European cities were run both by the church and by secular city governments. Those institutions within city walls generally took in the injured, chronically ill, infirm elderly, and poor expectant mothers, while patients with contagious diseases were sent to small pest-houses or infirmaries outside the city walls. The staff at such hospitals and infirmaries often had to swear oaths of loyalty and agree to follow all directives laid out for the day-to-day operations of the institution. From these oaths, we can tell what care for the ill was supposed to be like, though we cannot be sure if such directives were followed.

(Nuremberg, Staatsarchiv, Amts- und Standbuecher, Nr. 101, f. 160, 57, 294, 400. Translated by Merry Wiesner-Hanks.)

Oaths of the Couple in Charge of the Infirmary for Incurables [those with the plague]

The *Hofmeister* and *Hofmeisterin* in the *Lazarett* or hospital for incurables should give their oath, and swear to God that they will conscientiously work for the good of the *Lazaretthaus* carefully, and keep it securely closed up, especially at night. The things that have been inventoried and given over to them, such as bedding, covering, sheets, other linens and utensils, should be left in the rooms and chests exactly as they are and not moved whenever the house is locked up.

When the *Lazarett* is closed, they should use nothing for their own needs, or without the knowledge of the council, or the overseer of all the hospitals. They should not remove or use even the least bit, and should report to the *Lazarett* at least once a year, so that any beds, sheets, or other utensils that have been damaged or destroyed by snow, rain, or in any other way may be repaired or replaced, and all remains in good shape. If through the will of God a plague returns and the *Lazarett* is opened again, they are to stay in their office and follow any ordinances and rules that are given to them by the council, the overseer or anyone else. All this should be done faithfully and without deceit.

Oaths of Female Staff in the City Hospital

Custorin's Oath and Ordinance

A *Custorin* hired and taken on in the new city hospital is to give her oath of loyalty, and swear to God the Almighty that she will further the needs of the hospital, and guard against damages and injuries to the best of her abilities. She should pay special attention to the orders of the appointed director of the hospital so that they are carried out to the advantage of the hospital and the good of the poor patients without excuses. She should report any problems or shortages, or if she finds anything illegal, to the director of the hospital immediately, without delay, and should enforce his decisions about these. Without his knowledge and advice she should not undertake anything, for that is not her calling or office.

166

She should pay strict attention to all utensils and movable goods, like bedding, cushions, pillows, sheets, towels, and so on, that belong to the poor, and which are entrusted to her, so that all are well preserved and maintained. None of these are to be sold, given away, loaned or otherwise disposed of, or used for her own purposes.

She is to be sure that the maids appointed to help her reliably aid the poor patients, giving them support by night and day – changing their bedding, as often as necessary, lifting them or laying them down, carrying them to meals at the normal time, getting drinks and preparing the necessary foods, and whatever else has been ordered by the doctor. She is to report any maid that is disobedient to the director of the hospital.

Anything that she cooks or has cooked in her kitchen for the poor and sick people, like meat or other dishes, is not to be given to the pensioners [elderly people who paid the hospital for their care] or other healthy people who are not in need, neither for a payment, a gift or for free, but only to the poor weak people in the hospital for whom it is intended. Everything that she buys for such a use, such as salt, lard, eggs, milk, chickens, and so on, from the money provided by the director of the hospital is to be used for the good of the poor sick people, as called for, and nowhere else. She is to handle the money given her each week by the director of the hospital for fish and other things carefully and honestly, and not loan, take, or keep any of it, but buy the necessary things immediately as if it were her own business. Each week she is to give the director of the hospital an orderly accounting of all that she has purchased, and stand next to the tradesmen when they prepare and weigh out all goods so that all is weighed and handled truthfully. If she sees, tastes, or finds any problems or shortages, whether of salt, lard, meat, cabbage, vegetables, spices or anything else, she is inform the director of the hospital, so that the cook, or whoever is guilty, is forced to improve. She is to invite no friends or guests to her table nor prepare any special dishes for them nor have them prepared, but is to be satisfied with her salary and benefits.

She is to pay attention to those who should be in the hospital and who should not. If she finds some who have become healthy again, she should let them go, but otherwise give the poor people support, speak to them in a friendly manner and as often as necessary bring them refreshing drinks. If one of the sick people dies, she is to take custody of all that he brought into the hospital, like money, clothing, or other movable goods, so that nothing is taken from it to the detriment of the hospital, which has rights over all these goods. She should inform the director of the hospital of the death immediately, as she has sworn to do, and wait for his decision about this legacy, and then follow it. She should also provide the maids working under her with any necessities. All this should be carried out faithfully and without deceit.

Meisterin's Oath and Ordinance

Those who are taken on and hired as *Meisterin* in the new city hospital should give their oath and swear to God that they will be true and responsible to the hospital, serve its needs at all times, and watch for and guard against damages and injuries as much as possible, and care for the poor ill with the best attentiveness, giving out and distributing everything that the ordinance of the hospital calls for easily and graciously. She should pay special attention to the orders of the established director of the hospital, so that they are carried out to the benefit of the hospital and the good of the poor patients without delay. If she has any problems or shortages, or suspects or finds anything amiss, she should report it immediately to the director of the hospital, wait for his decision and then carry it out. Without his knowledge and orders she is not to venture or do anything, for that is not her position or office.

She should pay special attention to the kitchen and the things that belong to it, and order every day what should be cooked and served. At all times she should notice that the cooks and maids assigned to her pay attention to the cinnamon and other spices, taking neither too much nor too little. They should prepare the correct amount of meat according to the number of healthy people who can eat it and serve it at the correct time. All meat should be washed and cleaned, the pans and other kitchen utensils kept clean so that the food is properly and purely cooked. At the proper times she should test the food, to see whether it is correctly salted and has the right amount of fat. When it is time to eat, she should serve the food to the poor patients, sit beside the *Custorin* and both help each other dish up, giving each patient what he is supposed to get.

While she is serving, she should pay special attention to how many very ill people are in the hospital, that cannot eat meat or that sort of meal, so that on the next day she counts that number fewer and orders less food to be cooked. Nothing more should be cooked than needed for the number of people who want to eat it; all excess should be avoided. While the meals are being cooked she should not spin or sew for her own profit, or allow her maids to do it, so that the cooking is carefully looked after.

She should also go to the market during the regular, normal times, and buy whatever is necessary, or what the director of the hospital has ordered her to, as if it were her own business. The money that she has received for this from the director of the hospital is to be used for nothing else than the business of the hospital. She is to take, keep, or borrow none of it for herself, nor loan some of it to another, but give the director of the hospital an itemized accounting of her income and expenditures each week, or as often as he demands it. She is to be present and be sure when the butcher brings the meat, that it is good and suitable, without blemishes or a strong smell, and is correctly weighed and cut on a board.

From this hour on she is responsible also to go every Monday with the *Custorin* among the poor patients and see who needs to stay longer in the hospital and who not, and release the healthy again. Because she is responsible for the administration of the household furniture and movable goods for the servants, like beds, cushions, pillows, sheets, handtowels, tablecloths, keys, plates and the like, she is to care for them conscientiously, and anything else that is entrusted to her for the hospital, so that nothing is destroyed or lost.

She is not to prepare or give any food, be it fish, meat, spices or anything else, cooked or uncooked, for any of her relatives or strangers, whether for a payment, a gift or for free, but use it solely for the necessities of the hospital. She is not to invite any relatives or guests to her table, nor cook or have prepared any special dishes for them, but is to be satisfied with her established salary. All this should be carried out faithfully and without deceit.

Schauerin's Oath and Ordinance

The *Schauerin* in the new city hospital is to give her oath to the director of the hospital and swear to God that she will let no person be admitted to the hospital if he asks without the knowledge of the director of the hospital or *Meisterin*. But if someone asks to be let in, she should examine this person carefully and admit no one to the hospital who has a dangerous, contagious illness which could not be cured in the hospital, but only those who are suffering from moderate bodily weakness. All of these people should be citizens, children of citizens, or servants of the same, or journeymen who have worked a long time with a master here and are thus eligible to be taken into the hospital.

She should be careful when giving out wine and beer to the poor and aged, and also when distributing bread, that she give them only what they should have and what the hospital ordinances prescribe. Without the knowledge of the director of the hospital she is not to give or hand out anything, or use anything for her own needs. If she sees or experiences any shortages among the old people, the sick or others that could lead to problems for the hospital she is to report immediately to the director of the hospital or *Meisterin*. She is to take no bread that has been given to the sick and resell it to the pensioners nor to anyone else, but completely abstain from such trading, nor allow anyone else to do it, nor be silent if she finds anyone else doing it. She should do everything she is supposed to do when ordered to by the director of the hospital or *Meisterin*, without argument with all diligence, faithfully and without deceit.

169

21 Illustration of a bath maid, Germany sixteenth century

Public bath houses handled some of people's medical needs along with providing facilities for bathing, shaving, and washing hair. People generally did not have bathing facilities in their own houses, so that bath houses were the only places they could get a hot water bath. During the fifteenth century they were perfectly respectable, but during the sixteenth century they became more associated with prostitution; this decline in status plus an increase in the price of firewood (which made hot water more expensive) meant that many bath houses closed, and people were forced to resort to sponge baths for cleanliness. This is a woodcut by Wolf Dreschel; the verse reads: 'I, a bath maid, stand here alone,/ With naked arms and white legs/ I take care of people/ And do the same for young men/ There I am with my water in a hurry/ Young and old, and small children/ I whip them with branches and rub them off/ So that they go home clean.'

(Published in Walter L. Strauss, *The German Single-Leaf Woodcut* (New York: Abaris Books, 1975). Reproduced by permission.)

SERVANTS, SOLDIERS, AND SLAVES

22 Young woman places herself into service, France 1542

Large numbers of young people in early modern Europe were employed as servants in urban or rural households. A young person might place himself or herself into a household as a servant or apprentice, especially if her or his parents were dead or lived elsewhere. Although it was certainly more common for young men to place themselves, in the following document a young woman affirms her right to make such arrangements for herself. She signs up for two years of live-in employment as a servant and assistant to a merchant.

(Paris, Archives Nationales, Minutier central, Étude VIII/474, October 11, 1542. Translated by Carol Loats.)

Catherine Denis, daughter of the late Jehan Denis, who while living was a carpenter, living at Troussurt near Beauvais, the said Catherine aged more than 18 years, as she says, affirms that for her own benefit she places herself in service and employment.

[She places herself] from today for the next two years with and in the service of Nicollas Querin, merchant *mercier* [seller of fashion merchandise such as trims and accessories], living in Paris, rue St. Denis, near the culvert. [Querin], present here, has retained the said Catherine as his servant during the said time.

And the said Catherine, in making [this arrangement], has promised and promises to serve the said Nicollas Guerin well and loyally in his said occupation of *mercerie*, to sell and retail his merchandise, and she has promised and promises and guarantees to give a good account and balance of that which will be given to her by her said master to sell and retail, and of the profit which comes from it; and so promises to serve him in all his lawful and honorable business, work to his benefit, avoid losses to him; without serving elsewhere during the said time. For this service the said Nicollas Guerin has promised, will be obliged, and promises and guarantees to supply to the said Catherine what she needs in terms of drink, food, fire, bed, lodging, light, along with the sum of 10 *livres tournois* for the said time of two years, and which he has promised to pay to the said Catherine to the extent that she earns it, to the said value of 10 *livres tournois* for the said two years.

Because thus, etc., promising, etc., obligating, etc., each renouncing to the other, etc., Done the year 1542, Wednesday, the 11th day of October.

23 Man places his sister into service, France 1551

The care of those with disabilities, as with the care of orphans, was a responsibility which might be taken up by those in the kinship networks, or might fall to others. In the following case, an adult man appears before the notaries to place his sister, who is deaf and mute, into service and apprenticeship with a widow. This widow was

apparently related to the servant through the widow's deceased husband. The age of the new servant is not specified.
(Paris, Archives Nationales, Minutier central, Étude XI/31, November 9, 1551. Translated by Carol Loats.)

Didier Beaulse, *carrier* [stone-cutter in a quarry] living in the Courtille near and outside of the Porte du Temple in this city of Paris, affirms that he has given and placed as servant and *chambrière* [chambermaid] from today for the next 10 years, Benarde Beaulse, his sister, being deaf and mute.

[He has placed her] to and with Perrette LeFeure, widow of the late Estienne Beausse, who while living worked in vineyards, [the widow] living in Coipeaulx, in Paris, rue Saint Jacques, here present taking and retaining the said Bernarde as her servant. And [the widow] promises to provide and deliver what she needs in terms of drink, food, fire, bed, lodging, and light; and to maintain her with all her clothing and necessities whatsoever, well and respectably, as [Bernarde] is accustomed to.

And at the end of the said time, [the widow] will leave [Bernarde] respectably clothed, according to her standing. And also the widow promises and guarantees to give and pay to [Bernarde] or someone on her behalf, etc., the sum of 45 *sous tournois* for her wages and compensation, with the condition that the said Bernarde will be obliged to serve the said widow Beaulse in all things lawful and honorable during the said time, without taking flight nor serving elsewhere during the said time.

Promising, etc., obligating each in his own right. Done and passed in duplicate, in the year 1551, Monday, the 9th day of November.

24 Journeyman places his daughter into service, France 1540

The male artisan's life cycle was supposed to take him from apprenticeship to wage work as a skilled artisan, and then to adulthood as a master of a trade, but this did not always happen. Many men encountered difficulties in their own life course, being unable to achieve the mastership of their trades despite being married and having children old enough to learn a trade themselves. In this document, a man still a compagnon [journeyman] places his daughter in service in his own trade, for her to acquire skills sufficient to serve her well later.
(Paris, Archives Nationales, Minutier central, Étude XXXIII/25, May 10, 1540. Translated by Carol Loats.)

Jehan Couderet, *compagnon* maker of tennis equipment living at Saint Marcel in Paris in the area of the Clos Saint Genevieve, parish Saint Estienne du Mont in Paris, affirms that he has given and placed as servant, from the first day of this present month and year for the next two years, Jehanne Couderet, his daughter, present, aged nine years or so.

[He has placed his daughter] with Guyon Blondeau, of the said profession, living at the Clos de Chardonneret in Paris, here present, taking and retaining the said Jehanne as his servant during the said time.

[Blondeau] has promised and promises to supply and deliver to her the things she needs in terms of drink and food, fire, bed, lodging, and light; and to maintain her in footwear of wool as well as shoes, and further to maintain her with all clothing and other necessities during the said time, according to her standing; and at the end of the said time, to give her one bodice of a corset of the value of 50 *sous tournois*, with three shirts, three head-dresses, six caps, and six *gorgias* [a type of collar], all of hemp cloth, for the use of the said Jehanne and according to the standing of the said parties. And also, [Blondeau] promises to teach the said Jehanne to sew sacks for tennis balls, [to teach her] well and duly as is appropriate, and leave her as an *ouvrière* [skilled worker] at the end of the said time.

And therefore the said Jehanne has promised to serve her said master, obey his commands, work to his benefit, avoid losses to him, and warn him of problems as soon [as it comes to her attention]; without taking flight, etc., wanting, etc.; and in case of flight her father promises to seek her and search in the city and surroundings of Paris and bring her back, [if she can be found, to finish the time of her service.] And he pledges her loyalty, etc.

Thus etc., promising, etc., obligating, each in his own right, and the said Jehanne seized and held, etc. Done in duplicate, the said day and year [1540, the 10th day of May].

25 Theft by a servant, Denmark 1625

Most servants were employed on a permanent basis, but some were more temporary. The following court case dealing with a servant girl accused of theft reveals the hardship of a single woman trying to make a living by temporary employment and by running errands.

(*Sokkelund Herreds tingbøger, 1624–25*, ed. Poul Erik Olsen (Copenhagen: Landbohistorisk Selskab, 1980), pp. 22–23. Translated by Grethe Jacobsen and Pernille Erenfeldt.)

Thursday December 9th 1625

Hans Lauridsen in Virum brought forward aftersaid testimonies against a woman named Karen Pedersdatter, reports (she is) born in Jutland.

Then Doritte Nielsdatter in Virum came forward to testify and made her oath according to the law and recounted how she saw aforesaid Karen had an apron in a basket and with it entered the eastern room, to which aforesaid Karen Pedersdatter answered that she only had aforesaid apron one day. In the same way, Sofie Kristensdatter of the same place came forward and made her oath according to the law and recounted how aforesaid Karen took a shift from the girl of Steffen Bager in Copenhagen and aforesaid Sofie was one of those who took (it) from her.

Maren [wife of] Peder Hanssen who was a servant with aforesaid Hans Lauridsen at that time, likewise Bodil Mortensdatter who also served aforesaid Hans Lauridsen, aforesaid Sofie testified likewise about the apron that Doritte has testified about.

Rasmus Esborson in Buddinge also made his oath according to the law and recounted how aforesaid Karen came to him in his house wanting to borrow a pair of hosen of his woman and told how she wanted to go to Hans Lauridsen's (house) in Virum and furthermore asked his woman if she could borrow a food pouch and a knife and bring that to Hans Lauridsen. Sometime before that happened, she came to aforesaid Rasmus with a slice of pork and asked his woman if she could afford to pay her for this slice, then aforesaid Rasmus gave her 10 Shilling for it.

Likewise Laurids Andersen in Buddinge came forward, made his oath according to the law and recounted how his woman asked aforesaid Karen where she had been. Then aforesaid Karen answered that she had been to Copenhagen at Mette Islendriss with a goose, that aforesaid Hans Lauridsen supposedly gave her to bring to his sister and recounted that she got 12 shilling as a fee for this. Then she went home. A day or so later she returned bringing some pork, which were 2 hams, a shoulder and a piece of pork which she tried to sell . . . and Laurids Andersen said furthermore that she swore that she got aforesaid pork from Hans Lauridsen in Virum as a payment. And aforesaid Karen, when she had borrowed the pouch from Rasmus Esborson's woman, then when she returned, she had a loaf of bread, which she swore that Hans Lauridsen gave her. Likewise a loaf cut into four pieces, which she swore Hans Lauridsen's woman gave her.

Likewise aforesaid Laurids Andersen recounted that Karen said to his woman that if she could get hold of some hops, then she could supply her with some malt. Recounted further that she had a piece of green cheese.

Likewise aforesaid Karen confessed to have lain in aforesaid Hans Lauridsen's barn for an entire month since she left his service without the knowledge of Hans Lauridsen and his woman.

Rasmus Esbemson in Buddinge asked aforesaid Karen whether he and his woman had housed her knowingly overnight any time to which she answered no, [she] had not been lying at (the house of) aforesaid Rasmus . . .

Thursday December 16th 1624

Hans Lauridsen in Virum brought forth into the court a woman by the name of Karen Pedersdatter along with some stolen items, which are a shift, an apron and a button, made from bone, which aforesaid Hans

Lauridsen has found at Abelone's in Virum. Then came forward a witness from Abelone as she, because of her frailty, is unable to appear in court and testified according to the law that she for some time had been unable to leave her yard because of her frailty and that she had bought aforesaid button from Karen Pedersdatter outside the gate . . . Jens Persen and Hans Persen in Virum and Hans in Lyngby testified to this under oath. And aforesaid goods were assessed to $4\frac{1}{2}$ Marks for the apron, the shift and the button by these men, Peder Jorgensen, Hans Bendtsen in Emdrup, Soren Andersen in Utterslev, Thomas Persen in Gentofte Furthermore came forward a witness against aforesaid Karen Pedersdatter, who is Sisse Laurids Olsen's wife in Buddinge and made her oath according to the law and recounted how aforesaid Karen came to her in her house and had a piece of bacon and offered it to her for 10 Shilling and then for 8 Shilling and as she were not interested in cash, she offered her beer. And aforesaid Sisse inquired of aforesaid Karen where she got that bacon. Then she said that she received a side of bacon from Hans Lauridsen in Virum and there was paint on that bacon, to which Hans Lauridsen answered that aforesaid Karen never received any bacon from him neither as a purchase nor as a gift, which aforesaid Karen herself agreed with and said she received some bacon from Soren Ludhorn and that he would be able to confirm that under oath.

Then came forward a witness by the name of Ellen Laurids' wife in Buddinge and here in court confirmed what her husband testified here eight days ago and Hans Lauridsen firmly denied to have given aforesaid Karen the goose to carry to his sister and the other things in the testimony [of Karen] that he was supposed to have done, which is, given her bread.

Then came [Niels Jensen] forward to testify about the testimony of Sara Sorensdatter who has recounted to Laurids Mikkelsen in Copenhagen, and Niels Jensen in Virum was asked if it is the same shift which was taken off the body of aforesaid Karen Pedersdatter by the aforesaid women who testified before, to which Laurids Mikkelsen had answered that he does not know whether it is the same or not.

Finally, Ellen Laurids Andersen's wife came forward and complained about aforesaid Karen and recounted how aforesaid Karen stole 3 silver spoons from her and that two of her sieves disappeared while Karen stayed in her house which accusation aforesaid Karen denied but could not prove.

Having brought the case and offered testimonies to prove his case against aforesaid Karen, aforesaid Hans Lauridsen asked the judge whether or not aforesaid woman should be punished for her deeds according to the law which is the Jutish Law, Book 2 Chapter 95 and Chapter 102 and asked for a verdict.

[Jyske Lov 2-95: 'How a man shall search for his stolen property'; 2-102: 'How to pledge surety' (if accused of theft)]

26 Fornication with a servant, Denmark 1469

The oldest provincial laws of Denmark (compiled during the late twelfth and early thirteenth centuries) included punishments for fornication with a slave woman, for which a fine was paid to the owner. Slavery was abolished during the thirteenth century, but in 1469 a special appellate court in Jutland in Denmark determined that fornication with a housekeeper also constituted theft from the employer of the housekeeper if the lover was not in the same employ, and both treason and fornication if he was. The ruling of 1469 came to apply to housekeepers entrusted with the care of their employer's property, and the decision was cited in several subsequent court cases. It was made a formal law in 1562, though it only applied to servants of royal and noble employers and only in the case where both parties were in the same employ. The law was formally in force until 1866.
(Copy of original verdict in the Danish National Archives and in manuscript collections in the Royal Library, Copenhagen, Denmark. Most recent edition in *Danske Domme 1375–1662, De private Domssamlinger, I.' 1375–1553*, Det danske Sprog- og Litteraturselskab (Copenhagen: Reitzel, 1978), pp. 89–93. Translated by Grethe Jacobsen and Pernille Arenfeldt.)

We, Jens, by God's grace Bishop of Aarhus, [the names of 4 knights, 14 squires and 12 peasants] make known with this our open letter that we were summoned to Randers on the Tuesday after the Feast of Saint Gregory [March 14th] 1469 in the capacity of Bishop and Jury regarding the matter and dispute between Claus Steen, squire, on the one side, and Erik Sorensen Myrt and his oath-helpers of Onsild District [on the other] regarding a maiden with whom Erik Sorensen had intercourse [and who is] in the service of the aforementioned Claus Steen.

Upon address, reply and the circumstances of the case, letter and evidence, which was given to us from both parties, we declared this to be the law that a man who seduces or has intercourse with any man's or woman's maid or woman, who is entrusted with key and lock and responsibility over their property, whether a little or much and is found guilty of this deed, if they are in the same service then it is treachery and theft, but if the man or youth is not in the service [that she is, the one who does it] then it is theft, when such happens. We thus declare the verdict to be overruled and invalidated which has been pronounced by the oath helpers which the aforementioned Erik Sorensen Myrt gave aforementioned Claus Steen [stating] that he is not and was not a thief nor a traitor because he lay with Maren Mortensdaughter, who is in the service of aforementioned Claus Steen.

To witness that it so transpired and happened in all ways we have attached our seals onto this letter.

27 Soldier charged with bigamy, Spain 1598

Early modern Europeans were much more mobile than generally thought. Women left home to work as domestic servants, and men often traveled beyond the confines of their home towns as merchants and soldiers. While such travels were no doubt exciting, they could also lead to problems for men like Juan Pacheco whose love interests finally caught up with him when he was charged with bigamy in 1598.

(Relaciones de Causas, Archivo Histórico Nacional, Sección Inquisición, legajo 2042, no.35, f. 1 (1598). Translated by Allyson Poska.)

Juan Pacheco, a soldier in the fort of Viana in Portugal, 50 years of age, charged with being married two times, denounced himself [to the Inquisition stating] that 30 years ago, more or less, while living in the town of Pontevedra he made a promise of marriage in the present tense with Catalina Alvarez in the presence of many people that he named. He cohabited and lived with her for the period of two years and had a son by her. Afterwards, he went to Italy and Flanders where he served as a soldier until he became a captain in the kingdom of Portugal. Staying in the town of Viana [Portugal] he had become fond of Mencia Barriosa and he was married to her by a cleric in the church . . . He was sentenced to hear mass with the insignias of his crime, abjure 'de levi' and banished to the galleys for three years. He was not given the ordinary penalty of leaving the church and being publicly whipped since he came and denounced himself and named the witnesses of his first marriage. . . .

28 Woodcut of a field-cook and his wife, Germany 1568

Early modern armies did not have soldiers specifically responsible for provisioning, but men and women attached themselves to armies to find food and cook for them; women who engaged in such occupations are often called 'camp followers' and regarded as prostitutes, but the food and clean clothing they provided may have been more important for soldiers than sex. This is a woodcut illustration of a couple who were field-cooks (the derogatory term for them is Sudler, which implies slovenly or filthy) by the German artist Wolfgang Strauch. The verse reads: We come out of Frisia/ And are in demand in Braunschweig/ There we cook for the army/ With roasting, baking, steaming, boiling/ We furnish them with cows, hogs, lambs, geese/ Sausage, sauerkraut, greens, beans/ Because of this my slovenly cook-wife and I/ Can always stay with the soldiers.

(Published in Walter L. Strauss, *The German Single-Leaf Woodcut* (New York: Abaris Books, 1975). Reproduced by permission.)

Der Sudler vnd sein Sudlerin.

Auß Frießlandt rauschen wir da her | Mit Küen / Seruen / Lemmer / Gensen | Gedruckt zu Nürnberg/
Ihn Braunschweyg steet vnser beger | Mit würsten / kraut / kröß / leber / wensen | bey Wolff Strauch.
Ob wir ihm heer do möchten Sudlen | Auff das ich vnd mein Sudel Koch | 1 5 6 8.
Mit Braten / Bachen / Sieden /sudlen | Beyn Knechten möchten bleyben noch. |

29 Report on service to the court, Spain 1561

In Spain, the nearby towns of central Castile profited immeasurably from King Philip II's decision to make Madrid the capital of his kingdom in 1561. During the economic expansion that accompanied the movement of the court, service work such cleaning, washing, and cooking, was especially in demand, as Madrid grew from a tiny village into the center of an empire. In their response to King Philip II's question-naire, the town of Hortaleza noted that the people of the town had become quickly integrated into the economic life of the new capital.

(*Relaciones histórico-geográfico-estadísticas de los pueblos de España hecho por iniciativa de Felipe II: Provincia de Madrid*, eds. Carmelo Viñas y Mey and Ramón Paz (Madrid: CSIC, 1949), p. 319. Translated by Allyson Poska.)

To question number 35, they said that the way of life that they have in the said place is their labor as has been said. And many people of the said place have as their livelihood cooking for private persons, inhabitants of the town of Madrid and courtiers, and the women washing the linens of the said persons. . . .

30 Report on a slave hired by the Inquisition, Portugal 1581

The administration and management of the Inquisition took up a lot of effort and energy from many religious leaders in early modern Portugal. Not only were they concerned with converting or punishing the infidels, but religious leaders also had to deal with the daily demands of the infrastructure they upheld, including the provisioning and maintenance of jails where infidel prisoners were kept. The following document deals with the mun-dane yet telling task of cleaning the jails and sweeping some floors and stairways, a task for which some employees of the inquisitors had received an increase in their salary in 1579. Two years later this increase was rescinded because officials had invested in the purchase of a [male] slave who presumably did this work for no pay at all.

(Isaías da Rosa Pereira, ed., *Documentos para a História da Inquisição em Portugal* (Século XVI), vol. I (Lisbon: Serviços da Caritas Portuguesa, s.n., 1987), p. 117. Translated by Darlene Abreu-Ferreira.)

The Archbishop of Lisbon, Chief Inquisitor, etc., I send to you João Campelo, treasurer of the Holy Office of Lisbon, that from the first day of this month of January and from henceforth do not pay the eight thousand *réis* to the two guards that with another provision of ours we had you give per year in increase, for taking charge of the clean-up of the jails, nor the four thousand *réis* that were given to the gatekeeper of the dispatch, and the three thousand to the gatekeeper of the courtyard, for sweeping the houses of dispatch and the stairs, since they no longer have that task for the reason that we bought a slave to do the housekeeping. Execute it thus. Given in Lisbon the first of February of one thousand five hundred and eighty-one.

31 Note regarding a slave woman, Ottoman Empire
mid seventeenth century

The following brief note, undated and unsigned, was most likely written by the Ottoman queen mother Turhan, who assumed the regency when her husband died and her son was only six years old. It concerns the gift of a talented slave woman, which the queen mother was returning to the giver, the husband of an Ottoman princess. Not uncommon among the Ottoman elite was the practice of gifting highly trained slave women who might be expert in dance, musical performance (and sometimes composition), or the recitation and composition of poetry. During the early modern period, male and female slaves occupied the highest ranks in the Ottoman ruling class. In fact, all consorts of the Ottoman sultans from the mid fifteenth century on were Christian women – enslaved during war or purchased from slave dealers – who were then taken into the palace, converted to Islam, and trained in the Ottoman language, etiquette, and culture. In the incident recorded below, Turban shows her concern for a female slave such as she herself once was, though she had remained in the imperial household, rising through its ranks to become one of the dynasty's most powerful queen mothers.

(Letters kept in the Topkapi palace archives. Translated by Leslie Peirce.)

You sent us a slave woman trained in dancing. Bravo! May you prosper! We too are opposed to a Muslim's going to an unbeliever. We have sent the slave woman back so that you might give her to your companion, the princess, from us. May God bless you.

Questions for discussion

1 What types of goods were typically found in an early modern urban house-hold? In a hospital? How did people obtain these items?
2 How did merchants seek to increase their profits? In what types of activities, besides buying and selling merchandise, did they engage?
3 What were the main aims of craft guilds, as evidenced in their ordinances?
4 How did political authorities seek to regulate trade, production, and other aspects of economic life?
5 How would you compare the work opportunities for men with those for women?
6 What problems and benefits were associated with being a servant? With working on one's own?
7 What types of employment opportunities were provided by the military? By royal courts? How did these compare with being a member of a craft guild?
8 How would you compare patterns of work in early modern Europe with those of today?

6

RELIGION

Most people in early modern Europe were Christian, with a small population of Jews residing in many areas, primarily in eastern Europe. In the Ottoman Empire to the East, the dominant religion was Islam, but Christians and Jews also lived under Ottoman control. Throughout the European continent, religious minorities lived under varying – and never very secure – degrees of toleration and protection from the authorities.

One of the most important features of early modern life was the way in which religion permeated virtually every aspect of an individual's world. In an age of great uncertainty, when people died at all ages from a wide variety of illness and misfortune, it was easy to accept the notion of supernatural forces that were either arbitrary or beyond the comprehension of mere mortals. At the same time, such a power had to be placated. Thus the notion of a greater power was compelling and nearly universal. Vestiges of pagan tradition remained within the dominant Catholic tradition well into the sixteenth century and beyond. For example, people said prayers before eating, sleeping, harvesting, giving birth, and every activity in between. They often prayed to saints who had specific associations everything from fertility to finding lost objects, much as the ancients had prayed to specific gods and demigods.

The one leisure-time activity that families often engaged in together was worship. Well-to-do fathers often held morning and evening prayers, or after the development of the printing press read out loud to the entire household – servants included – from the Bible or other religious literature. Families attended church services together, the wealthier of them often sitting in special family pews. Religious ceremonies, such as weddings, baptisms, and funerals, marked major family events, and in Catholic areas the anniversaries of family members' deaths were also the occasion of special ceremonies. Particularly after the Reformation, time spent not working was supposed to be spent examining one's soul, whether in the family group, the larger congregation, or, if one were literate, reading and praying on one's own

Religious holidays also provided an occasion for community-wide festivals that were not very pious, particularly before the Reformation but also afterwards in many areas. Most areas celebrated specific saints' days, which were also often linked to important points in the agricultural cycle, such as harvesting or planting. The whole community would turn out for these festivals, which offered social companionship and a break from the bleakness of work. At festivals and weddings, people of all social classes often engaged in wild public parties and celebrations, wearing costumes and playing games. Protestant and Catholic reformers often criticized the drinking, gambling, and dancing that accompanied festivals and weddings, and occasionally succeeded in having festivals prohibited and weddings restricted to solemn ceremonies in a church. In a few instances, such as Geneva under Calvin's governance, they also banned certain leisure-time activities that occurred outside of festivals, such as gambling, card-playing, and plays.

In Catholic Europe, religious institutions played a central role in the social and economic structure of the early modern world. In many ways they functioned like a parallel government to the secular one run by a king. Like the secular government, the Catholic Church leveled taxes, or tithes. Ecclesiastical courts had their own jurisdiction over matters concerning priests and nuns, and Inquisitions as well.

Ecclesiastical and secular authorities could reinforce each other. For example, the initiative for public religious rituals often came from the political authorities, and civic processions frequently instituted by city magistrates. Even when undertaken to celebrate secular events (for example military victory), processions ended at a church. However, even a purely religious event was shaped by lay leaders to give it powerful secular overtones. So a celebration of the Body of Christ lent itself aptly to the objectives of magistrates who wanted to enhance communal solidarity by making all citizens feel like indispensable parts of the 'social body' – a body whose head or heart was embodied by the mayor or council. Religion, then, was an asset to municipal rulers. This sense of reciprocity and mutual interest was further reinforced by the familial relationships that could exist between secular and religious elites, as wealthy families placed their daughters in certain convents or sponsored their son's entry into the priesthood.

But church and civic governments in most European countries also had an uneasy relationship with one another. Often jockeying for power at the highest political levels, they also battled for the resources at the micro level, competing for the wealth of peasants and nobles alike through an elaborate system of taxation. These Church taxes, or tithes, along with the vast land holdings of the Church, led many to view the religious institutions as too worldly.

The religious landscape changed radically in western Europe with the Protestant Reformation, and the Catholic Reformation which followed it. City magistrates often made the ultimate decision to join Luther's (and later Calvin's) movement or remain Catholic. In this decision, they were influenced by a mix of community sentiment and the allegiance of their lords. In the early decades of the Reformation, cities often swung back and forth according to political climate. Europeans often hedged their bets by not embracing either faith too enthusiastically.

182

As Luther and soon after Calvin developed new ways of thinking about faith and salvation, and drew thousands of followers away from the Catholic Church, Europe erupted into war. These wars – concentrated in central and northern Europe – dragged much of the continent into near continuous, extremely bloody conflict for much of the sixteenth and seventeenth centuries. Some secular leaders also used these religious upheavals to further their political and territorial interests, which prolonged and intensified the fighting.

On a local, more personal level, the religious reformations affected virtually all Europeans. Many enthusiastically embraced the new alternatives that the Protestant faiths offered. In the process they risked their lives, and some found themselves imprisoned or worse for their beliefs by the Catholic Inquisition or by their secular, Catholic leaders. The reverse was true for Catholics living in what had become Protestant lands. For all of these faiths, the early modern period was a time of spiritual intensity and preoccupation with salvation.

Distinct differences emerged in the texture of religious life in Catholic and Protestant regions. Catholic towns, for example, boasted large numbers of resident clergy, as they always had. The Catholic reformation, which flowered largely in response to the sentiments driving the Protestant movement, stimulated the founding of new and more ascetic or more militant religious orders, such as the Ursulines, Capuchins, and especially the Jesuits. Religious processions continued through the streets of Catholic towns. Confraternities, such an important component of early modern social and economic life, continued to thrive.

By contrast, Protestant towns had fewer clergy, and monastic institutions disappeared in Protestant regions. Sometimes cathedral chapters and collegiate churches continued to function, but they had little impact on the life of the community. Compared to Catholic practice, the Protestant faith offered less variety of physical venues for religious expression. For the most part, Protestant religious life was confined to one's home and parish church. Even the architecture was different: church buildings themselves were more spare, in keeping with Protestant distrust of images and other physical aids to devotion. Street-corner shrines disappeared, along with the chapels that were so much of pre-Reformation topography. The traditional cycle of saints' days and religious festivals was scaled down or even reduced to the simple alternating of Sabbath and weekdays. Finally, the streets themselves lost much of their religious coloration.

One mission shared by Catholic and Protestant authorities alike was the eradication of witchcraft, which they perceived as a sinister and widespread threat. Across Europe, thousands of people, mostly women, were rounded up and tried as witches. Tens of thousands perished; by the end of the sixteenth century some villages in Germany had killed or driven away their entire female population. Some of the women accused of witchcraft did in fact believe they were witches, but they were the minority. Many accused witches were women who were socially vulnerable in some way, for example poor women, widows, or prostitutes. Others were women who were scolds, or healers whose techniques often drew on traditional folk medicine and raised suspicions in an age in which 'science' and scientific methods – as practiced by male doctors – began to gain prestige. Finally, women accused of witchcraft were often targeted by their enemies as a form of vendetta. The witchcraze that spread through Europe in the sixteenth and seventeenth centuries is a forceful reminder of the intensity with which people in this period struggled over, questioned, and asserted their spiritual convictions.

DEFINING AND MAINTAINING ORTHODOXY

1 An Inquisitor's report, Portugal 1542

The Portuguese Inquisition was established in 1526, and in its quest to eradicate Portugal of all non-Catholic practices, it left a legacy of intolerance and suspicion that is reflected in this record. Citizens, neighbors, and acquaintances were pitted against each other as New Christians vied for acceptance and survival. New Christians were those who had been forcibly converted to Catholicism from Judaism or Islam, and were often suspected of not truly adhering to the true doctrine. Inquisitors expected Old Christians to report on any signs of possible deviance.

(Francisco Sousa Viterbo, ed., *Trabalhos Nauticos dos Portuguezes nos Séculos XVI e XVII, Part I* (Lisbon: Typographia da Academia Real da Sciencias, 1898 [facsimile, Lisbon: Imprensa Nacional-Casa Moeda, 1988], p. 377 [341]. Translated by Darlene Abreu-Ferreira.)

And following this on the fifth day of the month of June of 1542 years, in Lisbon.

It. Isabel Fernandez, wife of Pero Reinel, who makes navigation charts, who lives in this city at the entrance way to the Misericordia at the rear of the terrace for old wheat, in the parish of *See*, was asked and testified under oath on the Bible if she knows of any person or persons who have said or done something against our holy Catholic faith, said she the witness that she did not know anything else except that in this last Lent, she the witness was going to the customs house and passing through the square of Pelourinho Velho [the old pillory], where items are sold at auction, they were selling some *tavoleiros* [special tins for baking cookies] and some women were buying the said *tavoleiros* who placed a bid on them and a porter, who was auctioning who is named Remedeo, carried the said *tavoleiros* to them to look at, and they took them in their hands and were looking at them and were not pleased with them and left them, so then the said Remedeo told them – in a harsh voice: these are the women who took the virginity from God!, and so then she the witness left and afterwards encountered the said porter and reprimanded him for having spoken those words and that he said that he was joking, and said she the witness that she does not know if the said Remedeo is a New Christian or an Old, and yet that he appeared to be a New Christian, and that there were many people present who she the witness did not know nor did she know the women who took the said *tavoleiros* for it happened that she was passing by and heard the above mentioned and said no more. Antonio Roiz wrote it with the two marks that were made in truth and requested me the notary that I sign for her for [she] not knowing how to write, she the witness said further that it was true that seven or eight months ago more or less that one day came to her house a certain Isabel Fernandez, New Christian, widowed woman, who sold olive oil in the Feraria, started to talk and that she the witness asked her and said that for what reason the New Christians when dead were laid in virgin graves, because the Old Christians rejoiced that the earth that ate the father and mother and grandparents would eat them and that the said Isabel Fernandez retorted that she was astonished that she did not know that, that the reason for which the New Christians did that was because if they lay in graves where other dead had already been that all the sins of those who were buried there would be transmitted to them, and that she the witness replied to her by saying that was the blindness in which they lived, and said no more.

2 Sexual relations and religion, Portugal early sixteenth century

The ordinances against king D. Manuel I (r. 1495–1521) deal with a multitude of what might be termed private matters, but the distinctions between public and private, church and state, were not all that clear in the early modern period. The following example deals with the prohibition of sexual relationships between Christians and non-Christians, the penalty for which was death.

(*Ordenações do Senhor Rey D. Manuel, vol. V* (Coimbra: Na Real Imprensa da Unversidade, 1797), p. 70. Translated by Darlene Abreu-Ferreira.)

Titulo XXI. Any Christian who has carnal union with any Moorish woman, or with any other infidel woman, or a Christian woman with a Moor or a Jew, or with any other infidel, shall die for it; and this when such union took place voluntarily and knowingly, because if any woman of a similar condition is forced, she shall not die, nor be punished for it; only he who committed it by force shall receive this punishment. And likewise he who does this sin in ignorance, not knowing, nor having just reason to know that the other person was from another doctrine, does not merit punishment for it, and only shall be punished that person who was aware of the said infidelity, or who had just reason to know it; that if some blame be for knowing it, or having just reason to know it, he shall be punished according to the offense in which he is found.

3 Explaining baptism, Spain sixteenth century

Over the centuries, even such basic rituals as baptism had become infused with local traditions that sometimes challenged Church doctrine. As a part of the Catholic Reformation, the Catholic Church worked to bring some uniformity to the religious practices of its parishioners. In this piece, Bishop Francisco Manrique de Lara admonishes the parishioners of his diocese to follow Catholic orthodox practice more carefully.
(From the diocesan synod of Francisco Manrique de Lara, bishop of Ourense (1542–1556), in Antonio García y García, *Synodicon Hispanum, vol. 1: Galicia* (Madrid: Biblioteca de Autores Cristianos, 1981), p. 236. Translated by Allyson Poska.)

Some people of this bishopric, either out of ignorance or out of malice, baptize their children one, two, and three times, and more, inviting new godfathers and godmothers each time to the said act. And another error accompanies this one: they do not take them to be baptized at the church where the font for holy baptism is, only baptizing them at home. And they fall into another great error. Many people leave their children without baptism for the period of one month, and even close to a year, because of certain vain and superstitious things; all of which is clearly in contradiction of the precepts established by the Church of faithful Christians.

4 Work and the Sabbath, Spain 1566

The Christian tradition that no work was to be done on Sundays or holidays was a source of regular conflict between parishioners and the ecclesiastical hierarchy. Bishops wanted their parishioners to attend Mass and study on holy days, business owners wanted the additional income from being open on Sunday, and parishioners often preferred to spend the day socializing in bars. In this excerpt from a visit to a parish in northwestern Spain, a delegate from the Bishop attempts to encourage parishioners to attend Mass by ordering the tavern owners to close until Mass is over.
(*Libro de Visitas, Santa María Amarante*, Archivo Histórico Diocesano de Ourense, 24.1.13, Folio 9–10 (1566). Translated by Allyson Poska.)

His majesty is informed that on past visits Gregorio Gómez and Alonso Galente, inhabitants of Dacon, Juan de Momdian and Juan Bernáldez, inhabitants of Toscana, and Gabriel de Dacon all tavern owners, were admonished not to open the taverns nor sell wine, bread or meat to the parishioners on Sundays and holidays before High Mass. They have not wanted to comply, opening the taverns and selling wine and meat so that the parishioners quit coming to Mass in order to be there playing and drinking. Being compassionate with them he has fined and fines each one of them three reales for the fabric of the church for this first time, except Alonso Galente who is fined only one and a half reales on account of his poverty. Henceforth, they will be fined one ducat for each time that they open them during Mass.

5 Villagers cope with religious change, Denmark 1543–1544

The first Lutheran bishop of the Danish island of Zealand travelled widely in his diocese and wrote his experiences down in 1543–1544, including stories and episodes that he could use didactically, but which also reveal how his audience needed to be reminded of the religious change that had been introduced in 1536 with the establishment of a Lutheran Church and state in Denmark. The church in Kippinge, mentioned in the following text, had contained a chalice, reputed to be bleeding, which made it a popular destination for pilgrimages.
(*Peder Palladius' Visitatsbog*, ed. by Lis Jacobsen, Copenhagen: Gyldendal, 1925, pp. 130–131. Translated by Grethe Jacobsen and Pernille Arenfeldt.)

Another great abuse has been the visits to dead saints while forgetting the living saints . . . A good and honest man has become the parish minister in Holmstrup and Kippinge. Whoever arrives there in his ungodly business he directs back to whence he came. Flames have consumed St. Severin and his statue has been taken away. You will not find what you are looking for. Last year, in Flakkebjerg County, a woman dropped her child by accident and it broke its neck. Her husband was not home. Fearing her husband's reaction, she took the dead child in her arms and ran to Kippinge, five miles away. As the parish minister realised that she had come as a pilgrim, he lectured to her about the proper belief and she laid her child in the cemetery and went home again. Still, I had to read her out of her belief in that and more when I visited here. Stay with your parish church and learn there what will benefit your soul and leave such ungodly ideas behind.

6 Legal opinion concerning the religious training of a woman accused of infanticide, Germany 1787

Though all Christian denominations in early modern Europe mandated religious instruction, and some was available in most cities and villages, many people, especially the very poor, had no opportunity to attend. In this legal brief, which was part of the documentation of a case of infanticide, the jurist noted how superficial and scanty the religious training of the accused was; his explanation was not enough to bring about a reduction in the sentence of the accused, however.
(Wilhelm Wächterhäuser, *Das Verbrechen des Kindesmordes im Zeitalter der Aufklärung*, Quellen und Forschungen zur Strafrechtsgeschichte, vol. III (Berlin, 1973), p. 108. Translated by Merry Wiesner-Hanks.)

The unfortunate accused had enjoyed as good as no religious instruction, in that when she was six she went to a school run by the village sexton for fourteen days, and after that she learned a few catechism questions and readings by heart from one of her companions without understanding their meaning. At her confirmation she did not receive any further religious instruction, but some questions were put to her by her pastor, which he answered himself and simply admonished her. It was clear from the examination before the court, that in terms of religious and moral matters she has a completely miserable understanding and incorrect notions; in particular, in terms of the unlawfulness and liability to punishment of the deed she has done, and its seriousness, she has only a little and incomplete understanding and conviction, and no idea about the meaning of the words that she learned by heart in her youth: thou shall not kill.

RELIGIOUS ACTIVITIES

7 Religious bequest, Denmark 1415

In a will from 1415 the religious interests of an urban woman are mirrored in her bequests to religious institutions and persons in three cities, reserving the largest bequest, valuable urban property, for the cathedral of St. Lawrence, the archiepiscopal cathedral of medieval Denmark.
(*Testamenter fra Danmarks Middelalder indtil 1450*, Udgivne for Det kongelige danske Selskab for Fædrelandets Historie og Sprog af Kr. Erslev (Copenhagen: Gyldendal, 1901). Translated by Grethe Jacobsen and Pernille Arenfeldt.)

Will of Katrina Laurensdatter, wife of Laurens Jensen. 1415.

In nomine Domini, amen. I, Katerina Laurendsdatter, wife of Laurens Jensen, have a body that is not well but a soul that by the help of God is well; with the will of my dear husband and several of our true friends I now bequeath the goods that God has lent me accordingly:

First I donate to the Church of St. Lawrence in Lund, half of a stone house, situated in Malmø, which yields 3 solid marks in yearly income, which house I lawfully and honestly inherited from my parents, whose names were Lasse Skytte and Katerine Laurenses, on the condition that a memorial mass be said in aforesaid church for me and my aforesaid parents after the fest of St. Canute the King [July 10]. One mark of the annual rent of aforesaid stone house to be distributed thus: the canon is to have 3 shillings, the bell-ringer 2 'grot', and the rest goes to the building of the church.

Item I donate 3 marks in Scanian money to my parish church of St. Olaf. Item for my confessor, Master Benedict Jensen, priest, 1 silver spoon. Item every monastery in Lund 4 'grot.' Item Mistress Benedicte in the convent

1 shilling. Item for the monastery, parish church and Holy Spirit Hospital in Landskrona each 4 shillings. Item the Black Friars in Helsingborg 4 'grot.' Item my sister a red tunic with a black sleeve with metal ornaments. Item my sister's daughter Estrid a red cape and a hood with metal ornaments.

This is my will and final desire which I ask my dear husband, Laurens Jensen aforesaid, and Peder Saxtorp, esquire, to fulfil for the benefit of my soul which I trust them to do and to answer to God.

For further witness the seals of honest men who are Master Benedict, my confessor, Sire Peter in Resløf and Peder Saxtorp, esquire aforesaid, have been attached to this.

Datum Agård, Billeberg parish, anno domini 1514, *crastino visitacionis beate Marie virginis gloriose.*

8 A Catholic woman writes of her faith, England 1610

During the period of the Protestant and Catholic Reformations, individuals who were not members of the clergy debated religion orally and occasionally published pamphlets and treatises detailing their ideas on religious matters. It is very difficult to find information about oral discussions, but occasionally one of the participants shared his or her experiences in letters to others. The following is a portion of a letter from Luisa de Carvajal (1566–1614) to Joseph Creswell, the director of the English Jesuits in Spain and Portugal. Carvajal was a wealthy Spanish noblewoman orphaned at a young age who developed a strong sense of religious calling. In 1605 she went to England, which had become Protestant many decades before, to minister to Catholics there and attempt to convince people to convert to Catholicism. She was arrested and jailed for a few days in 1608, and again in 1613, and died shortly after her second release from prison.

(Elizabeth Rhodes, *This Tight Embrace: Luisa de Carvajal y Mendoza (1566–1614)*
(Milwaukee: Marquette University Press, 2000), pp. 265–279. Reprinted by permission.)

1. I receive great mercy and consolation from Your Grace's letters, and I hope that Your Grace has received consolation with my last correspondence, seeing the great constancy of the holy martyrs Garves and Fludder [two Catholic martyrs]. And of me, I can tell Your Grace that I have walked between the cross and holy water, as they say there, because I have been in prison, and since it was in the public jail, it would be useless for me to keep silent about it.

2. The reason was because, arriving one day at a store in Cheapside [a part of London], leaning on the door sill from outside, as is my custom, the occasion offered to ask one of the young attendants if he was Catholic presented itself, and he responded, 'No, God forbid!' And I replied, 'May God not permit that you not be, which is what matters for you.' At this the mistress and master of the shop came over, and another youth and

neighboring merchants, and a great chat about religion ensued. They asked a lot about the mass, about priests, about confession, but what we spent the most time on (over two hours) was whether the Roman religion was the only true one, and whether the Pope is the head of the Church, and whether St. Peter's keys have been left to them [the Popes] forever in succession.

3. Some listened with pleasure, others with fury, and so much that I sensed some danger, at least of being arrested. But I thought nothing of it, in exchange for setting that light before their eyes in the best way I could. And in these simple matters of faith there are known methods [of convincing] which are very handy for anyone, and with which one can wage war on error. And although they might not take it very well at first, in the end those truths remain in their memories, to be meditated upon and open to holy inspirations, and God's cause for their salvation or condemnation is greatly justified. And there are very many who never manage to find out even where the priests are, and among the lay Catholics, not many want to run that risk [of contact with priests] without a guaranteed benefit. And the merchants of Cheapside exceed the rest of the city in malice, error, and hatred for the Pope, as well as in the quantity of its residents and money. And some of this can be observed in the fact that, when I have spoken on several occasions with others about exactly the same things, they have always taken it affably.

4. The mistress of the shop tried to stir everyone to anger, as did another infernal young man who was there, younger in age but with greater malice. The woman said it was a shame that they were tolerating me and that, without a doubt, I was some Roman [Catholic] priest dressed like a woman so as to better persuade people of my religion. Our Lord saw fit that I speak the best English I've spoken since I've been in England, and they thought I was Scottish because of the way I spoke and because I showed affection for the King, because one of the eldest men came over to me and asked whether he [James] wasn't quite wise for not making his entire kingdom continue in error. I responded that it wasn't a question of the King, who had been left as a child, without his saintly Catholic mother, in the power of the Puritans, and that they had a truer and more legitimate King now than they had had in Queen Elizabeth.

5. Thus I tried not to evade the truth and make them forget the malicious question about the King, about which they are extremely touchy? And so then they asked why it was that the King was truer. And I said that because he was the great-grandson of the eldest daughter of Henry VIII and Elizabeth, his daughter, was born during the life of Queen Catherine, Mary's mother. And from that they inferred that I was calling her a bastard but, since it had already happened and she left no sons, it wasn't a matter

190

of importance. And we got through that with few words and returned to questions about the true religion once more.

6. And hearing behind me that someone calling Mr. Garves a traitor, and my Ann [one of her English companions], [insisting he was] a martyr, were disputing, I prohibited her from continuing, fearing that she might say something impolitic? And I asked him to tell me why Garves had died. He said only because he was a Roman Catholic. 'And for no other reason?' I replied. He said yes. 'Well then,' I said to him, 'don't be shocked that he is called a martyr.' And he seemed to take it well.

7. With this I returned to my house and I left them like lions against me. And two weeks later they managed to spot me, for it was necessary for me to go out, which I do but few times without a very specific need to buy necessary things or to go see the felicitous confessors of Christ in the prisons, or something similar, and never to visit anyone (for my natural condition so inclines me and my poor health and strength require it. And in the end they surrounded me, looking at me like basilisks [small, snakelike creatures believed to kill with their sight and breath] and with a sheriff they brought, they said I had to go to Sir Thomas Bennet's house, the justice of the peace, not far from there. And although they had no warrant, I didn't resist, so they wouldn't grab me by the arm or raise a ruckus right in the middle of the street. And it wasn't a bad moment for my soul either. And all three of us went along agreeably, I mean Ann and Faith, my companions, and myself (for the other two [companions] had stayed at home). And our servant, who is an old and virtuous man of honor and long-standing Catholic faith, went with us.

8. We found the judge seated beneath a little roof on his patio, where he probably conducts his business, and he had us there, examining witnesses and questioning people from six in the evening or a bit later until around nine, when it started to get dark. The witnesses swore on their Bible what truths they said, with a few lies, but more or less within the limits of what I've already touched upon, without inventing anything else. And they talked so much nonsense sometimes that they made me recall that line [from the Bible], *Et testimonia convenientia non erant?* [But their witness agreed not together.] And there were two or three of them stirring up the people of the nearby streets against me, saying I was a priest in a woman's clothes who was walking around persuading people of my faith, and since it was something so unheard of, I believe in half an hour there were more than two hundred people, so they were saying, at the judge's door, with the street full of a great, confusing noise. And among them they were already saying that there were three priests, with their long black gowns, which is our garb? The judge got up to calm them down a few times, because they were trying

hard to get in. And he told me that if he were to send me to the jail then, the people would go at me. I told him I thought he had more charity than that.

9. He asked my homeland, name, address, and the reason I was in England, and by telling the truth I cut it short, saying my name was Luisa de Carvajal, and I was Spanish, and I lived close to don Pedro's house, where I went to hear mass, and that I had come to follow the example of many saints of the holy church who voluntarily exiled themselves into foreign lands, being unprotected and poor. And although it was all gibberish to the pitiful old man, that was the best answer, without a doubt.

10. He laughed as if he were crazy and asked me if it was the case that I affirmed the Pope to be the head of the Church and his religion the only true one. I said yes. He asked me if I wanted to remain in said opinions. And I responded that yes I did, and that I was prepared to die for them . . .

13. The judge's daughters kept coming in and out, as well as his wife; it must have been so they could see us. In the end they took us to the jail, after we had been in a lower room adjoining the same patio since nightfall, sometimes walking about, and sometimes with my kneeling in one of its corners to pray that God help us. And we could not leave until after eleven thirty, so as to depart without there being a lot of people, and even so about twenty from the neighborhood followed us. The judge's secretary was among them, one of good Thomas's cousins, who is now imprisoned, much needed by all our friends. He told the jailer to treat us well, but that must not have been able to happen that night, and so they put us in the highest part of a narrow little attic, with a lit candle and the door locked with a key the jailer took with him, without our being able to get so much as a drop of water or beer or even a bite of bread. And what with this and not being very well, and without being able to get into a bed, I slept little indeed, but with notable consolation, and this diminished when I considered what little the whole business amounted to.

14. I had asked them if, for money, they would put me close to the jailer's wife and female servants, even though it were less comfortable than that lodging. And in the morning they put us in one of her rooms, around ten o'clock, and although dingy and without air, it was reasonable, and the women were all courteous and affable. . . .

15. We were in there for four days, from Saturday until Wednesday at ten at night, when the Council sent orders for them to set me free, with the judge having sent them my papers. . . .

16. While in jail I spoke about religion much more than I had out of it, with all the jailers and officials and their families and friends whom, with my permission, they brought to speak with me. And they listened nicely.

192

And I didn't want to let the chance slip by, remembering the Holy Apostle who says that the word of God is not tied down?

9 Family praying, Germany c. 1550

Both Protestant and Catholic authorities recommended individual and family prayer as an important spiritual activity, and diaries and letters indicate that people did pray frequently. In this single-sheet broadside by the German printer Wolfgang Strauch, a family – probably the man who paid for the broadside, along with his wife and children – is depicted in prayer before the cross. Such broadsheets were designed as aids to prayer, to be read or hung on a wall.

(Walter L. Strauss, *The German Single-leaf Woodcut, 1550–1600* (New York: Abaris Books, 1975). Reproduced by permission.)

10 Religion and revelry, Spain 1606

Religious processions and festivals were central to early modern people's social and devotional lives. These events meant a day off from traditional work and an opportunity to celebrate with friends and family. As pious as many people were, religious processions could easily get out of hand, with people eating and drinking to excess. In this case, a night of revelry led to a fight and an audience with the Inquisition when Pedro de Islas was accused of blasphemy.

(Relaciones de Causas, Archivo Histórico Nacional, Sección Inquisición, legajo 2042, no. 43 f. 11 (1606). Translated by Allyson Poska.)

Pedro de Islas, a peasant from San Victorio, Tierra de Lemos, forty years old . . . four years ago, the accused was in a shrine where many people had gathered in pilgrimage. Next to the high altar, a certain person with a crucifix in his hand began to scuffle with the accused. And the accused with a sword in his hand went against the said person [with the crucifix in his hand] and slashed him with the iron and some of [the slashes] hit the Christ [on the crucifix] and that caused a great scandal in the said shrine. On the same occasion, the accused sat on top of the high altar in front of an image of Our Lady that was there with his back to the image and stayed that way for most of the night. He was reprimanded and exiled for one year from this city [Santiago de Compostela] and his parish and fined six thousand maravedis.

11 A young woman healed through a pilgrimage, Germany 1580

For all Christian Europeans before the Reformation, and for Catholic and Orthodox Christians afterwards, pilgrimages to holy places were quite common, either to give thanks for blessings or to make special requests. In this broadsheet published by the Catholic university printer Johann Mayer, a young woman lame since birth is miraculously healed through a pilgrimage to the church at Einsiedeln. In the first scene, the young woman is bent over walking on the road, in the second she meets Christ who touches her legs, in the third she becomes more erect through Christ's touch, and in the fourth she runs toward the church, carrying what looks like a rosary. Individuals who had been healed on a pilgrimage frequently left (and in some pilgrimage churches, continue to leave) models of the healed body part for later pilgrims to contemplate.

(Walter L. Strauss, *The German Single-leaf Woodcut, 1550–1600* (New York: Abaris Books, 1975). Reproduced by permission.)

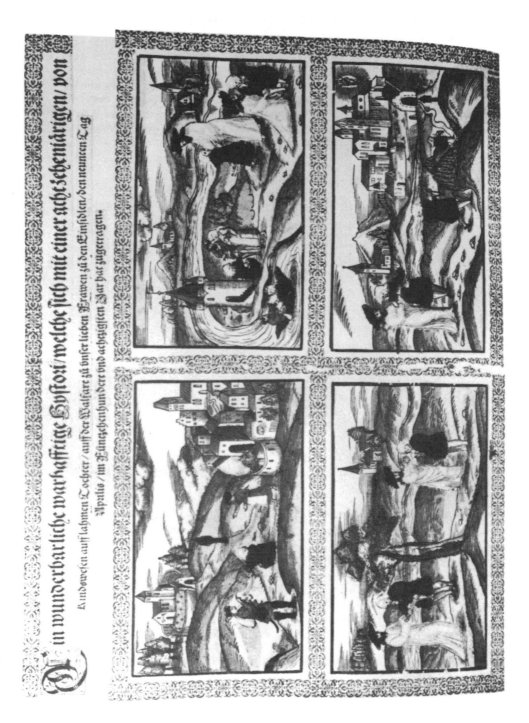

12 A daughter's memory of her mother's piety, Germany 1750

During the seventeenth and eighteenth centuries in many parts of Europe people sought to deepen their spiritual experiences in a variety of ways. Organized movements developed that promoted more intense piety, such as pietism in Germany and Methodism in England, and followers were encouraged to engage in frequent individual prayer. In this selection from a letter, Katharina Stolberg describes the intensity with which her mother, Christiane Charlotte Friederike Stolberg, prayed.
(J.H. Hennes, *Aus Friedrich Leopold von Stolberg's Jugendjahren. Nach Briefen der Familie und andern handschiftlichen Nachrichten* (Frankfurt, 1876), pp. 7–8. Translated by Merry Wiesner-Hanks.)

My mother was a true prayer. She did not start a trip or any undertaking without praying; she did not start reading a book or writing a letter without praying. Wherever she went, she took the first moment that she was alone to drop on her knees or sit down, and with closed eyes – she opened them only to cast devout glances at the heavens – and folded hand she prayed. The presence of her children or her servants did not bother her; I am also certain that few of her friends have not seen her in prayer; yet it occurred to no one to become annoyed at this or to wonder about it. Her whole demeanor was so open and so natural, with no doubts in her belief and with such joy in her prayer. Her whole being was so lively, so cheerful, that it was impossible to have any doubts about her. I do not know if she ever wished to have a miraculous sign of belief, but a child-like belief was her element. From childhood on she had a very special view of providence whenever she listened to prayers, and she wished only that her dear Father would fulfill her requests, not give signs or miracles.

13 A daughter's letter to her father on her confirmation day, Germany 1778

Young people who were Catholic or members of many Protestant denominations including Lutherans and Anglicans went through a ritual of the confirmation of their faith when they reached adolescence. Until they had been confirmed, they were not allowed to take Holy Communion, a central ritual in Christianity, in which bread and wine represent – or in Catholicism, are transformed into – the body and blood of Christ. Until they were confirmed, Catholic young people did not make their confessions, a necessary prerequisite to Communion. In this letter, Susanna Maria Jakobina Loeffelholz asks her father's forgiveness and blessing before her confirmation; such a request was probably encouraged by her priest, or expected as a normal prelude to Communion.
(Franz Erich Mencken, ed., *Dein Dich zartlich liebender Sohn. Kinderbriefe aus sechs Jahrhunderten* (Munich, 1965), pp. 43–44. Translated by Merry Wiesner-Hanks.)

Today is one of the most important days in my whole life, because with God's support I will go into a confessional booth for the first time in my

life, and afterward will be invited to the atonement and holy meal of our
lord Jesus. So that I might appear in a more worthy way, it is my duty and
obligation as a child, to first appear before you, my gracious father, with my
thanks and debts . . . because my conscience is also convinced that I have
often offended you my dear Papa both consciously and unconsciously, and
have brought you to anger, so I will not only attest to this, but will ask you
obediently with my whole soul to forgive me my youthful errors and sins
from your heart. If you do not bear these in mind any more, I will attempt,
with the help of God, to transforms these errors into virtues. I ask in
closing only this, that you include me in your Christian and fatherly prayers,
and ask for God's grace and help for me, to which God will undoubtedly
listen. For this I will be, for the duration of my life, My gracious Herr
Papa's humble and obedient daughter.

14 Jewish prayers, Eastern Europe seventeenth century

Prayer was a common religious activity for people of all religious persuasions in early
modern Europe. Many prayers were spontaneous, and there is no way to reconstruct
them, but others were published, and people were encouraged to memorize and then
recite them. This selection comes from two *tkhines*, supplicatory prayers for women
written in Yiddish, the everyday language of central and eastern European Jews.
Most *tkhines* were probably written by men, though some are known to be written by
women, and they often concern issues that were important in women's lives, such
as childbirth, family, and widowhood. Some were written specifically to be recited by
a woman as she carried out the three special women's religious duties in Judaism:
separating out a portion of dough in memory of priestly offerings, lighting the Sabbath candles, and remaining apart from her husband during menstruation until she
had taken a ritual bath.

(*Tkhines* (Amsterdam, 1658) co. [5c] and *Shloyshe she'orim*, translated in Chava
Weissler, 'Prayers in Yiddish and the Religious World of Ashkenazic Women', in
Judith R. Baskin, ed., *Jewish Women in Historical Perspective* (Detroit: Wayne State
University Press, 1991), pp. 159, 174–175. Reprinted by permission.)

[The woman] says this when she puts the loaf of *berkhes* [braided Sabbath
bread] into the oven: Lord of all the world, in your hand is all blessing. I
come now to revere your holiness, and I pray you to bestow your blessing
on the baked goods. Send an angel to guard the baking, so that all will be
well-baked, will rise nicely, and will not burn, to honor the holy Sabbath
(which you have chosen so that Israel your children may rest thereon) and
over which one recites the holy blessing – as you blessed the dough of
Sarah and Rebecca our mothers. My Lord God, listen to my voice; you are
the God who hears the voices of those who call to you with the whole
heart. May you be praised to eternity.

I, Sarah bas Tovim, [the woman traditionally regarded as the author of this prayer] I do this for the sake of the dear God, blessed be he and blessed be his name, and arrange, this second time, yet another beautiful new *tkhine* concerning three gates. The first gate is founded upon the three commandments which we women were commanded: [The acronym] *Hanna"h* is their name . . . that is to say, separating dough for *hallah*, observing menstrual avoidances [*niddah*], and kindling Sabbath lights [*hadlaqat ha-nerot*]. The second gate is a *tkhine* to pray when one blesses the New Moon. The third gate concerns the Days of Awe.

I take for my help the living God, blessed be he, who lives forever and to eternity, and I set out this second beautiful new *tkhine* in Yiddish with great love, with great awe, with trembling and terror . . . May God have mercy upon me and upon all Israel. May I not long be forced to be a wanderer, by the merit of our Mothers, Sarah, Rebecca, Rachel, and Leah. And my own dear mother Leah pray to God, blessed be he, for me, that my being a wanderer may be an atonement for me for my sins.

COMPETING TRADITIONS

15 A queen combats Protestantism, Portugal sixteenth century

In most parts of Europe, people's religious practices had to accord with those of the rulers, or they risked arrest, imprisonment, or even death. Rulers worried when divergent religious beliefs and practices were allowed in areas close to their own territory, as in this letter from the Queen regent of Portugal, D. Catarina (reigned 1557–1562). One of her many concerns was the spread of Protestantism in northern Europe. This document is one of her letters to Count Castanheira in France asking his advice on how to proceed with a possible diplomatic mission to talk over this problem with France's Charles IX.
(Joaquim Veríssimo Serrão, ed., *Documentos inéditos para a história do reinado de D. Sebastião* (Coimbra: Universidade de Coimbra, 1958), pp. 46–47. Translated by Darlene Abreu-Ferreira.)

Count, my friend, I the King send you many greetings as the one I love. From letters dated September 16 that I have now received from João Pereira de Antas my ambassador in the court of the King of France, I have learned of the great role in that realm that the ministers of the Lutheran sect and their followers have, and the regard and authority enjoyed by very important persons in said realm, and how close it is there for the loss of our holy Catholic faith if our Lord [Charles IX of France] does not deal with it, as you will see from the summary I am sending you along with this, taken from said letters to better inform you, and from other letters by Andre Tellez my uncle and my ambassador in the Court of Castile, I have learned of the good work that he ordered done on this matter with the King of France by the Seigneur de Samze, nobleman of the Upper House of said King of France, who for his part was sent to said King of Castile, as you will also see from the summary of it that I am sending you, from which and from the state of these religious questions you will understand how it behooves us to take great care in a remedy for it and because it seems that I am obliged to take up the matter with the King of France, they [religious questions] being of the type that they are and that they very much affect the honor of Our Lord, peace and tranquillity of all Christianity. I would greatly appreciate you writing to me with all haste if I should do it, and what on this matter should I say to him, and if it should be by a particular person that I send and whom should I choose, and of what station should he be, for I want to resolve this thing immediately, since to delay could create great harm. Written in Lisbon, on the 22 of October of 1562. The Queen.

16 Letters from and a hymn about two Anabaptist martyrs, Netherlands 1552

During the period of the Protestant and Catholic Reformations, individuals of many religious denominations were arrested, tried, imprisoned, tortured, and sometimes executed for their religious beliefs. The harshest treatment was accorded to Anabaptists, who denied the efficacy of infant baptism and often rejected other teachings accepted by most Protestants and Catholics. Many of the documents regarding the persecution of Anabaptists were collected into large volumes, and their stories were also told orally or formed the basis for hymns designed to be sung by the faithful. The following is an exchange of letters between a husband and wife, Jeronimus Segersz and Lijsken Dircks, who were executed as Anabaptists in Antwerp, and a hymn detailing and praising their brave acts. Segersz was burned at the stake in 1551, and Dircks was drowned several months later; her execution was delayed because she was pregnant at the time of her trial and the court waited until the child had been born to put her to death, a common practice for women who were executed. Both the letters and the hymn include references to specific verses of the Bible; the Bible was extremely important to Anabaptists, and many of them had memorized large sections of it.
(Hermina Joldersma and Louis Grijp, ed. and trans., 'Elisabeth's manly courage': Testimonials and Songs of Martyred Anabaptist Women of the Low Countries (Milwaukee: Marquette University Press, 2001). Reprinted by permission.)

Here follows another Letter from Jeronimus Segersz to his Wife [excerpts]:
Grace, peace, a joyful heart, through the confession of Jesus Christ, be with you, my dear wife Lijsken in the Lord. I wish you, my dear Wife Lijsken,

a passionate love for God, and a joyful spirit in Christ Jesus. Know that I remember you *Rom 1:9* day and night in my prayers, beseeching and sighing to God on your behalf; I am in great sorrow on your count because you will have to be imprisoned there for such a long time. I would have wished, had it been the Lord's will, that you would have been out of your bonds, but now the Lord's will was different, because he wants to test you, and to reveal his power and might through you, against all those who stand against truth. Therefore I cannot go against the Lord's will, so that I might not tempt him, but rather I will praise and thank him all the more because he has made us both *Acts 5:41* worthy to suffer for his name; for those whom he has chosen for that are all especially selected Lambs, for he has *Rev 14:4* redeemed them from among mortals as the first-fruits of God.

Further, my dearest one, therefore I have been very joyful up to this time, thanking and praising God, that he has made us fitting for this. But when I heard from you that you were more sorrowful than your tongue could express, that caused me to shed many a tear, and to have a downcast heart, for that is a great sorrow. I also understood that this might be so because you had told me so often to stop heeding Assverus [a silversmith who was a leaders among the Anabaptists], and I didn't do that; this has caused me many a tear, and I am very sorry about it. *Rom 9:19* Still, I can do nothing against the will of God, and if it had been his will, he would have given us a way out. But he has given us *Job 14:5* our measure, and we will not exceed it. Hence we cannot escape *Tob 13:2* from the Lord. Therefore let us not be sad because of the workings of the Lord, but much rather (as *Mt 5:12* Christ says) rejoice and be glad . . .

So I beseech you, my love, that you should not be sad any longer, for the Lord will keep you as the *Zech 2:8* apple of his eye; yes, '*Is 49:15* as little as a mother might forget her suckling child, so I will not forget you', says the Lord; yes, '*Job 10:27* my sheep hear my voice', (says the Lord), 'and they follow me, and no one shall take them from my hand'. Therefore, my very dearest, be content, and trust in the Lord, and *Heb 13:5* he will not forsake you. I also understood, partly from my sister, that you were also sad because you had not been more tolerant towards me. Listen, my dear lamb, you were not antagonistic towards me, and we lived with one another no differently than we were obliged to live, why would you then be sad? Be satisfied, for Christ will not count it against you, *Ezek 18:22* for he will not remember our sins. And I thank the Lord that you did live so submissively with me; I would be gladly imprisoned instead of you for a year on water and bread, indeed, and then would gladly die tenfold, if you were released. O, if only I could help you with my tears, and with my blood, how willingly would I suffer for you! but my suffering cannot help you. Therefore be at peace, I will beseech the Lord even more for you. I wrote this letter in tears, because I had heard that you were so sad. And I ask you to write me about how things are going with you. With this I commend you to the Lord.

This is a Letter from Lijsken, Jeronimus's wife, which she wrote to him in the prison in Antwerp.

. . . My dear Husband in the Lord, whom I married before God and his congregation, about which they say that I have committed adultery because I was not married in Baal's temple. But the Lord says: *Mt 5:12* 'Rejoice when everyone speaks evil of you for my name's sake, then rejoice and be glad, for you will be rewarded in heaven.'

Know that I cried a great deal because you were sad on account of me, because you had heard that I had so often said to you that you should forsake Assverus and you didn't do that; rest your mind about that, my dearest in the Lord, if the Lord had not wanted it so, it would not have happened thus. *Mt 6:10* For the Lord's will must be done for the salvation of both our souls, for he does not let *1 Cor 10:13* us be tempted beyond our ability to endure. Therefore be comforted, my dearest in the Lord, and rejoice in the Lord as you have done from the beginning, praising and thanking him that he has so specially chosen us that we may be imprisoned for so long for his name's sake, and were found worthy for that *Acts 5:41*, he knows what he foresaw with that. Although the children of *Num 14:8* Israel languished long in the wilderness, if they had obeyed the voice of the Lord, they too would have entered the Promised Land with Joshua and Caleb. Just so also we are now in the wilderness among these devouring animals who daily spread their *Ps 7:15, 57:6* nets to catch us with them. But the Lord who is so mighty, and who does not forsake his own who trust in him, those he will keep from all evil, yes, as the *Zech 2:8* apple of his eye. Therefore let us then be at peace in him, and take on our cross with joy and patience, and await with firm faith those promises which he has made us *Rev 2:13*, not doubting them, for he is faithful who has promised it. This is so we might be crowned on *2 Esd 2:41, Rev 7:9* Zion's mountain, and be adorned with palms, and might follow the *Rev 14:4* Lamb. I pray you, my love in the Lord, be comforted in the Lord, with all the beloved friends, and *1 Th 5:25* pray to the Lord for me. Amen.

Here follows yet another Letter from Jeronimus Segersz to his Wife:

. . . I wish my beloved wife, whom I married before God and his holy Congregation *1 Cor 7:2* as my own wife, just as *Gen 11:29* Abraham took Sara, and *Gen 24:15* Isaac Rebecca, and *Tob 7:14* Tobias his uncle's daughter as his wife, exactly so I took you, too, as my wife, *1 Cor 7:2, Mt 19:5* according to God's word and command, and not like this horribly blind world. On account of this I praise and thank the Lord night and day, that he spared us so long that we could get to know one another a little, and that we have had knowledge of the truth. Because of this they say that we have lived in adultery, because we were not joined in that idolatrous, mortal, vain, proud, gluttonous institution, and with that adulterous generation, which is nothing but an abomination before the eyes of God. That's why they lie about us, just as they lied about *Mt 11:19* Christ. And even if they said that you should tend to your sewing, that will not deter us, *Mt 11:28* for Christ has called all of us, *Jn 5:39* and led us to search Scripture, for it testifies of him. Further, Christ said that Mary *Lk 10:42* had chosen the best part, because she searched Scripture. . . .

And further I am letting you know, my beloved Wife in the Lord, that I am sorry that you cried, for when I heard that you were being questioned, I prayed to the Lord day and night all the more passionately for you. Know for certain that he will keep you as the *Zech 2:8* apple of his eye. I praise the Lord always, that he has made us both *Acts 5:41* worthy to suffer for his name's sake, for which reason I rejoice greatly. And when I read your Letter, and heard how things were with you, and that as a greeting you wished me the crucified Christ, so my heart and my soul sprang in my body for joy. Yes, so much so, that I could not finish the letter completely, I had to fall to my *Eph 3:14* knees before the Lord, and praise and thank him for his might, comfort, and joy, even though I was still sorrowful because of our Brethren, and for your sake, that you will have to be imprisoned there for so long. I have commended you to the hands of the Lord together with the fruit of your womb; trust him, and do not doubt that he will give you the same joy that he gives me, and will keep you *1 Pet 1:5* to the very end.

Another letter from Lijsken, Jeronimus' Wife [to friends and to her husband: excerpts]:

. . . I cannot thank nor praise the Lord enough for the wonderful grace, *Sir 43:27* and for the endless mercy, and for the great Love which he has shown to us, so that we might be his *2 Cor 6:18* sons and daughters if we overcome *Rev 3:21* just as he overcame. Oh, truly, we might well say *Heb 11:1* that upright faith reconciles itself to that which is not seen, *Gal 5:6* that which is working through love, that which shall bring us to glory, *Rom 8:17* provided that we suffer with him. Let us note, beloved

Friends in the Lord, how great a love worldly people have one for another. There are those in the Steen [Antwerp's main prison] (it's been said), who rejoice when they are brought to the rack, because of those whom they love, so that they can be closer to them even though they cannot come together in person. Do hear, my beloved Brothers and Sisters in the Lord, if the world has such love, oh, what love ought we then to have, who are expectant of such wonderful promises! I see another beautiful image before my eyes, of a Bride, how she adorns herself to please her Bridegroom of this world. Oh, how then ought we to adorn ourselves, that we might please our Bridegroom! [. . . .] I pray to the Lord night and day, that he will grant us such burning love, so that we do not care what torments they might inflict on us [. . . .]

Know, my dear Husband in the Lord, when I read that you were so very joyful in the Lord, I could not finish the Letter, I had to pray to the Lord that he would grant me, too, the same joy, and keep me to the very end, so that with joy we may present our sacrifice to the glory of our Father who is in heaven, and to the edification of all dear brothers and sisters. *Acts 20:32* With this I want to commend you to the Lord, and the word of his mercy. Know that I thank you very much for your Letter which you wrote me. The grace of the Lord be with us always.

Another Letter from Lijsken written to her Husband [excerpts]:
[. . . .] I wish us both the crucified Christ as a Protector and Shepherd of our Souls. He himself will keep us in all righteousness, holiness and truth to the very end, and he will also keep us as his sons and daughters, if we keep our *Heb 3:14* Devotion to his being until the very end, indeed, as the *Zech 2:8* apple of his eye. Therefore let us trust in him, and he will not *Heb 13:5* desert us in eternity, but will preserve us as he has done for his own from the beginning of the world. Let us not *1 Cor 10:13* be seized by any temptation except those which are human. The Lord is faithful (says Paul), he will not let us be tested beyond our ability. *2 Cor 1:3* Thanks be to God the Father of our Lord Jesus Christ, who has made us *Acts 5:41* worthy to suffer for his name a short mortal suffering for such beautiful promises that he has made to us, together with all those who remain stead-fast in his teaching. *Wis 3:5* In little we may suffer here, but in much will we be rewarded.

My dearly beloved husband in the Lord, you have prevailed through some trials; in those trials you have remained steadfast, the Lord be given eternal praise and glory for his great mercy. And I also pray the Lord, with weeping, that he will make me, too, fitting for that, to suffer for his name's sake [. . . .]

203

A Song about Jeronimus Segersz and his Wife Lijsken
To the Tune: 'O Sion wilt thou gather'

1 Most faithful is the Lord our God
   2 Cor 1:4 Comforts his own from morn to night.
   When Jeroen, together with his Wife,
   From evil suffered sorrow great,
   So they *Jos 1:5, Heb 13:5* were not forsaken
   By God, in their sad, dark affliction,
   Ps 91:15 Who in their need did come to aid them,
   Through his spirit most wondrously.

2 The Markgrave and his fellow Sophists,
   put on a good show with their wares,
   But Jeroen spoke, with no dissembling,
       'And should the fool stand up right now,
       And say: "The power to leave is in your hands",
       All you need say is: "I regret it":
       From my course I would not want to stray,
       For I possess the truth, I know.'

3 Then *Markgrave* he spoke with fury wild:
   'I'll have you thrown into the fire
   Alive, if you won't hear!'
   Jeroen laughed at all the ranting,
       Spake bravely: *Acts 21:13* 'I'll gladly suffer all
       Of what you might do unto me,
       For this my faith!' (For doing battle
   Well armed that Champion was).

4 Two Priests he once took on, together,
   Punished them so, with God's own word,
   That they ought well to've been ashamed;
   For that they were angry and enraged,
   They burned with fury at Jeroen,
   Smashing their fists upon the table,
   Insisting that Peter had begun
   The papacy, the first mass held by Andrew.

5 Well, these finally quit the field,
   But Jeronimus to the rack was brought,
   Much he suffered pain and torment,
   Gileyn's helper racked him long,

And while he lay there, bound up tight,
With water Gileyn poured him full;
The cruel Wolves about him stood,
Expecting his need to make him speak.

6   When he had suffered all of this,
And lay in strong walls imprisoned,
He was indeed so much at peace,
All his burden up and left him,
For he could hardly get to sleep
Through rejoicing and joy so great,
Which he gleaned while in the Emperor's chair,
Granted to him by the Lord.

7   Thus did the Sheep the Wolf escape;
But then he turned his craft on Lijsken,
Thinking he make that woman recant;
But her pillar was the word of God,
And she endured, remained *Mt 24:13, Mk 13:13* fast standing
Against the Anti-Christ's rough rabble,
Who so harshly did pursue her,
Even coming around to Scripture.

8   *Priest* 'And you, you think to use the Scriptures?
Go on, be gone, sew your own seam.
The Lord's Apostles (so it seems)
You seek to follow in their deeds,
But where is then your Tongue?
Acts 2:4 For right off they spoke through the Spirit,
With greatest passion, altogether,
God's authentic word, in tongues.'

9   'Ah, but *Acts 2:41* all those who were baptized
By the Apostles, they did not
Speak in tongues, before the crowds.
It is enough, as Scripture says,
That in Christ we do believe,
Jn 5:39 Who commanded us to search and study
The Scriptures plain brought from above;
For *Lk 10:42* Mary had chosen the best part.'

10 *Priest* 'We people here, we have been Sent,
And Moses we do represent!'

Lijsken 'Then you, as Scripture does report,
Will earn with it all the afflictions,
As in Matthew's gospel we do read.'
Priest 'And has he then been sent by God,
The one who you all this has taught?'
Lijsken 'Indeed, I know that surely and most finally.'

11   The Sophists and the Hypocrites,
So very much were angered,
That they could not tear to bits
God's children through their teachings false.
And so the Council did decide
That those dear lambs so sweet they would
Cast out, away, to their deaths.
That's how they quenched their cruel hearts!

12   Jeroen, going to the sacrifice,
Was very well prepared to die;
Big Hendrik, standing there as well,
Patiently waited for death with him.
They stepped together, the two of them,
Thus to the stake, and had no fear,
For their Father they did long,
Ps 31:6, Lk 23:46, Acts 7:59 To whom they did commend their Spirit.

13   Jeroen had to leave his love,
That was for him a sorrow great;
For she was fruitful with their child.
And when she had borne that child,
In torment, with great labour,
They threw that small sheep in the Scheldt.
Take this example to further spread
God's praise to all tormented Brethren.

17 Fighting demonic possession, Russia 1659

Religious institutions and services offered pre-modern women and men an alternative system for the treatment of physical and emotional illnesses. Recipients of healing through the ecclesiastical system sometimes made formal statements attesting to their 'miraculous' cures. This statement by a woman named Solomonia, describes her healing of demon-possession through the intercession of Saints Prokopii and Ioann of Ustiug. Ustiug was a major commercial center of Russia in the seventeenth century, and Sts. Prokopii and Ioann became the center of a popular cult. Solomonia's statement is found in a cycle of miracle tales compiled by the clergy at the saints' shrine, appended to a longer and more detailed account of her sufferings. It was edited to suit the genre of the miracle-tale, but retains Solomonia's first-person voice.

According to this account, she had been afflicted by demons since her wedding night over a decade earlier. The demons raped her, forced her to bear demonic children, made her attack her father, carried her off from home, and tried to hang her from the rafters and then to drown her. Or, as modern people might put it, Solomonia engaged in promiscuous sex, rejected her children, became violent with her father, ran away from home, and attempted suicide. Her despairing family sent her to the cathedral in Ustiug for treatment, and after two trips and months of residence, she received healing from the saints through their direct intercession.

(Excerpted from the original version published in *Pamiatniki starinnoi russkoi literatur*, N. Kostomarov, ed., vyp 1 (St. Petersburg, 1860; reprint: The Hague: Mouton, 1970), pp. 153–168. Translated by Eve Levin.)

In the past, in the year 167 [=1659], because of my sins, the Devil Satan, who from time immemorial hates humanity and fights it, settled a demonic force in me. This force ruled me for eleven years and five months, and during that time, I was tormented by all sorts of unspeakable tortures, as have been described already. I, a sinful one, did not see the natural world and the rays of the sun truly, but for me day was like night. I went to God's churches as though a prisoner tied up, sometimes into the holy church itself, sometimes to the entryway. [In early modern Russia, sinners under penance were forbidden to enter the church building and take their places among the congregation, but instead stood on the porches outside the doors of the sanctuary.] I did not listen to the voices singing or reading; my eyes were blind to holy things and by ears deafened by the terrifying demonic yearnings. From the first day when I sensed the hostile demonic blue flame, from then until now my ears were filled with a great noise during the chanting of God's words.

On the eve of July 8, the feast day of St. Prokopii, a desire entered me to go to the all-night vigil in the church in honor of St. Prokopii, the miracle-worker, to hear about his marvelous miracles. Before that, I had had no desire to do this. I went and stood outside the church, at the north doors. At that time, inside the church they were reading the vita of St. Prokopii. I stood there for a short time, and my brother started to send me into the church. Whether because of my brother's fear, or because of the gaze of all the people standing there, I entered the church with great difficulty, and the demonic force was forbidding me . . .

I began to cry out as much as I could, 'Don't bring me into the church of St. Prokopii!' They dragged me by force, but I broke away from them, and I went into the church of St. Ioann the miracle-worker. I sat down, and I saw the grave of St. Ioann as though it was shaking. I greatly feared this terrifying vision, and I held onto the grave of St. Ioann with my sinful hands. I dozed a little, and I saw an ineffable light, and in this light a maiden saintly and very wonderful; I cannot tell how beautiful. She came into the church of St. Ioann through the noon doors [Russian churches were always oriented on an east–west axis, with the altar on the east or 'sunrise' wall. The 'noon doors' were located on the south side of the sanctuary] past the icons standing there, and came to me. She took me by the right shoulder, and said, 'Lord Jesus Christ, son of God, have mercy upon us!' I did not answer anything. She said to me, 'Solomonia, say "Amen".' I did not answer anything. She repeated the prayer a second time and a third, and this most holy maiden said to me, 'Solomonia, say "Amen".' I was barely able to answer 'Amen!' She said, 'Answer twice more, "Amen".' I answered twice, 'Amen! Amen!' She said to me, 'Do you know who I am?' I said to her, 'My lady, I do not know you at all. I am a sinful person in great distress from the demonic force living inside me.' The most holy maiden adorned in light said to me, 'How can you not know me? You have been coming to my house unceasingly for five years!' I, sinful person, said, 'Where is your house, my lady?' She said to me, 'My house is the cathedral church. I am called the most holy Mary, who gave birth in the flesh to Jesus Christ, my creator and God. Today I shall reveal a great miracle through you, thanks to Sts. Prokopii and Ioann of Ustiug, the miracle workers, my representatives and supplicants to me. Pray to them unceasingly for healing. In your womb now there are seven hundred demons, and another thousand and seven hundred demons will enter you. Do not fear these wicked ones, for the miracle-workers Prokopii and Ioann will stand by you, and rescue you from the demonic force of illness. . . . You should promise to observe all the instructions they tell you.' Having heard this, I, a sinful person, could not answer her anything. Then the Most Holy Mother of God said, 'Peace be upon you, Solomonia!' And she departed by the same path by which she had entered.

I awoke from that wondrous vision and terrifying apparition, and I wanted to run from the church. I saw my brother standing nearby, and I was afraid. Then I gathered my strength, and I sat down, and I dozed off. I saw a great light in the church, unlike anything I had seen before, and St. Prokopii came into the church by the western doors. When he was near the grave of St. Ioann, St. Ioann got up from his grave. They came to me, a sinner, and the saints stood before me and said, 'Depart, accursed ones, from the servant of God Solomonia!' The saint said to me, 'Solomonia, pray from the depths of your heart to the intercessor of Christians, the most pure Mother of God and to Sts. Prokopii and Ioann, and you will be healed on this day. And give us your promise that you will not return to your former husband, and will not attach yourself to another one. You will still suffer a evil torment for three hours this day, but then you will be healed . . .'

This was St. Prokopii's appearance: long red hair, a simple red beard, not too short, short clothing, boots on his feet, pokers in his hands. St. Ioann was the same sort, as he is depicted on the icon in the local fashion. Then they said to me, 'Peace be upon you, Solomonia!' And they left her, and became invisible.

I, a sinful person, awoke from this wondrous vision, and came to; and I left the church. My brother and someone else took me, leading me then to the church of St. Prokopii. I cried out as much as I could, 'Do not bring me to St. Prokopii!' They did not listen to me, but dragged me by force into the church . . . My spiritual father and the priest Simion of the cathedral church began to read the Psalter over me. And I began to suffer the worst torment from the demons living inside me, and I, a sinful person, could not listen to the words they were saying. I began to cry out to them not to read the psalter over me. And so it was with me for three hours . . .

I went out of my mind and saw a wondrous and terrifying vision. On the right side, the ranks of priests and deacons came, and sang, with cross and Gospel and candles and incense. On the opposite side I saw a multitude of demons; and in appearance the wicked ones were black and blue and savage and terrifying. They were like a great cloud, and these wicked ones spit and sneezed in my face. I came to those terrifying and savage ones and did not suffer at all, thanks for the prayers of the most holy Mother of God and Sts. Prokopii and Ioann . . .

Suddenly, an ineffable light shone on the place where I lay. I saw a youth coming into the room with a candle, and behind him came Sts. Prokopii and Ioann. They stood by my head, and the holy men spoke among themselves. I do not know what they said. Then St. Prokopii came up to me, and made the sign of the cross with his hand over my womb. St. Ioann held a little spade in his hand, and he came up to me and cut open my womb and took a demon out of me and gave it to St. Prokopii. The demon began to cry out in a loud voice and wriggle in his hand. St. Prokopii showed me the demon, and said, 'Solomonia, do you see the demon, which was in your womb?' I looked at it, black in appearance and having a tail and a wide and terrifying mouth. He put the wicked one down on the floor and whacked it with his pokers. . . . St. Ioann said to St. Prokopii that while cutting me, a sinful person, not to bloody my chift, and not defile God's church. St. Prokopii replied, 'Solomonia will not allow herself to be bloodied, and my house will not be bloodied by the hostile force.' St. Ioann began to remove the demons from that same wound, as before. St. Prokopii took them, threw them to the floor of the church, and stomped them with his foot. St. Prokopii said to St. Ioann, 'Is Solomonia's womb clean of the demons living inside her?' St. Ioann replied, 'She is clean, and there is no corruption in her!' Then St. Prokopii himself looked into my womb, to see that it was clean. St. Prokopii said, 'Glory be to God!' And St. Ioann also said, 'Glory be to God!' Then the saints said to me, 'Solomonia, you also should say "Glory be to God!"' My tongue moved, and I said, 'Glory be to God!'

Then St. Prokopii said to me, 'Solomonia, from this day you will be healed of that great demonic torment of illness. You will still suffer from hostile imaginings, but you should not fear them.' And then St. Prokopii said to me, 'Be well, Solomonia, until God's day of judgment!' He blessed me with his hand and said, 'May our blessing be upon you now and forever!' And he said, 'Solomonia, go to the right side, and recite the Jesus prayer, and say, "Glory be to God!"' And after this speech, the saints became invisible.

I returned to myself after this wondrous vision, and I saw the light of the sun in the church, and I looked around the whole church and icons. I asked my brother in the church, 'Am I standing here, or am I seeing a vision?' My brother answered me, 'You are standing in the church of St. Prokopii at the liturgy, and the holy Gospel is being read.' Then I looked at the grave of St. Prokopii, and I rejoiced greatly, and bowed to St. Prokopii's grave. I fell down there and began to pray and call for help, 'O saint of God Prokopii, you did not overlook me, a sinful person, but searched for me, like a lost sheep, and you rescued me from hostile oppression.' I did not sense in my womb any hostile force, and I did not suffer even a little; and the sores from the evil devilish abrasions healed. From now on I am healthy, just as the saint told me.

18 Vision of soldiers, Bohemia 1580

The visions recounted in the previous source were clearly regarded as extra-ordinary in early modern Europe, but they were not uncommon occurrences. People seeing visions, and the religious authorities who had jurisdiction over them, had to determine if the visions were divine or demonic, and try to interpret their meaning. Such visions were the frequent subjects of pamphlets and single-sheet broadsheets, so that people who did not see the vision directly could also debate its interpretation. This is a typical example, printed by the Czech printer Buryam Walda in Prague in 1580. The text describes the vision of the soldiers in detail, names the individuals who saw it and vouches for their trustworthiness, and then ascribes a general religious meaning to it, as a sign from God to avoid fighting and discord.
(Walter L. Strauss, *The German Single-leaf Woodcut, 1550–1600* (New York: Abaris Books, 1975). Reproduced by permission.)

Wunderzeichen vnd seltzam geschicht / so am Himel den dien-
stag nach Maria Himmelfahrt / in der Kron Böhaimb / zu Alten Knin / vier Meil von Prag
gelegen / In disem 1 5 80. Jar / von vilen glaubwirdigen Personen ist gesehen worden.

Anno 1 5 80. am dienstag nach Marias Himelfahrt / morgen frue vor der eylfften stunde nach der gantzen vhr/ ist die Sonne ain Himmel gantz rohr erschinen / darinnen zwen geharnischte Männer in gantz schwartzen Kürissen gewapnet mit nider gelassnen armen / neben einander stehendt gesehen worden / vn darnach auß der Sonnen / nach der seyten von Mittag gegen Mitternacht gestritten / der erste geschwinder als der ander gegangen / wie sie aber alle beide auß der Sonnen gegen Mitternacht gewichen / seindt sie alle beide verschwunden / vber ein kleine weile hernach / ist widerumb in derselben Sonnen / ein ander gewapneter Mann / glich den vorigen gesehen worden / welcher mit dem kopff bis auff die schuldern in der Sonnen / der ander theil seines leibs vnter der Sonnen gewesen / vnd gleich wie die zween ersten / nach der seyten anß der Sonnen nach Mitternacht gewichen / vn als baldt von wegen deß Vebels nicht mehr gesehen worden / ist von was nun dises Wunderzeichen bedeutet / weiß der Allmächtig Gott am besten / solche gesicht vnd wunderzeichen / ist von vilen glaubwirdigen Personen gesehen worden / Insonderheit / vom Fürsichtigen Merten Prstach / Carl Karel / Bergmais ster desselben Bergwercks auffm Knin / welches vier Meil von Prag gelegen / Adam deß Großen Rabe Son daselbsten / vnd Anna mit Namen die alte Packo Waale / wonhafftig dasell sten / von disem Wunderzeichen hat Prophecey / der Welt berembte Astronomus M. Codicellus / in seiner heurigen Practicken / da er schreibe vom September / man werde ein Wunder zeichen sehen / welches ergentlich also geschehen / denn diß gesicht ist geschehen worden / den sibenden tag deß Monats September / dem schein nach zurchten. Christlicher Leser merck auff / wider diß die gantze geschwinde vnd sehr gefährliche zeit / die mir armen erlebt haben / denn kein wunder wer / wo vns die Barmhertzigkeit Gottes nit schützet / das wir lengst alle sampt außgerottet vnd verschunden weren / von wegen vnser großen Sünd vnd Misserhat / bedenck derhalben ein jeder seine sünde vnd gebrechen / vnnd wende sich zu Gott mit gantzem hertzen / wie vns Joel im 11. Capitel vermanet / ehe der All mächtige Gott seinen gefaßten zorn vber vns ergehen lasse / denn sein zorn ist groß / vnd sein grim ist wider vns gerichtet / Item 36. Cap. Vnd die Gott von gantzem hertzen vnd festen glauben / er wolle sein gefaßten zorn auff die Heyden vnd vn glaubigen / vnd auff die / die seinen heiligen Namen nit anruffen / wenden / vnnd vns zu vnsern zeytenden fride senden / vmb welchen Esaias im 30. Cap. gebetten / gib vns O Herr deinen friden / vnnd deine war heit / der meinen zeiten / also hat auch Jeremias die gefangen Juden in Babolonia / durch sein sterben vermanet / das sie vns den friden suchen / vnd vmb die heilige statt Gottes beten / Irem: 29. Cap. Sucher der statt hail / darein ich euch hab füren lassen / vnd bitter für sie / denn vnder ge statt Gottes beten / Irem: 20. Psalm / Bittet vmb frid der Stadt Jerusalem / welchs Gasstlichu die Christ Item fride werdet ir auch fride haben / Im 122. Psalm / Bittet vmb frid der Stadt Jerusalem / welchs Gasstlichu die Christ liche Kirche verstanden wirdt / derhalben so wir vns mit gantzem hertzen vnd vestem glauben zu Gott bekeren / so wirde vns der Barmhertzige Gott auch solches alles warhafftiglichen wider faren lassen / 2c.

Getruckt zu Prag / inn der Alten Statt / bey Burpam Walda.

19 Healing spells, Italy sixteenth century

Among the popular classes of early modern Europe, developments in modern medicine remained remote, and many continued to rely on a mixture of religious devotion
and folk medicine when ill. Folk medicine typically consisted of the use of certain
herbs and other substances, alongside chants invoking saints, Jesus, and the Virgin
Mary. One of the most striking aspects of these beliefs is the variety of beliefs in
supernatural forces and invisible powers. The Madonna of the High Seas (Madonna

211

dell'Alto Mare) was often invoked as the source of dream prophesies. In the prayers below we see how closely linked were matters of health, the supernatural, food and agriculture.

(Cecilia Gatto Trocchi, *Magia e medicina popolare in Italia* (Rome: Newton Compton, 1982), p. 234. Translated by Monica Chojnacka.)

O Madonna of the High Seas
Come to me in my dreams, for I must speak with you
Doors of gold and keys of silver
Bring me this dream for my salvation
O, of evil and of good
Beautiful Mother, you must warn me
If there is evil
Sharp needles, rushing water and burning fire
If there is good
A table is set
The church is lighted
And the vines are full [of grapes]

Men who suffered from 'hysteria' were considered victims of Mal di matrone, or 'illness of the strong woman'. In the region of Abruzzo such a condition was treated with a chest massage and the chant below. (Cecilia Galto Trocchi, *Magia e medicina popolare in Italia* (Rome: Newton Compton, 1982), p. 234. Translated by Monica Chojnacka.)

I will defeat you, Mother of the Strong Women
You have ninety-nine mouths
Cold like the snow
Sharp like needles
Your mouth like that of a serpent,
Your throat like that of a mare
Do not destroy this servant of God
I point you to the Virgin Mary
In the company of Saint Gregory

20 A woman is accused of witchcraft, Italy 1625

Religious traditions overlap in this Inquisition trial record from seventeenth-century Venice. Christina Collari was accused both of witchcraft and of having a sexual relationship with a Jewish merchant. Below is the testimony from one of the witnesses in her trial, a former lover named Nicholas who was fifty-five years old.

(Archivio di Stato di Venezia, Sant'Uffizio, Processi, B. 80, no. 2, doc. #3, December 1625. Translated by Monica Chojnacka.)

Inquisitor: Do you know a Christina who starches collars for a living?

Resp.: Yes, I know her; for three years we had carnal relations because my wife is ill, and it's been one year since I haven't had anything more to do with her, since I have reconciled myself with God's majesty.

Inqu.: Do you know that said Christina has practiced any kind of witchcraft?

Resp.: That I ever saw, no. But I did hear talk from Mr. Antonio, the husband of Mrs. Cattarina . . . that about a year and a half ago he told me that I needed to free myself of said Christina, telling me that she was a witch because she had brought about the death of his nephew, a grown man. This was also told to me by Cattarina his wife, who is still alive, though the husband is now dead. And some clients of mine also told me this, though I can't remember who was present when they told me. Nor did they tell me what particular sort of witchcraft said Christina practiced.

Inqu.: Do you know that said Christina practiced witchcraft to pressure her lovers?

Resp.: I don't know anything else, if not that once a year ago, about a month before I left her, I found a piece of cord in a little envelope for combs [probably a makeshift small bag for small things, made of a folded piece of paper] near the bed, whose color I don't remember. It wasn't made of silk, but of some thread, and it was wound around so that I don't know its length, and it had various knots with pins. . . . And when I asked her what she was doing with that cord, she answered that she tossed that to see what would be [i.e., to divine the future], and that she was doing no harm by using it. Then I threw it into the fire, and I left her, very angry, after reproaching her for engaging in such slothful, bad behavior. No one else was in the house when this happened, but outside of the room, in the entry way I saw a woman who rented one of the other rooms in the house, she was called the Fiorentina [the Florentine, i.e., from the city of Florence]; I don't remember her real name, who is the wife of Zanella the linen maker. And to this woman (she's about forty years old), I showed said cord [editor's note: how did Nicholas show Fiorentina the cord if he had just thrown it into the fire?], and I told her how I had found it in the envelope. And she, without saying a word to me, shrugged her shoulders.

Inqu.: If you know that said Christina had domestic relations with any Jew

Resp.:   Yes, my lords, a Jew from Ferrara named Bonforno, a man of thirty-six years. Actually I caught him, and I saw him in the house, and before, when he used to come by wearing a black hat, I thought he was a Christian. But once I discovered the deceit by finding his red hat [Jews had to wear special red or yellow hats to distinguish themselves from the Christian population] in her storage chest, she confessed to me that this Jew had slept with her.

Inqu.:   If you know whether that Jew brought things to eat to that Christina, and whether she ate them, and what sorts of food it was?

Resp.:   Before I learned that he was a Jew, one Sunday we were eating together at Christina's house, who in those days lived in the parish of San Marcuola [near the Jewish Ghetto]. He brought two fowl, cooked in a pan and a pan of meat cooked with cloves, and he gave me to understand that he was staying in [the parish of] San Boldo in the home of a well-born friend of his. And other times, she told me that this Jew had brought her other cooked things, but at that point she had not yet told me that he was a Jew, because I learned of it from the hat, and when I found the hat, she and he confessed to me that he was a Jew, and after reproaching them I never returned, and that happened about a month after the said Sunday.

Inqu.:   If you know whether said Christina ate meat on Friday or Saturday that was brought to her by said Jew, and did you hear talk of this?

Resp.:   No, my lords.

21 Witchcraft pamphlet, Germany 1566

The upsurge in beliefs about the danger of witches was both fueled by and fueled a huge number of publications of all types, from single-age broadsheets and small pamphlets to learned treatises. Many of these were illustrated, often with woodcuts or engravings taken from other publications, so that certain images became very well known and contributed to the creation of stereotypes about witches. This is the title page from Johann Weier's *De Praestigiis Daemonum*, a treatise on witchcraft that went through many editions. The illustration on this page was also used in many other works on witchcraft, and conveys many of the standard beliefs about witches: the women are old, unruly (symbolized by their flowing hair), sexually insatiable (one is riding a goat, a symbol of sexual excess), and engaged in a standard women's activity (cooking) that will no doubt have dreadful consequences.
(Johann Weier, *De Praestigiis Daemonum* (Frankfurt, 1566).)

DE PRÆSTIGIIS.
Der Erste Theil.
Von den Teuf=
eln/ Zaubrern/ Schwartzkünst=
lern/ Teuffels beschwerern Hexen oder
Unholden vnd Gifft=
bereitern.

Erstlich durch D. Johan Wei=
er in Latein beschrieben/ nachmalen
verteutscht von Johanne Fuglino/ vnd jetzt wide=
rumb nach dem letzten Lateinischen Original im
66. jar außgangen vbersehen/ an vielen orthen
mercklich gebessert/ vnd mit einem nützli=
chen Register gemehret.

Getruckt zu Franckfurt am Mayn/ 1566.

Questions for discussion

1 What differences do you find between Catholics and Protestants in these documents? How does their religion affect the ways in which they discuss their problems and concerns?
2 What was the relationship between magic and religious conviction in the early modern period? How did that change over time?
3 What was the relationship between religious institutions and what we might term private life in this period?
4 What might draw a woman or man to a particular faith in early modern Europe?
5 Discuss the relationship between religious belief and power (first, you must define these two terms).

7

NETWORKS

.Early modern Europeans lived out their lives by working within a number of different, overlapping networks. These webs of sentiment, obligation, reciprocity, and dependence helped individuals navigate through a complicated, dangerous, and often arbitrary world. In fact, the term 'individual' itself has a different meaning when we talk about the past. People thought about themselves in relation to their collective, multiple identities. A typical city woman could think of herself in relation to her place within her natal family, her marital family, her neighborhood and parish, and her city, of which she was a citizen. She might belong to a secret community of Protestants or Catholics in a region where the other religion was dominant. She might associate with other women of her profession, either at home, as a weaver, for example, or in the marketplace as she sold her wares. Likewise, a man's identity was shaped by his identity as a father, a brother, and a son, but also by his profession and the professional community to which he might belong, most likely a guild.

The most basic community was that of the family. The family provided early modern Europeans with the tools they needed to survive in society. These included the skills necessary for a profession and the contacts to pursue that profession. Families arranged for their daughters to enter domestic service and for their sons to contract an apprenticeship. Family status and strategies determined not only what sort of profession a son or daughter might practice, but also the sort of marriage he or she might make. Once married or settled in a profession, sons and daughters maintained contact with their families, both parents and siblings, bound by ties of obligation and often financial interest as well.

But the family was not the only source of support for early modern Europeans. Personal friendships were also crucial. In addition, the wider informal community of the neighborhood or parish often provided an important complement or even substitute for the family network. Neighbors might feud, but they also constructed webs of assistance, friendship, and economic exchange that fueled early modern society. The early modern world was not a private one; neighbors moved easily in and out of one another's homes and took an unabashed interest in one another's affairs.

Neighborhood and friendship networks could provide daily support as well as help in extraordinary circumstances, like death, arrest, or natural catastrophe. They were also the source of much leisure activity: guilds, parishes, and neighborhoods all sponsored commemorative processions and festivals. Often these were theoretically linked to religious holidays but were in fact opportunities to socialize and break up the daily routine of work.

More formal sorts of communities existed as well. Guilds were important complements to the civic and ecclesiastical infrastructure of early modern society. These professional and religious organizations helped local members (and families of members) in times of need. They also organized charitable endeavors, and theoretically protected their members from danger through their association. Not to belong to such an organization was to be extremely vulnerable in early modern society. Another institutionalized form of community was the confraternity. Confraternities were devotional organizations for laymen, sanctioned to a degree by the Catholic church. With the Catholic reform movement, many of these organizations, traditionally linked to a profession or an area of the city, became more inclusive, even welcoming women into their ranks. Alongside them sprang up other religious organizations, specifically for women, which offered those who did not take religious vows to nevertheless live a life of piety and sacrifice without relinquishing ties to the outside world.

Religious organizations, both for layfolk and the more formal institutions of convent and monastery, offered early moderns important alternatives to the traditional secular life of marriage. Convents, sometimes derided as sites of illicit sexual activity and general corruption, were in fact centers of great intellectual and spiritual activity. It is true that some women were forced into convents by their families for reasons of familial strategy (such as not having the money to pay for a daughter's dowry). But many others found such a female community to be a source of inspiration and an opportunity for collective independence and creativity that would have been nearly impossible to achieve as a married woman on the 'outside'.

Communities could also be sites of discord and destruction. Neighbors squabbled, and kept a close eye on each other, sometimes with the attention of reporting real or invented dangerous activity to the appropriate authorities. The success of guilds depended on their exclusivity, so artisans attempting to open business without the proper license were quickly crushed. Convents, such an important center of female community, could also be places of bitter conflict, both between the convent and the church authorities who supervised it, and among the nuns themselves.

Above all, early modern European identified themselves by their relationships with others. Such connections gave meaning and purpose to their daily activities, and helped them understand and negotiate the wider world. What follows is a sampling of the ways in which men and women understood these relationships, and worked within them.

FAMILY BONDS

1 Female relatives share a business interest, Italy 1585

This is a petition to the Venetian High Court of Appeals, called the Pien Collegio, by a group of female relatives with common business interests. The 4 ducats the family was to pay in taxes was a considerable sum; the annual rent for a modest apartment in Venice at this time was about 8 ducats.
(Archivio di Stato di Venezia, Pien Collegio, Suppliche di Dentro, B. 8, n. 92, December 12, 1585. Translated by Monica Chojnacka.)

Your Serenity [i.e., the Venetian State] has never wished that any person should have to bear more than he is capable of, but we poor daughters and niece of Mr. Balissere Balbi appear at your feet, to recount to you that in 1566, when the above named [Balbi] was alive, he owned and ran a few fruit orchards, and this was reported to the Tax authorities, and it seemed that, for these orchards and what we were able to glean from them, we owed four ducats to the Tax gentlemen, with two more ducats added to that. While we continued to live and work the orchard, after a while the Lord our God chose to call [Balbi] to Him, along with two of our brothers, his sons, which left us poor women without capital or any industry. The said orchards passed into the hands of others who had paid their taxes plus the added tax, and it seemed just to Your Serenity that they could pay the taxes on our property as well [and thus take possession of it], but with every reverence.

2 Siblings apply for a patent, Italy 1568

This petition, or *supplica*, was presented to the Venetian high court in 1568, by a family of one brother and four sisters, plus another man. They claimed to have invented a device that enabled a person to remain underwater for several hours, which they wished to patent. This supplica suggests that it was possible for unmarried women to participate in the financial and creative life of the natal family in the sixteenth century. None of these sisters appears to have been married at the time of the petition, since none is identified by a husband's surname. The equal status of the five siblings is indicated by the way in which all five are presented as equally responsible for the device's creation.
(Archivio di Stato di Venezia, Pien Collegio, filza 3, no. 100, November 1568. Translated by Monica Chojnacka.)

It has always been the custom of Your Sereneness to welcome those who with their ingenuity discover new and important inventions which can contribute to the public and the private good. In this spirit come we Salvador di Gradi g. Marc'antonio citizen of this your Illustrious city, Laura, Isabetta, Simona, Chrestina, sisters of the above named Salvador, and Francesco Cavanei your most faithful servants. Considering how great the damage is to ships, both armed and unarmed, when they sink under water, and how useful it would be to recover the goods and weapons and all the other things [in the ships] . . . after great effort and expense we have discovered two important secrets and inventions, the first something that allows a man or men . . . to go underwater . . . and remain able to breathe, without these men needing to enclose themselves in anything, the other to give them light so that they can see, and remain under said water for the space of approximately three hours, and they will be able to recover all of the things that they wish to (from the ship). (This is) something truly of great service and utility because, having both air and light, the men will be able to enter the submerged ship, and with the time allowed can easily recover as we have described all of the goods that they wish. . . . We Salvador, Laura, Isabetta, Simona, Chrestina and Francesco the above-named ask Your Sereneness to graciously grant us . . . the rights (to this invention) for fifty years.

3 Kinship and employment, France 1547 and 1551

Extensive networks of kinship were clearly an important source, though not the only source, of support for orphaned children. People in many parts of Europe in this period went to notaries to formally arrange for the care and future of such children. In the following document, a man takes on responsibility for a young girl, his wife's sister, without monetary compensation, while explicitly expecting free use of her labor. Note that by the time she is 15, she is anticipated to be qualified to earn a living for herself.
(Paris, Archives Nationales, Minutier central, Étude LXXXVI/10, September 1, 1542. Translated by Carol Loats.)

The honorable Jehan Carranne, merchant *fripier* [a seller of used clothes], *bourgeois* of Paris, affirms that he has promised and promises to Anthoine Martygnat, master joiner [a craftsman who worked with wood], and Henry Paquet, merchant bookseller, *bourgeois* of Paris, present here, acting in the name of and as guardians for Geneviefve LeBe, daughter of the deceased Pierre LeBe, who while living was a merchant, *bourgeois* of Paris, and of [the deceased] Collette Preudhommie, previously his wife. [Carranne has promised] to keep the said Geneviefve, aged 9 to 10 years or so, with him, to

220

raise and house her very suitably and respectably, according to her standing, from today for the next 5 years; and this without the said Geneviefve or anyone for her being obliged to pay anything to the said Carranne because of this [arrangement].

This promise is made as much for the considerable love that the said Carranne bears toward the said Geneviefve LeBe, who is the sister of his wife, as also for the consideration that neither the said Geneviefve LeBe nor anyone for her will be able to ask anything for her wages and compensation during the time that she will reside with him.

And during the said time, the said Carronne will be obliged to send the said Geneviefve LeBe to school to learn her service, and equally to have her taught a respectable trade to earn a living if she so desires; and the said Martignat and Paquet, in the said name, will be obliged to pay the money that it will cost to pay for the said schooling and apprenticeship in a trade.

And also the said Martignat and Paquet, in the said name, will be obliged and promise during the five years to maintain the said Geneviefve LeBe with her clothing of wool, linen, footwear, and other clothing, respectably, according to her standing.

And if during the said time the said wife of the said Carronne departs from this life, these present [arrangements] will remain null for the time which remains of the said five years.

Because thus promising, etc., obligating, each in his own right, the said Martignat and Paquet in the said name renouncing, etc. Done and passed in duplicate, in the year 1542, Friday, the first day of September.

> While the above contract shows the role of kin in the care of a child, the next one shows an arrangement for companionship of a godmother by her goddaughter. A man went before the notaries to place his daughter with his widowed sister. Clearly, however, even an arrangement such as this had economic implications as well as personal and emotional ones.
> (Paris, Archives Nationales, Minutier central, Étude LIV/149, June 16, 1555. Translated by Carol Loats.)

The honorable Loys Mayet, merchant goldsmith, *bourgeois* of Paris affirms that he has given and placed [his daughter] to and with the honorable Jacqueline Mayet, his sister, widow of the late Pierre Belin, who while living was a merchant and *bourgeois* of Paris. [Jacqueline], present here, has taken and retained, takes and retains [the child] with her to give her company.

[She takes] Jacqueline Mayet, daughter of the said Loys Mayet, from today until the said Jacqueline will be settled in marriage or otherwise.

And this widow promises to provide and deliver to [the girl] what she needs in terms of drink, food, fire, lodging, and light, and to treat her as is appropriate; to have her taught her duty [the word *service* used here could instead refer to religious practice; the meaning is ambiguous], along with the art to sew in linen or in wool, as [the widow] sees fit; and also the widow promises to maintain the said Jacqueline with all clothing, footwear, and linen during the said time, respectably, according to her standing.

This present arrangement and promise [is] made as much in consideration of certain clothing and leases made between the said widow and Loys Mayet, all today before the notaries named below . . . as for the considerable natural love that the said widow has and says she has for the said Loys Mayet and for the said Jacqueline, [the widow's] goddaughter, and also because it is [the widow's] wish and pleasure to do so.

And if the said widow departs from this life during the said time, in this case the widow wants and intends that one of [her] children will take the said Jacqueline, her said goddaughter, with [him or her] to raise and support her as is said above, up to when she will be settled in marriage or otherwise; and [whoever takes her in that case] will not be able to ask anything of the said Louys Mayet nor of the said Jacqueline in any way for all the raising and support.

Also, neither the said Jacqueline [the child] nor anyone for her will be able to ask anything of the said widow nor of her children as her wages and compensation that she might be able to [earn] during the said time that she will have been with the widow.

And further, if the said Jacqueline [the child] departs from this life [within] ten years after the said Jacqueline has been with [the widow] or one of her children, the widow can give to the other child of the said Mayet, [that is] the oldest after the said Jacqueline, the sum of 10 *livres tournois* to aid in providing for [him or her].

Because thus promising, etc., obligating, each in his own right renouncing, etc. Done in the year 1555, Sunday, the 16th day of June.

FRIENDSHIP NETWORKS AND NEIGHBORHOODS

4 A noble widow writes to her friend's daughter, Denmark 1534

Letter from Anne Meinstrup to Sophie Krummedige, December 19, 1534.
This letter from a noble widow to the daughter of her long-time friend was written during the civil war, which preceded the introduction of the Reformation in Denmark. The war had developed into a class war between the nobility on the one side and peasants and burghers on the other. Sophie was residing in Norway, while her

husband had been captured in Denmark, and rumors spread that nobles all over Zealand were to be killed by the soldiers of the peasants. Anne had sought refugee with her grandchildren, who were in her charge, at her estate, Vallø, south of Copenhagen.

(Original in the Danish National Archives. Collection of Private Archives. Translated by Grethe Jacobsen and Pernille Arenfeldt.)

Sisterly and loving greetings, my dear sister, as always hoping that God be with you.

My dearest Sophie, I can never repay you for the great good you have shown me in so many ways, especially the great and good deed you showed me when we were together last. The good Lord will impress upon me my debt to you and rest assured that I shall never forget that as long as I live. My dearest Sophie, I will inform you that this past Wednesday some soldiers came from Germany to this country, which your messenger will also tell you. My dear Sophie, I can never describe fully the sorrow and the fear I have had and still have for these people. I will inform you that I am now at Vallø and have been here for 14 days and I don't know how long it is God's will that I remain here. My dearest Sophie, I hope that with God's help you will get good news about your dear husband and all our good friends, and may you know that at this time, Duke Christian and the Count are meeting for negotiation; my hopes rest with God that he may reconcile them. My very dearest Sophie, I only ask that you would write when you have a messenger to this country, and I thank you for the letter you have written me and for the sugar candy you sent me and for all the good things you have done to my grandchildren and myself. May the eternal God grant me an opportunity to repay you and you will not find a woman on earth more willing and ready than me for as long as I live. My dear Sophie, Oluf Glob and Anne and Sophie ask me to thank you greatly for all the good you have shown them and they pray to God that they will be able to repay you anytime you will need it. My dear Sophie, I know no other news than your messenger won't be able to tell you. Hereby I recommend you and all yours to God. Command over my powers and me as you would any person you have done much well.

From Vallø Saturday after Lucia Day anno domino 1534. Anne Meinstrups daughter

[Shortly after, Anne Meinstrup heeded the call to all noblemen and women to come to a great meeting at Ringsted with Count Christoffer. At the meeting, where she was the only noble, she was brutally murdered by some soldiers. The murder aroused great anger and distress among nobles as well as commoners who eulogized her as a very capable and good woman.]

5 How women should socialize, Russia sixteenth century

In sixteenth- and seventeenth-century Russia, women of the urban elite led secluded lives in the women's sections of the house. Although they did not attend most public functions or socialize with men, respectable women were permitted, and even encouraged, to associate with each other. But because such gatherings took place outside the purview of men, moralizing male authors worried that the women might misbehave. So the male author of *Domostroi*, a guide to household management, provided instructions for a wife's proper conduct in the company of her friends.
(Translated version from *The Domostroi: Rules for Russian Households in the Time of Ivan the Terrible*, ed. Carolyn Johnston Pouncy (Ithaca: Cornell University Press, 1994), pp. 132–133. Reprinted by permission.)

When she visits or invites people to her house, she must still obey her husband's commandments. While entertaining guests or visiting, she should wear her best clothes. During meals, she should not drink alcohol. A drunk man is bad, but a drunk woman is not fit to be on the earth.

With her guests she should discuss needlework and household management, discipline and embroidery. . . . A good woman monitors herself. She asks politely about good things she does not know. She refuses to listen to or to indulge in bad, mocking, or lecherous speech. Instead, she looks for evidence of good management: well-prepared food; unusual dishes or needlework; a good, thoughtful, and intelligent hostess; intelligent, polite, orderly, handy, and thoughtful servants. She asks politely and demurely about those things that are new to her; she must be submissive in that way. Then, having returned to her own home, she tells her husband all she has learned, to bring repose to his soul.

Such good women make suitable friends, not because of the food they offer, but because of the benefits of their conversation and their knowledge. Each woman should take stock of her own behavior and should not mock. She should not gossip about anyone. If others ask questions about someone, even if they sometimes torment her, she should answer, 'I do not know anything about that. I didn't hear about it and don't know about it. I do not talk about inconsequential things, or pass judgment on princesses or boyars' wives, or on my neighbors, either.'

6 Two noblewomen correspond, Denmark 1560s

This letter was written c. 1563–1565 by Sibylle Gyldenstjerne (1540–1611) to Birgitte Gøje (1511–1574), both members of the Danish nobility. The two women were related through the mother of Sibylle Gyldenstjerne, thus the address 'my dear mother's sister' which was used for almost all female relatives on the mother's side. In all parts of society people turned to friends and relatives for help in conducting their daily lives. In this letter the younger Sibylle Gyldenstjerne turns to her aunt, who had been in charge of her upbringing from the time she was two until she was around fourteen and who also had been involved in arranging her engagement to Eskild Gøje (d. 1573). Sibylle Gyldenstjerne would, therefore, expect help in finding an adequate number of capable servants – as a mother would be expected to offer, especially when a woman was about to give birth. The letter also indicates that the need for good servants was felt more strongly by noble women than by their husbands, who often spent the majority of their lives away from their fiefs and estates and thus left their property under the authority of their wives and/or bailiffs. In the letter, reference is made to a number of maids; unfortunately, it is not possible to differentiate clearly between them in order to determine who had committed which sins. However, it seems that the 'bad sins', referred to, were associated with the pregnancy of an unmarried maid, thus the rush to see her marriage take place and the need to replace her in the household.

(The original document is kept in the Danish National Archives, Copenhagen. It has previously been published in *Breve til og fra Herluf Trolle og Birgitte Gjøe*, ed. by G.L. Wad, Copenhagen, 1893. Translated by Grethe Jacobsen and Pernille Arenfeldt.)

My very kind and loving greeting now and forever sent with our Lord. My very dearest mother's sister, of my good will and pleasure I thank you for all the goodness and honor that you always have shown and demonstrated towards me in many ways, and particularly for your kind letter that I now have received from you, for [all this] you will throughout my life find me willing, and [as] I consider it my duty to owe you everything I can, to do everything I can to serve you well. My very dearest mother's sister, you write to Eskild and me about the housekeeper that you are willing to send to us and I thank you for this and for all other good [acts], and I implore you to allow her to come here at the first opportunity. And may you know that Eskild will be departing from here Wednesday to my Lord [: the King], and if it seems reasonable to you and possible for you to do so, I would very much appreciate it if she could come here while Eskild is in Zealand, so the one who is here now could be sent away before he returns, for he does not intend to stay there long, but will return shortly. And as you write about this maid that you will give me when Johanne's wedding has taken place, then Eskild also said that we have had enough of such bad sins. And I beg you to talk to Eskild regarding the same girl and tell him that she is honest and capable, and praise her sufficiently [and] then he will probably be satisfied. I do not care that she is not so beautiful, for I know well that her capability is not to be found in her beauty. I would very much appreciate it if you would send the girl to me together with the woman, and if I can have them at the first given occasion, for I have great need of them when I now let go of this girl, who is to be married very soon, then I do not have anyone except Johanne and one more, who I got [: employed] before I

225

went to Zealand. And I will not let go of Johanne until God has allowed me to deliver [the child], for I have no one who can bring me food or anything else that I need, before the others can get into the routines[.] I will, however, allow the riding master and her [Johanne] to be joined together [: also to get married] at this girl's wedding who is to have our curate [in marriage]. May God grant that you could ask your good friends to obtain some favors from the King for his long service, so that he may have somewhere to live. Dear mother's sister, I can never fully write you how much I would like to talk to you, may God grant that we can see each other soon. I will no longer burden you with this my poor letter but throughout my life you shall find me, as if I was your own daughter, [willing] to do everything I can to serve you that you may benefit from. I truly beg you to send me those women folk here while Eskild is in Zealand. Hereby you are commended to God the Almighty. Please send Herluf many good wishes on my behalf. In Nyborg Friday after the Feast of Saint George. I implore you to burn this letter when it has been read.

Sibylle Gyldenstjerne

(Address:) To my [. . . .]st mother's sister Lady Birgitte [wife of] Herluf Trolle of Herlufsholm, very kindly written.

7 A trial reveals neighborhood loyalties, Italy 1608

(a) This is testimony of Betta Buranelli, in an Inquisition case in which her two sisters-in-law were accused of witchcraft. Betta enthusiastically denounced them, and described in her testimony how she placed neighborly concern over familial loyalties. Her connections to the neighborhood (and those of her sisters-in-law) are illustrated by the list of witnesses appearing at the trial.
(Archivio di Stato di Venezia (ASV), Sant'Uffizio, Processi, B. 70, no. 16, doc. 2, 1608: Translated by Monica Chojnacka.)

I denounce the sisters Dionora and Vicenza Buranelle as witches and blasphemers who live sinful lives, because I have frequented these sisters for about twelve years, and as I am ill, their sister Giulia said to me 'Betta, watch out, something may have been done to you', and I said 'who would do me harm?'. And Giulia explained 'Look, it's my sisters, who are evil, because one day Dionora beat up one of her nieces, who was Giulia's daughter.' And the girl said 'shut up witch, you have worked witchcraft on Betta,' and this was said to them many times, and Father Girollamo [a priest] sent them away, because they are witches, and women of bad behavior, and they always insisted to him that they were good, devout Christians. So that your Reverend Lordships may know if these bad women know that Pater Noster, the Ave Maria, the Creed and the ten commandments, and for testimony about their bad reputation and evil ways, you may question the witnesses listed below:

Mrs. Camilla, wife of Agostino Cavallaro
Mr. Bernardin dal Gallo
Angelo Rigo and his wife
Mr. Zuanne Carise
Paulina de Vico
Mrs. Luchina Scalabrina, wife of Frantine de Bei
Mrs. Marietta, wife of Mr. Bastian Carise
Girollamo Sparese
Mrs. Bettina wife of Mr. Agostina Zenaro
Mrs. Virginia, wife of Menego Spane
Mrs. Cecilia Penza, wife of Master Domenico Carese
Mrs. Cecilia, wife of Mr. Benedetto Caime.

> (b) Cecilia Penza, a young matron, was a neighbor who defended the two sisters. One of them, Dionora, was Cecilia's comare, a term used in Italian to describe both godparents and close friends. In this case, Cecilia reports that Dionora was present at her baptism, so Dionora was likely Cecilia's godmother. This means that Cecilia's family and that of Dionora had long been linked by bonds of friendship and obligation.
> (Archivio di Stato di Venezia, Sant'Uffizio, Processi, B. 70, no. 16, doc. 15, 1608. Translated by Monica Chojnacka.)

It may be twenty-four years or more that I have lived in the Mureri neighborhood where these women, whom Your Lordships have named to me, also live. They live in the home of Father Gieronimo Pagan [a priest], and they are considered evil and sinful women by all of the women who live near them. Mrs. Dionora is my *comare*, who baptized me, nor have they ever done anything bad to me.

As for the accusation that they have blasphemed God's name, by the Holy Mother I have heard them when they yell in the neighborhood, and on occasion they start dancing, both of them, and the Priest reproaches them. And when I'm minding my own business, if they start screaming with the neighbors, I let them scream, and one day Mrs. Dianora was yelling with Mrs. Appolonia, the mother of Giacometto del Bello, the stonemason, who had been injured. She [Dionora] had visited [Appolonia], and given her a bracelet and a jug of wine, with which Appolonia says Dionora cursed her son, who then died, so they were yelling at each other for a good while. I have said that Dionora is my *comare*, nonetheless I have told the truth.

8 A parish census, Italy 1590s

Below is an excerpt from a parish 'soul count' taken in Venice at the end of the sixteenth century. Soul counts, or 'status animarum', were surveys of homes, often conducted by the parish priest or an assistant, to note the occupants of each household in a particular parish and verify that they had all been given the appropriate sacraments, particularly baptism and confirmation. The result is a fairly complete list of the inhabitants of such neighborhoods, including servants and children. In the register excerpted below, the record-taker proceeded house by house, noting the residents in order of their relationship to the head of the household, who was always listed first. Note the high number of women heading households and the makeup of their homes; many of them took in boarders, male and female, to help make ends meet.

(Source: Archivio della Curia Patriarcale di Venezia (ACPV), Archivio Segreto, Status Animarum, S. Giovanni Novo. Translated by Monica Chojnacka.)

Street: Courtyard of the hospedaletto
Maria of Padua
3 children: two are hers (10 and 13 yrs old), a 2-year-old belongs to the boarder Caterina
Caterina, a widow from Zara [a Venetian Greek colony]
Zuanmaria, a cobbler
Silvestro, a tailor

Street: Courtyard of the hospedaletto
Marina, a widow
1 child: Laura, an orphan who is 7 years old
Caterina, from Vicenza
Girardo Zaratin, a captain

Street: Courtyard of the hospedaletto
Franceschina Sagreo, widow
1 child, a nephew who is 12 years old
Vicenzo, a Greek tailor
Thomaso, a Greek haberdasher

Street: Courtyard of the hospedaletto
Marzia, a widow
A widow

Street: Courtyard of the hospedaletto
Antonio, a delivery man
His wife
2 children (10 and 8 years old)
Simon, a basket maker

Street of the Broken Courtyard
Ambrose, a delivery man
His wife
Leandra a widow from Concordia
Anzola
Madelena, a German
Pietro Antonio, a delivery man
Zuan, a German baker

Street of the Broken Courtyard
Michele, a stonemason
Julia [not identified as his wife]

Street of the Broken Courtyard
Bortolo, a carpenter
His wife
1 [adult] child: Domenego, his nephew, a carpenter
Hippolito, from Modena, scabbard maker

Street of the Broken Courtyard
Geronimo, a carpenter in Cha Zane
His wife
Dario, from Brescia

Street of the Broken Courtyard
Agnola, a widow
Maria, a widow
Agnolo, a basket maker

Street of the Broken Courtyard
Marutio, a dealer in dry goods
His wife
His aunt, a widow

Street of the Broken Courtyard
Zuane, cobbler
His wife
2 children (ages 12 and 10)

Street of the Broken Courtyard
Alessandro, a boatman
His wife
3 children (ages 16, 13, and 7)
A carpenter, a mason

Street of the Broken Courtyard
Andriana, a widow
1 child

PROFESSIONAL NETWORKS

9 Guild ordinance, England 1346

Craft guilds controlled most of the skilled labor in early modern Europe. Along with organizing and regulating work, and providing job security, guilds also provided their members with a social identity, complete with a meeting place and often an array of activities only loosely associated with a profession. The ways in which guilds sought to increase a sense of community among their members can be seen in the following ordinances for the white-tawyers guild in London. White-tawyers were persons who prepared skins into leather with salt, alum, and other substances, giving it a white surface

(Edward P. Cheney, editor and translator, *Translations and Reprints from the Original Sources of European History*, vol. II, no. 1 (Philadelphia: University of Pennsylvania Press, n.d.), pp. 23–25.)

In honor of God, of Our Lady, and of All Saints, and for the nurture of tranquillity and peace among the good folks the megucers, called white-tawyers, the folks of the same trade have, by assent of Richard Lacer, mayor, and of the aldermen, ordained the points under-written.

In the first place, they have ordained that they will find a wax candle, to burn before our Lady in the church of Allhallows, near London wall.

Also, that each person of the said trade shall put in the box such sum as he shall think fit, in aid of maintaining the said candle.

Also, if by chance any one of the said trade shall fall into poverty, whether through old age or because he cannot labor or work, and have nothing with which to keep himself, he shall have every week from the said box 7 pence for his support, if he be a man of good repute. And after his decease, if he have a wife, a woman of good repute, she shall have weekly for her support 7 pence from the said box, so long as she shall behave herself well and keep single.

And that no stranger shall work in the said trade, or keep house for the same in the city, if he be not an apprentice, or a man admitted to the franchise of the said city.

And that no one shall take the serving-man of another to work with him, during his term, unless it be with the permission of his master.

And if any one of the said trade shall have work in his house that he cannot complete, or if for want of assistance such work shall be in danger of being lost, those of the said trade shall aid him, that so the said work be not lost.

And if any one of the said trade shall depart this life, and have not wherewithal to be buried, he shall be buried at the expense of their common box. And when any one of the said trade shall die, all those of the said trade shall go to the vigil, and make offering on the morrow.

And if any serving-man shall conduct himself in any other manner than properly towards his master, and act rebelliously toward him, no one of the said trade shall set him to work, until he shall have made amends before the mayor and aldermen; and before them such misprision [misconduct] shall be redressed.

Also, that the good folks of the same trade shall once in the year be assembled in a certain place, convenient thereto, there to choose two men of the most loyal and benefitting of the same trade, to be overseers of work and all other things touching the trade for that year; which persons shall be presented to the mayor and aldermen for the time being, and sworn before them diligently to inquire and make search, and loyally to present to the said mayor and aldermen such defaults as they shall find touching the said trade without sparing anyone for friendship or for hatred, or in any other manner. And if any one of the said trade shall be found rebellious against the said overseers, so as not to let them properly make their search and assay, as they ought to do; or if he shall absent himself from the meeting aforesaid, without reasonable cause, after due warning by the said overseers, he shall pay to the Chamber, upon the first default, 40 pence; and on the second like default, half a mark [80 pence]; and on the third one mark [160 pence]; and on the fourth, 20 shillings [240 pence], and shall forswear the trade forever.

Also, that if the overseers shall be found lax and negligent about their duty, or partial to any person for gift or for friendship, maintaining him or voluntarily permitting him to continue in his default, and shall not present him to the mayor and aldermen, as before stated, they are to incur the penalty foresaid.

Also, that each year, at such assemblies of the good folks of the said trade, there shall be chosen overseers, as before stated. And if it be found that through laxity or negligence of the said governors such assemblies are not held, each of the said overseers is to incur the said penalty.

Also, that all skins falsely and deceitfully wrought in their trade which the said overseers shall find on sale in the hands of any person, citizen or foreigner, within the franchise shall be forfeited to the said chamber, and the worker thereof amerced in manner aforesaid.

Also, that no one who has not been an apprentice, and has not finished his term of apprenticeship in the said trade, shall be made free of the same trade; unless it be attested by the overseers for the time being, or by four persons of the said trade, that such person is able and sufficiently skilled to be made free of the same.

10 Letter reporting on a journeyman's unpaid debt, Germany 1540

Craft and journeymen's guilds regulated the conduct of their members in both work-related activities and other matters. Those who were judged at fault could be banned from working, or otherwise punished. Particularly in the case of journeymen, who often travelled from city to city, letters were sent warning guilds in other towns against hiring certain people and asking them for assistance in enforcing punishments. This is a letter sent by the journeymen saddlemakers of Regensburg to the saddlemakers in Nuremberg, warning them about a journeyman who had been tossed out of the guild in Regensburg for not paying a debt.
(B. Schoenlank, 'Zur Geschichte des altnürnbergischen Gesellenwesens', *Jahrbücher für Nationalökonomie und Statistisk* N.F. 19 (1889), p. 375. Translated by Merry Wiesner-Hanks.)

Our friendly greetings and willing service to our dear honorable guild-brothers. We would like to let you know about a journeyman saddlemaker who is reputed to be working with you who calls himself Jacob Paur from Dinkelsbuhl, who was also at Schwäbisch-Hall. A journeyman saddlemaker here with the name of Reichart of Regensburg loaned the same Jacob two gold gulden in coins, and Jacob of Dinkelsbuhl promised and said that he would pay the same Reichart the money he had loaned him back before he left town, or he would be a thief and a rogue in his craft. An apothecary and a packer were there and heard him say [he promised] to repay this. But Jacob moved away without the knowledge or agreement of the same journeyman Reichart, and did not repay the debt or live up to his promise. In addition, he also harmed good honorable people in Regensburg in other ways, which we will write to you about shortly. If you wish to keep yourselves from harm, be careful [of him]. So our request to you is that you hold this same Jacob until he lives up to his promise and repays the debt; this will earn you much. If he is not with you, send [this letter] on. This same Jacob wears a combed coat and a Belgian hooded cloak open in the front. If it is him he knows all about this. God be praised.

11 Servants denounce one of their own, Spain 1587

Class expectations and living situations meant that servants often socialized together. While their collegiality brought them solace from their lives away from their families, it could also have dangerous repercussions. In this summary of a case brought before the Spanish Inquisition in 1587, the idle chatter between servants

232

led to a young girl's exile from the community after her fellow servants denounced her heretical statements.

(Relaciones de Causas, Archivo Histórico Nacional, Sección Inquisición, legajo 2042, no. 19, f. 5 (1587). Translated by Allyson Poska.)

Marina de Cedeyra, a single woman from the town of Cedeyra, 18 years of age, being one night in a house in the said town with other servants of the said house and talking about men and women, the said Marina de Cedeyra said that it was no sin for a single man to have carnal access to a single woman . . . as they might marry . . . she said that she had said it as a simple and ignorant girl and without knowing what she was saying. [She was sentenced to] wear the clothing of a penitent . . . to abjure 'de levi' and exiled from this city and town of Cedeyra for two leagues and three years. They did not punish her more as she was a simple girl of little intelligence.

12 Networks among cloth dealers, Denmark 1537

This short probate notice reveals an extensive network of merchants and cloth dealers. The deceased, Mette Tydemands, was a draper as was her sister, who received her account books. Both were customers of the merchant Ditlev Enbeck whose wife audited the books for the probate court together with a female mercer, also a customer of Enbeck.

(*Malmø rådstueprotokol (Stadsbok) 1503–1548*. Edited by Erik Kroman in conjunction with Leif Ljungberg og Einar Bager (Copenhagen: Selskabet for Udgivelse af Kilder til dansk Historie, 1965), pp. 129–130. Translated by Grethe Jacobsen and Pernille Arenfeldt.)

Anno ut supra [1537] on Friday before Egidius [31st August] here at the City Hall in the presence of the mayors, city council and the king's reeve, did Thale Tysk and Karine, Ditlev's wife, hand over the account books and keys of Mette Tydemands to her sister, Magdalena Peder Overskaerers.

13 A father places his daughter with a colleague, France 1541

Networks centered on a common trade could be the basis for the placement of a child into another household. In the following document, a father places his daughter into apprenticeship with a man in his own trade, though the trade was generally practiced by men, and though he could have taught her himself. Note the young age of the girl, and the long duration of the apprenticeship, which hint at an element of foster care.

(Paris, Archives Nationales, Minutier central, Étude LXXXVI/9, November 28, 1541. Translated by Carol Loats.)

Francoys de Callonne, master pin-maker, living in Paris, affirms that he has given and placed as apprentice and servant, from today for the next

10 years, Blandine de Callonne, his daughter, aged 7 to 8 years says the said Francoys de Callonne, the said Blandine accepting and with her consent.

[Her father places her] with Jehan Guillemart, also master pin-maker living . . . in Paris, present here, taking, and retaining the said Blandine as his apprentice and servant, to whom he has promised and will be obliged to show and teach, to the best of his ability, the said trade and profession of pin-maker and all in which he is involved because of it.

And during the said time [he has promised] to supply and deliver what she needs in terms of drink, food, fire, bed, lodging, and light; and with this to maintain her with her clothing and other necessities whatsoever, honorably, according to her standing.

And because of the service that the said Blandine will be able to do for the said Guillemart during the said time, Guillemart promises and guarantees to pay to the said Blandine, or to someone on her behalf, the sum of 10 *livres tournois*, at the end of the said ten years; and to leave her at the end of the said ten years honorably clothed according to her standing.

And in consideration of this the said Blandine, on the authority of the said person placing her, her father, promises to serve, etc., work for his benefit, etc., avoid losses, and warn, etc., without absenting herself, etc.; and in case of absence the said [de Callonne] promises and will be obliged to seek her in the city and outskirts of Paris and bring her back, etc., and however pledges her to complete loyalty and integrity.

Promising, etc., obligating each in his own right, etc., even the said apprentice renouncing her body, etc. Done and passed in the year 1541, Monday, 28th day of November.

RELIGIOUS COMMUNITIES

14 Nun's description of relations within the convent, Germany 1678

As with many aspects of early modern life, there are many more records about the way communities and networks were supposed to operate than about the way they did. This is certainly true for religious communities, for which there are large numbers of rules and regulations laying out the structure of the day and prescribing the way people were to treat each other, but few actual reports. Those that exist were generally written for a specific purpose, often to defend or attack the monastic way of life, so they do not present an objective picture. Despite their subjective nature, however, they can still give us a glimpse of the ways in which people actually related when they lived in the very close quarters that were common in convents and monasteries. The following is a discussion of some interpersonal relations in the Ursuline convent in Erfurt, Germany, written by a nun who had left the order, Martha Elisabeth Zitter. This is a section of her much longer book describing the reasons

she had left the convent, published by a Protestant pastor; it thus highlights the negative in convent life, yet also captures the intensity of close relations.
(Merry Wiesner-Hanks and Joan Skocir, *Convents Confront the Reformation: Catholic and Protestant Nuns in Germany* (Milwaukee: Marquette University Press, 1998), pp. 91–97. Reprinted by permission.)

The commands of the leaders of the order often run contrary to God and his holy commandments, which I can demonstrate with many examples. Among the many I will only cite a single one, and ask: Whether it is in accordance with the will of God, when the mother superior commands one of the nuns that is under her authority to bring forth invented truths as if they were truths about another [nun], towards whom she is not well disposed, in order to accuse an innocent [person]? And imposes on another, that she support the one who first brought up the slander, and help damn the innocent to punishment through false witness? Commands like this happened often in the convent, which God's goodness has led me out of in strange ways. Those Christian hearts and sincere souls who were often painfully punished through such slanders can testify to this upon request. From the bottom of my heart, I wish them the same enlightenment of the merciful God as I experienced, and the same means to save themselves – with both their souls, which have been bought through the dear blood of Christ, and their bodies – from the barbarous tyranny of Dr. Hunolt [the nuns' confessor] and the French nuns in Erfurt. And [I wish] that they would come to such a place where they could edify and console themselves with me through true teaching from God's Word and the good example of righteous evangelical Christians. For I know only too well, how much it hurts when one must see and experience in the aforementioned convent, how pride and ambition, envy, slander, anger, untruth, unfairness and other deadly sins reign there.

I deliberately began above with pride and ambition, for all the others spring from these. Pride and arrogance make the four oldest [nuns] who are still there hateful and bitter toward each other (though otherwise they are very harmonious when it serves to the detriment of the younger [nuns]). They will not grudge anyone advantage in office, and even make an alienation from conversation and living together out of the alienation of their hearts. Yes, it has certainly been a half year that they have not come together, and spoken nothing but prickly and quarrelsome words to each other or told very annoying things about each other that are uninteresting to everyone. [They did this] even though such works themselves prove truthfully how far the desire to rule had driven the one and the other. It was not enough for them that one party made the other despised through the disclosure of their godless life in the convent, but they troubled themselves scrupulously to write letters to other convents and also to Mainz to his Electoral Grace [the bishop of Mainz, who had charge over the convents in this area], so that he was obliged to send three [nuns] from Erfurt back to another convent that is almost one hundred miles away. Despite sending the one party away, the remaining four who are still ruling could not lay down or turn away from their pride and ambition. This is proved by the cunning invented means and slanders with which they belittle and despise those whom they presume are gaining preference over the others, making them suspect to the highest authorities and others whom they presume can do something about this. Nothing would stun [me] about their violence and unbelievable pride.

Through such a life the nuns still want to glorify themselves, [saying that] they follow Christ's example closest in the convent. How well their life may be compared with their supposed glory may be seen also in the shameful envy that they have for one another. Not only in preference for offices, but in all things and especially in natural gifts. If one [of them] is somewhat more intelligent, more gifted in delicate work, more experienced, more loved, has better friendships, is given a preference or something special in clothing, or something else, then she has almost as many envious haters around her as there are sciences. They apply all sorts of tricks, [telling her] how she should hide such gifts and turn away from further recommendations and promotions.

From this springs the third [thing] I have mentioned above, that those who are envied in such a way are made suspect and despised through outrageous untruths. The most unchristian, however, is that some of them smash each other to pieces, and bear false witness about the others, that this one or that one is supposed to have said or done such things. For they know, that [the others] will not leave unless there are evil slanders and punishment. Therefore they bring the innocent to correction and punishment. It is not surprising that the nuns who have been through this are engulfed in the pain and desolation caused by such unfairness. I have experienced, and therefore can certainly write about and judge, how the poor distressed souls in the clerical order find themselves.

They have not spared their distinguished authorities – both outside and inside of the convent – from this evil defamation if they didn't do all that they wanted. I long [to see] what sort of poison arrows of evil defamation they will shoot after me, as is their habit. I don't fear these in the least, because along with my good conscience, my honest soul will be found [in my actions] both inside and outside the convent. I will prove that I have behaved through all of the persecutions and unfairness, and that they can not accuse me of a frivolous life. No one has heard me complain while

in the convent about the severity of the order, but certainly about the im-
measurable anger, unfair judgments, unearned punishments, the rages and
furies of Dr. Hunolt and the French nuns, directed against those who did
not speak well of their evil life. And also about the less than praiseworthy
conversations, which one or another of the spiritual directors of the convent had with some of the nuns, who adjusted all their actions so as to
please them [i.e., the spiritual directors] the best. Sometimes these talks –
which I heard with my own ears – sounded like lovers' conversations that
went on for a few hours or more. They went on during preparations for the
mass so that they [they priests] often forgot to consecrate the host and
those who wanted to take communion had to turn away from the church.

I said a few words about such things from time to time – though I
confess I was sometimes silent in order to prevent scandal – which cost me
dearly afterwards, from which it may be concluded that I could not value
such an estate [That is, the clerical estate], in which such a terrible life was
lived, as highly as one is supposed to.

15 Monitoring a confraternity, Spain 1655

Confraternities were an important aspect of lay piety. Some were single sex, while
others included both men and women. Under the guidance of parish priests, parishioners paid special devotions to certain saints and performed acts of charity, including burying the dead. In many communities, these organizations were the center of
members' social and religious lives. However, sometimes they lost their religious
focus, as this confraternity in northwestern Spain did, and the Church had to intervene to put an end to their revelry.
(Libro de Visitas, San Juan Abruciños, Archivo Histórico Diocesano de Ourense,
2.1.3, f. 1 (1655). Translated by Allyson Poska.)

In as much as the confraternity serves for nothing except to eat and drink,
his Illustriousness mandates that unless they make a half chapel in honor
of the saint and the brothers come [to worship there] and unless the
confraternity is growing every year, the priest does not want to have it and
his Illustriousness gives him the power to terminate it.

16 Member of a third order, Italy 1598

Along with enclosed orders of monks and nuns, and orders of friars, there were
religious groups generally known as 'third orders' or 'tertiaries' whose members
chose a life of religious contemplation and charity, but did not join convents. This is
an illustration of one such woman, from Cesare Vecellio, *Habiti antichiet Moderni de
tutto il Mundo*, published in 1598. Vecellio's description reads: 'In Venice there are
many types of *pizzochere* (tertiaries), as many as there are different religious mendic-
ant orders, whose clothing style these women have adopted. Most of these women

are widows who, having retired from the world because of devotion or necessity, find themselves reduced to this, so that they depend on aims and their own honest work. These women, since they do not observe the strictures of enclosure [i.e., the convent], cannot really call themselves nuns. Their official duty is to accompany the dead to their burial, to pray, and do other pious works'.

17 Letters between two sisters who were nuns, and their brother, Germany 1523

Protestants rejected the value of celibacy and the monastic life. During the Protestant Reformation one of the first moves of an area rejecting Catholicism was often to close the monasteries and convents. Authorities either confiscated the buildings and land immediately or forbade new novices, allowing the current residents to live out their lives on a portion of the convent's old income. Monks and nuns were expected to move to other houses run by their religious order in areas that remained Catholic, or – much better in Protestant eyes – to leave the religious life for one that involved marriage and a family. In many areas there is little record of what monks or nuns themselves thought about this process, nor sources that provide information about what happened to displaced monks or nuns. Sometimes individuals or whole institutions fought this process, which might alienate them from their families, particularly if the rest of the family had decided to accept Protestantism. The following is part of an exchange of letters between Katherine Rem, of the Katherine convent in the south German city of Augsburg, and her brother Bernard, who addressed his letter to both Katherine and his daughter Veronica, who was also in the convent. Several of Bernhard's earlier letters to them were printed, and this exchange was first printed as a small pamphlet in 1523. Pamphlets like this, from educated but not especially prominent people, sold well in the early years of the Reformation, when people were trying to sort out their own religious convictions.

(From Merry Wiesner-Hanks and Joan Skocir, eds., *Convents Confront the Reformation: Catholic and Protestant Nuns in Germany* (Milwaukee: Marquette University Press, 1998), pp. 27–37. Reprinted by permission.)

The answer of two nuns in the Katherine Convent of Augsburg to Bernhart Rem and afterwards his answer to this.
Isaiah 33
God is our lawgiver.
Job 8
The hope of a hypocrite melts away.

My brother Bernhart,

You have wished us the correct understanding of Jesus Christ. We thank you for that. We hope we have the correct understanding of God. God will fortify us because we praise and favor him. You have sent us two letters, which I am returning to you. We regard you as one of the false prophets that Jesus warned us against in the Holy Gospels when he said 'Guard yourselves against prophets who come in the form of a sheep and are ravening wolves.' Therefore you have also come with many good words and wanted to lead us astray and make us despondent. You should not think that we are so foolish that we place our hope in the convent and in our own works. Rather we place our hope in God. He is the true lord and rewarder of all things. Him do we serve more willingly in the convent than in the world, with the grace and help of God. You do not have to worry at all about our bodies and souls. You do not have to go to heaven or hell for us. God the Almighty will judge all of us at the Last Judgment, according to his justice. We all know that for certain. Therefore think about yourself, that you will become and be a good Christian and that you keep to your station in life rightly and that you do not swear by God's name and by his bitter martyrs. I know that you certainly can do this, and not eat meat on Friday or Saturday. These things are not the teachings of Jesus Christ. You will pull a splinter out of our eye, while you yourself have a large log in yours. I certainly know that you have said that your daughter and I are to you more as if we were in a brothel than in a convent. You should shame yourself in your heart to think [such a thing] to say nothing of saying this. Whoever hears this from you cannot think very well of you. There we certainly see the brotherly love that you have for us. And that you allowed [the letter] from us to be printed! The printer certainly does not think very well of you, even if he asked you with good words, 'Don't you have anything else to be printed about the religious [orders], what they are doing and how they are?' You should have given [up] the money through God's will. Why didn't you have [things written] by you and others like you printed? But I certainly know that you and those like you always do the right thing, and that the religious [orders] delivered enough to you. No one is sorry for this. There will still come a time when you will suffer. We will gladly suffer for God's sake with the help of God. He has also suffered greatly for our sake. God forgive you for everything. That is our angry message, [that] the bitter suffering of Jesus Christ press in your heart. It would be better for you if you mulled this over. You are a good fellow and happy. I wanted to answer your letter more fully, but I will commend it to God the Lord. You have shocked us because you actually wanted to come to us. If you don't come in kinship, stay out. If you want to straighten us out, then we don't want your [message] at all. You may not send us such things any more. We will not accept them. We also [already] have many good books.

Here follows the answer to this letter. Bernhart Rem wishes his sister Katherine and daughter Veronica Rem peace and grace in Christ.

I have received your answer but have viewed with little pleasure [the fact] that you have scorned my letter, written in all Christian faith, and that you have sent my admonition back to my house, and this in anger that I certainly did not anticipate. [You] insulted me and called me a false prophet. To these words I will say nothing harder than that you do not yet know or do not want to know, what a false prophet is. For a false prophet uses fine words to deceive simple hearts, which he cunningly separates from the healing words of Jesus Christ with his own illusions and human teaching. This I have – God is my witness – never done, but simply out of Christian faith, held before you not human teaching which confuses, but God's teaching, for your spiritual peace and the pleasure of your conscience. Human teaching destroys and confuses the heart, and pulls one away from the true and simply teachings of Christ our Savior (2 Cor. 11), just like the snake deceived Eve through its cunning. My letter to you is clear in all things. I also notice that no true Christian could have rejected it with cause. But you are still badly ensnared in your rule and human sins, so that you cannot grasp the self-evident evangelical truth. I therefore pray to Christ [that] he will enlighten your hearts to the true understanding of his costly freedom that he earned for us through a hard and scornful death. I have done this as your brother in Christ. I cannot give you grace, but so much is on me [that] I have given you a true warning. I do not repent this even though you are now enraged against me in the bitterness of your hearts. You write that your hope stands alone in God. I am glad to hear that and ask God that he increase such hope in you. However, that you [say you] want to serve God willingly in the convent, makes me fear that things will not go as smoothly with you as you say, for I have given you enough reports from Isaiah 29 and Matthew 15 that God does not want to be honored with human teachings and laws. I am concerned that you are still on the old path and [that you] make God very angry with works that you have thought up yourselves, that precious time is consumed in a destructive way, and that you are very troubled without joy and happiness in your conscience, and without fruit of your body [i.e., children], and that you do not want to understand what 'the world' means. Truly, because we live in the weak shelter of our mortal bodies, we always carry the world with us, in the fields, in the convents, and wherever we are. What did Saint Paul complain about as much as his mortal, sinful body, in which original sin raised itself so strongly and fought against the spirit of God day and night, in the convent and outside of the convent, as you have in Romans 7 [and] Galatians 5. Be on guard not to be sleepy and too secure behind high walls. You are truly in the world, and if you don't yet see as much wickedness as I do, so you still have sin and the fruits of sin near and in yourselves. For you are not holier than Paul who complained about this in himself many times. This part of your letter does not sound good; it suits the hypocrite well who was not like the others (Luke 18). You also desire that I do not bother myself about your body or soul, or [go to] heaven or hell for you. Here I notice that unfortunately you don't yet know what a Christian life is and what a Christian person's duties are. For you suppose that no one should take on anyone else, and everyone take on only themselves. Where then is Christian faith and love, that fulfills all commandments (Rom. 13)? I am nevertheless responsible, according to God's commandments, to warn you and give you good advice as my fellow human beings, even if you were not related to me (Matt. 18) . . .

Lastly, expose yourselves willingly to slander, just as if it might be called slander when one admonishes you in a friendly way in writing. Oh, if you want to become like the suffering Christ, you must suffer in a different way. If you are not in the world, why does the Word of God sting you so badly, making you question your life a bit? I wish you had used all the arts to answer my letter. You answer only the angry words; the letter itself is not so easy to answer. Take all your books and give basic answers if you are so learned. You don't want to accept any writings or admonitions from me. In this I see that you are angry. Whoever has anger and envy is still in the world. You have anger in you; therefore you have not yet escaped the world. I admit, however, that you have many books, but I request that you read only the Bible with diligence and fear of God, and let the other books go. Then you will certainly see, for what reasons I have written to you and [you] won't call me a false prophet anymore. You will learn composure and your vanity go, and also not despise the worries and prayers for you [which come from] the worst sinner, as you have done to me, even though I wanted to do this for your benefit. In conclusion, be angry, but do not sin; do not let the sun go down on your anger (Ps. 4, Eph. 4). And let a sinner and mortal say one thing to you out of Christian faith: This is that you arrange your life according to the word of God, which is our only light and rule. Live in a godly manner and let human teachings lie. I would rather be counted as carnal with the open sinners in the temple (Luke 18) than be religious with you and those like you. Nevertheless I wish you for once the correct knowledge of Jesus Christ, that the spirit that brings life would write in your hearts the overflowing good works of Christ, so that you know why he in human nature was fastened to the cross. When you know that, your little human discoveries and trust in your own works, habits, convent, fasting, and such things will soon fall away. It will be looked upon as very serious, for one does not presume to buy God's grace with spiritual simony. Who has ears to hear, let them hear. It is a secret vice rooted deep in our sinful nature. Such presumption, that always presumes one is more facile than God and can achieve God's grace through one's own work. It might be that a person could, with effort, ward off such godless error, but I will say nothing about the convents, where many different types of work – all of it self-chosen – are practiced with the fine glitter of holiness. And it is worthless straw, whatever one makes of it. But read with serious attention the 5th and 13th Psalms as Paul inserts [them] in Romans 3, so that you can recognize human works more easily. The grace of God be with you all. Amen. Date: Friday, September 11, 1523 in Augsburg.

18 Dispute in a convent, Denmark 1569

This is a letter from Margrete Urne to Mogens Gyldenstjerne (1481–1569), both members of the Danish nobility, written at Maribo Convent on February 22, 1569. Margrete Urne was at this time the abbess of Maribo Convent, a former Bridgettine convent, which was one of the religious institutions granted permission to continue after the Danish Reformation (officially introduced in 1536) on the condition that it accept the new Church Ordinance issued by the King in 1537. This permission was granted to a number of formerly Catholic convents during the 1550s to satisfy the demand from noble families who needed institutions to which they could send their daughters for an honorable upbringing and where noble women could live out their lives if they did not marry. Among these, Maribo Convent survived for the longest time even though it was the subject of much dispute. Soon after its transformation into a Protestant institution, complaints arose that the women led immoral lives and also maintained Catholic practices. In an attempt to restore order, new statutes were issued in 1572 and again in 1596, but without bringing the wanted peace and, as a consequence, the convent was dissolved in 1612.

The letter concerns a conflict between Margrete Urne and Mogens Gyldenstjerne, the father of one of the cloistered women. Gyldenstjerne was a politically very influential man whose support Margrete Urne could not afford to lose. The letter also reveals the problems of keeping order in the convent.

(The original is kept in the Danish National Archives, Copenhagen. It has previously been published in *Breve til og fra Mogens Gyldenstjerne og Anne Sparre*, ed. by E. Marquard (Copenhagen, 1941). Translated by Grethe Jacobsen and Pernille Arenfeldt.)

My very kind greeting now and forever sent with God. Dear Lord Mogens, particularly good friend, I thank you for all the great honor and good [services] you always have shown and done me, and particularly for the great good you truly sent me lately, when I wrote to you with my own messenger, for which I am not able to thank you fully, and all my days I will be found to be willing to serve you with all the best that my ability allows me. Dear Lord Mogens, as you write to me that your dear daughter Lady Sofie has written to you about what has been blamed on her as a result of what supposedly was said by the thief who was executed here, dear Lord Mogens then I kindly proclaim to you that it is an obvious lie that has been said about her, so may God punish the one who did this, and I never heard such talk before the thief was dead, as truly help me God. And [when] I have asked the people who were with this same thief while he was in prison if he said such words, then they all said no and took it on their souls' salvation that they never had heard such words from him. Dear Lord Mogens, I beg you for the sake of God and for what I may deserve from you, that you will not experience grief from this[;] I hope with the help of

243

God, that whoever has told this bad lie about her eventually will take it in their throat again for she is completely innocent, this I know for sure. Dear Lord Mogens, as you also write to me, your dear daughter has been badly struck here by sister Karina Fritzdaughter, and it is well known to me that she has been hit and that it has done great harm to her hearing, and completely without [her own] guilt or fault; for your dear daughter did not do anything to her for which she deserved slapping or striking, and I have never been shown greater disrespect since I entered into this service than this, which this sister Karina Fritzdaughter did me both by striking your dear daughter and in other things she did around the same time, which God the Almighty will punish her for in due time. Dear Lord Mogens, I beg you not to blame me for her hitting your dear daughter, God knows that if she had hit me myself, then I would not have felt as much pain as it causes me that she hit her. And I do not know what to do about her [Karina Fritzdaughter] and her supporters, for they are very disobedient in all ways. And I have heard that they have written a petition to His Royal Majesty and complained harshly about me, which God forgive them, but when good people come here to listen to their complaints, then I hope with God's help that I will well defend what I have done. But I fear that if it goes as they intend, then this convent will eventually be destroyed, for no one can stop them, as they behave exactly as they wish in all ways. Dear Mogens, I beg you to please take everything in the best meaning in this matter[;] I do hope that your dear children [Lady Sofie] and I will be given a complete apology for what has been done to us in this time. Dear Lord Mogens, I will no longer burden you with this my poor letter, but will now and always commend you to God the Almighty and Eternal, and [may God] protect you long and well from everything evil. Your daughter sends you many good greetings as do I. Written in Maribo Convent the Tuesday next after Lent Sunday anno domini MDLXVIIII.

S. Margrete daughter of Urne.

(On the back: Seal, address and Mogens Gyldenstjerne's note:)
Honest and wellborn man and upright knight Lord Mogens Gyldenstjerne of Stjernholm, my particularly good friend, very kindly written.
Received the 24th of February [15]69.

CONFLICT

19 Confronting an outsider, Portugal, 1440

As the previous document makes clear, networks and communities were not always harmonious. The example provided here, from a council meeting in Porto on June 10,

1440, deals with the question of an outsider who was believed to be the root of many troubles in the local community. The record begins with a list of thirty-eight 'good men,' that is, upstanding [male] citizens many of whom were connected to one another through socio-economic rank and family ties, twenty-six of whom signed the declaration proposed.

(J.A. Pinto Ferreira, ed., *Documentos e Memórias para a História do Porto, XL, 'Vereaçoens' Anos de 1401–1449* (Porto: Câmara Municipal do Porto, 1980), f. 42 [91–93]. Translated by Darlene Abreu-Ferreira.)

In the year of one thousand four hundred and forty on the tenth day of the month of June in the . . . city of Porto there were these good men that follow . . .

And other good men neighbours and residents in the said city. It was resolved all together for the honour and benefit of the said city for as much as it was said that those before them always lived very well and in great tranquility always serving the former Kings and likewise to our Lord the King in peace and harmony for being all thus and since they are all residents of the city joined in lineage kinship and marriage And that now not long ago came to live in this city Pedro Alvarez originally from Galicia procurator of a number that Pedro Alvarez created many quarrels between the residents of the said city enticing one and another to make accusations and famous libels for which some residents of the said city were imprisoned and ruined by it that having and continuing in his maliciousness though he was told not to engage in such things nevertheless once again he incited Alvaro Vaasquez de Sousa to accuse Branca Pirez his wife of committing the sin against him of adultery with Luis Affomso resident of the said city For which accusation Alvaro Vaasquez de Sousa [was] undoubtedly solely moved by malice and a great lie. For that Branca Pirez never did such a thing nor even imagined and even less that Luis Affomso. And for how many of these things we have to endure and could in the future lead to revolt among those of the city that it was resolved that this Pedro Alvarez not live anymore among them and go live outside of the city to remove the scandal according to what is said. And that moreover that they write to our Lord the King and to his council this which they ordered thus. And that it be his will to not consent such a man to live among us that they understood that if he could it would be a disservice and ruin to the city.

20 A local feud, Russia 1623

Conflicts among ordinary people often began with a minor offense on the part of one party. When the person with the grievance retaliated, a vendetta with repeating cycles of violence could result, with more and more family members and neighbors

245

drawn into the conflict. This petition, filed by a Russian peasant named Antonko
Fedorov, asks local ecclesiastical and secular authorities at a nearby military post as
well as neighbors to intervene in a dispute involving escalating violence.
(Published original, *Akty kholmogorskoi eparkhi, bk. 2*, Russkaia istoricheskaia
biblioteka, vol. 14 (St. Petersburg, 1894), pp. 662–664. Translated by Eve Levin.)

In the year 7131 [1623 in the Western calendar], Antonko Fedorov petitioned and made deposition to the ecclesiastical elder of Tarnaskaia gar-
rison and the commander Vasilii Feopentov's son Chetvertovo and to all
the peasants of Ust'-Uftiuskaia and Shevdenitskaia districts, against Larion
Iakov's son Drugov in regard to the following matter:

Our lords, it happened in this year, 7131, on Wednesday in the second week
after Easter, St. George's Day. On that day, I had gone past Kholmogory
[the major commercial and administrative center of that region of north
Russia] by raft with rye, along with Eufimii, the elder of St. Nicholas' [This
probably refers to the local church or a small nearby monastery, named
in honor of St. Nicholas], to the Markusha River. While I was away during
that week, lords, on the first Friday after St. George's Day after sunset,
my little wife Ogrofenka went looking for her cattle. And my little wife
Ogrofenka looked for her cattle at the portage in Shebenskie, nearby the
house of Iakov Drugov. My little wife Ogrofenka drove her cattle home to
Demidovskaia village. As soon as she reached the pasture by the pine forest
at the end of the field of Demidovskaia village, there Larion Iakov's son
Drugov caught up with my little wife Ogrofenka. He seized her by the hand
and by the collar and dragged her to the side of the road, and he robbed my
little wife Ogrofenka and insulted her impudently. In his robbery, he took
her silver earrings with red stones from her ears, and he ripped off her
silver cross from her throat, and from her throat a pouch with two rubles in
cash, and he removed from her hands two silver rings. He took in the
robbery property totaling three and a half rubles in all.

In this current year, 131, lords, on July 20, the holiday of the prophet
St. Elijah, Iakov Matveev's son Drugov invited me, Antonko, to his house
in Igumnovskaia village to drink beer. In accordance with his invitation, I
went to his house in Igumnovskaia village, and I brought my little wife
Ogrofenka with me, and I drank beer at Iakov's. Then that same Larion, in
his father Iakov's cottage, quarreled with me and with my little wife and
insulted us with every kind of improper, illicit language. He struck me on
the shoulder with a board, and dislocated my right arm from my shoulder.
He beat my little wife Ogrofenka about the ears. And having beaten us, that
same Larion bragged out loud that he would beat and rob me and my little
wife, and that he would insult us at shearing and haymaking, robbing and

insulting us impudently: 'Next time, you won't get the same from me, Antonko; beware, for I will beat and rob you and your wife at shearing and at haymaking and in the woods and in deserted places.'

Our lords, Church Elder Ivan and Commander Vasilii, and all the peasants of Ust'-Uftiuskaia district, listen to our great need and concerning Larion's great oral bragging and his impudent insults. May this be known and testified to you, our Lords, Elder Ivan and Commander Vasilii and all the peasants. Accept my deposition and order that it be recorded and by investigated immediately. I petition you and all the peasants earnestly.

21 A woman is accused of slander, Denmark 1551

For women especially, honor and an unblemished reputation was of utmost importance and a hasty word or a quarrel among friends and relatives could, if spread in public, result in a court case in order that the accused might have her honor and reputation restored. Another possibility was a settlement out of court with a public retraction of any accusations uttered, although this rarely came about with the king and his chancellor mediating as is the case in the following source. The women involved came from the higher bourgeoisie and the temperamental Helle, who was accused of slandering a friend, asked her husband as well as her brother, both important members of the new non-noble clergy of the Danish Lutheran church, to defend her. (*Kjøbenhavns Diplomatarium: Samling af Dokumenter, Breve og andre Kilder til Oplysning om Kjøbenhavns ældre Forhold før 1728. I–VIII*, ed. O. Nielsen, vol. IV (Copenhagen: Gad, 1872–87), pp. 534–535. Translated by Grethe Jacobsen and Pernille Arenfeldt.)

We, Christian etc., hereby announce to all that in the year 1551 after the birth of Christ the day after Saint Gallus (October 22nd) was presented at our castle at Copenhagen in our own presence and that of our dear Johan Friis of Hesselager, our loyal subject, Councillor and Chancellor, our dear Johan Guldsmed, burgher in our town of Copenhagen, on behalf of our dear Anne, widow of Oluf Hansen, burgheress of the same town, on the one side, and had summoned before us our dear Peter Dringelberg, canon of Lund, together with his wife on the other side, and Johan Guldsmed recounted how the aforementioned Anne, widow of Oluf Hansen, had taken accommodations with aforementioned Peder Dringelberg in Lund on the recent day of Saint Lawrence, and at that time Helle, his wife, uttered useless nonsense about her and accused her in front of her husband, saying that she (Anne) had not acted as she ought to and with this and more useless nonsense had run into the street and there spoken ill of her, so that she had gotten a bad reputation at home as well as abroad, and she asks that because aforementioned Helle had made up and spread such useless lies about her, that could not be proven, she (Helle) be punished according to the law. To this our dear master Jesper Brochmann, Archdeacon in Aarhus, answered on behalf of his sister, aforementioned Helle, and recounted that aforementioned Helle never openly had told any tales about Anne, widow of Oluf, which could damage her honor or reputation because she knew nothing but that she (Anne) openly and secretly had behaved as an honest women should do and if anybody would say something contrary to this then she (Helle) was the one who ought to respond as they are close relatives and if Helle should have uttered a hasty word about her then she should not be upset about that. Then, having heard the accusations, responses and considered the issues of the case and because aforementioned Helle stood in from of us and denied that she had ever accused her of anything dishonest and had given her an apology, as mentioned before, by saying that she knew of no dishonesty connected with her. Then we ordered that they should be reconciled and be friends, relatives and kin, as they ought to.

22 Women fight over a mercenary, Germany 1568

Jealousy and romantic quarrels were not solely subjects of literature, but no doubt occurred on a regular basis among ordinary people. The German printer Wolfgang Strauch shows a quarrel between two lower-class women over a mercenary, with one seeking to cut off the nose of the other. The German expression for not watching someone too closely is 'looking through your fingers at someone', which is just what the mercenary is doing here.

(Walter L. Strauss, *The German Single-lead Woodcut, 1550–1600* (New York: Abaris Books, 1975) Reproduced by permission.)

The Mercenary's Wife
[To the other woman] You wash-tub, you won't get away from me.
You want to go away with my husband?
You must leave this plunder of yours alone
Or I will cut off your nose.
[To her husband] And what kind of loose man are you,
Who takes on another piece of baggage?
Even though I have gone through
War and peace, good and ill with you.
The Beer Woman
[To the other woman] Leave me alone you old wrinkled hag,
Leave me go and don't insult me so.
If you had treated your husband right
He wouldn't have turned to me.
[To the man] Oh, help me, my dear Claus,
So that your wife leaves me in peace,
And does not bring me to shame.
Then I will go with you to Belgium.

Mercenary

Whatever is vexing you both, I'm leaving it alone,
And not watching you too closely.
Both of you are cross and ill-tempered,
I swear I won't help either one of you.
Whichever one of you sets aside the quarrel,
I'll say thank you,
And be favorable toward you,
And the other can go off to a tavern.

Questions for discussion

1   How do the subjects and writers of these documents describe their networks? What do their descriptions tell you about their assumptions and expectations regarding networks?
2   What sorts of networks would be particularly important to men or to women?
3   What sorts of networks would be particularly important to an early modern woman or man as s/he aged?
4   How are the types of communities described above different from contemporary ones? What sorts of networks are important today, and why? Are the reasons we need communities today different from those of earlier days?

8

WIDOWHOOD AND OLD AGE

Widowhood was a fact of life for early modern men and women, especially women. In a world of uncertainty and danger, Europeans buried spouses with alarming regularity. Thus, widows were a substantial part of the early modern population. The image of the widow as ugly crone is a legacy of this period, when European society was filled with older widowed women on the margins. But not all widows were old. Women often married older men (especially among the upper classes), which meant that they might find themselves still young, with small children to support. Women might also lose their husbands to disease, accidents, and violence.

The death of a spouse and old age are usually linked in the modern world, but this was not necessarily the case in early modern Europe, for people became widowed at all ages, and might easily be widowed several times during their lives. The death of a spouse brought a more dramatic change in status for women than it did for men. Women's link to the world of work often depended on their husband's professional identity, so that his death affected his widow's opportunities for making a living while the death of a wife did not. We can see this distinction in the fact that the word for 'widower' in most European lan-guages derives from the word for 'widow', whereas the more common pattern is for the female designation to derive from the male – princess from prince, actress from actor. The word 'widower', in fact, does not enter common usage until the eighteenth century, when people began to think about the loss of a spouse more as an emotional than an economic issue.

Imagery of widows in this period falls into two broad categories: widow as an ugly, old crone, dressed in rags and either vaguely or explicitly sinister; and widow as an avaricious, sexually rapacious woman eager to sink her claws into another man. Both images reflected society's anxiety over this large population of 'displaced' women, whose role in society was so problematic because they did not automatically fall under the authority of a man.

Such imagery was powerful, but the reality was more complex. Widows often found themselves in difficult circumstances. Whether or not she had children to support, a widow often had to scramble to make ends meet once her husband, the primary source of financial support, died. But widows also developed ways of coping. Some had to resort to begging or charity, but others rented out rooms or continued the occupation they had practiced while their husband was alive, such as sewing, laundering, or huckstering. For women who had worked alongside their husband in his profession, another option was to continue running his business, insofar as the authorities permitted them to do so.

In many parts of the world women who lost their husband returned to their birth families or entered the household of a brother or brother-in-law. In most areas of Europe, however, widows became heads of households themselves and were forced to find some way to survive and to support their dependent children. Not surprisingly, widowhood generally brought a decline in a woman's economic status, with the poorest households in towns and villages those headed by elderly widows; because the death of his wife did not mean a man had to change occupations, widowers did not become significantly poorer. During times of economic hardship, crime by widows, mostly petty theft, increased, though authorities tended to treat them less harshly than other lawbreakers.

Though widowhood often brought economic adversity for women, it also gave them some new opportunities for independence throughout most of Europe. Widows who had inherited money or property from their husbands or who had received their dowry back at his death were often relatively free to invest it or dispose of it as they wished. Aristocratic widows were often very active managing their families' business affairs, and identified the rights and privileges attached to their position as *theirs*, and not simply belonging to them in trust for their sons. Widowhood could also place a woman in a position of great power over her children, deciding the amount of dowry for her daughters and assisting her sons in gaining positions of political influence.

This social and economic independence was disturbing to many commentators, who viewed men being in charge as the norm, and they recommended that widows remarry. Remarriage was also troubling, however, for this lessened a woman's allegiance to the family of her first husband and could have serious economic consequences for the children of her first marriage, and might also give a wealthy widow what was seen as an inappropriate amount of power over her spouse. Laws regarding widows often reflect this ambivalence. In many parts of Europe laws made remarriage more attractive by requiring a widow to have a male guardian co-sign all financial transactions, even religious donations, and giving him power over her own children. The same law code might also make it less attractive by stipulating that a widow could lose all rights over her children through remarriage, including the right to see them. Not wishing to contemplate either the independence or remarriage of their wives, lawmakers were thus attempting somehow to keep a widow dependent on the family of her first husband.

In addition to simple financial security, a few widows from elite classes achieved much more, exercising a degree of power and authority that had been denied them as married women. They managed their households as well as real estate, and arranged marriages for their children. Queen Dowagers, as we see in the examples from Denmark and the Ottoman Empire, could run their countries in their son's stead.

Widowhood therefore was a third, sometimes final stage in a woman's life – a stage most women would only experience once, and sometimes more often. It was a stage of life in which she could confront the greatest hardship and vulnerability, both economically and socially, but it could also offer her the greatest opportunity for social and financial independence.

In actual practice, whether a widow remarried or not was more determined by her economic and personal situation than by laws or theoretical concerns. Younger widows remarried much more readily than older ones, and widows with few children more readily than those with many. The opposite is true in the case of widowers; those with many children were most likely to remarry, and to remarry quickly. In general, widowers were far more likely to remarry than widows; French statistics indicate that 50 percent of widowers remarried, while only 20 percent of widows did so.

Widowhood was a clear legal status, but 'old age' in the early modern period is harder to define. For women, the best marker might be menopause, which usually occurred somewhere in a woman's forties; the mean age at which women in northwestern Europe bore their last child was forty. Because life expectancy was less than it was today, however, even if people stopped having children before forty they still had children in their households for most of their later years of life. Older men and women whose children had all left home generally continued to live on their own as long as possible. Evidence from England indicates that middle-class children were more likely to assist their elderly parents by providing them with servants so that they could stay in their own households rather than taking them in; the elderly lived with their married children only among the poor. Though we often romanticize earlier periods as a time when the elderly were cherished for their wisdom and experience, this was not necessarily so. In many parts of Europe, parents made formal contracts with their children to assure themselves of a certain level of material support, or included clauses about this in their wills, as in the will of a man from the small English town of Cranbrook from 1477 reprinted here. The French author Christine de Pizan, in her advice book for women written in 1407, reminds young women that 'you owe honor to the elderly, so it follows that at all costs you must avoid mocking them and doing or saying injurious, derisive, or outrageous things, or bad things of whatever kind. Do not displease or find fault with them, as some wicked young people do who are very much to be reproached for it, who call them "old boys" or "old biddies."'

Older women were generally more in need of public support than older men, in part because their spouses were less likely or able to care for them than were the wives of older men, who were generally younger or had no way to leave an ailing spouse. Younger relatives were also more willing to take in elderly men than women; older women often formed joint households with other older female relatives or simply acquaintances to pool their resources and expenses, a practice almost unknown among men. The higher percentage of elderly female welfare recipients may have also been partly due to the fact that there were simply more older women than men around. Despite the dangers of childbirth, female life expectancy seems to have been gradually growing longer than male throughout this period; by the eighteenth century in France, female life expectancy at birth was about thirty-four and male about thirty-one.

Aging brought physical as well as economic changes, and there is evidence that these were viewed as more of a problem for women than men already in the sixteenth century. Post-menopausal women were widely believed to experience increased sex drive, which might even lead them to seek demonic lovers in order to satisfy themselves. They were held to emit vapors from their mouths that could cause nursing women's milk to dry up or animals and children to sicken. They were thought to be especially concerned with the lessening of their physical attractiveness, for a Spanish physician's remedies to combat wrinkles were all directed to women. At the very end of life, both men and women were viewed as physically and mentally infirm; many illustrations of the ages of man show the man in the seventh (and last) stage as bent over and supported by a cane, and in Shakespeare's play *As You Like It*, the character Jacques describes this stage as 'second childishness and mere oblivion'.

CARRYING ON THE FAMILY BUSINESS

1 A widow takes an apprentice, France 1612

The early death of a spouse was common in this period, and since the primary way of identifying a woman in a marriage contract was by her husband, even if dead, it is easy to tell that these contracts involved many women who were widows. An artisan's widow often had the right to carry on her deceased husband's trade, though that right was increasingly restricted in many trades during this period. In the following notarial contract, a young man in his twenties confirms that he has previously placed himself in an on-going apprenticeship with the widow of a merchant book seller. Note how the apprentice agrees to 'renounce' his body and possessions. This is consistent with the obligation of a person who joined a household to devote herself or himself completely to the household head.

(Paris, Archives Nationales, Minutier central, Étude XXXIII/240, February 17, 1612. Translated by Carol Loats.)

Was present in person Martin Collet, son of Pierre Collet, farm worker, living at Baudeville near Saint Merehoult on the borders of Lourne and of Jehanne Serve, his wife, [Martin's] father and mother, aged 23 to 24 years. [Martin Collet] voluntarily acknowledges, affirms, and declares that for his own benefit, from the 1st of January of last year, 1611, he has given and placed himself as servant and apprentice, from that day for the following three years, to and with the honorable Catherine Nivet, widow of the late Claude Montreil, while living merchant book seller in the University of Paris, living there, rue Saint Jehan de Latran, parish Saint Estienne du Mont. [Nivet], present here, has also declared that she has [back] then taken and retained the said Collet as her servant and apprentice for the said time. And [she] has shown to the best of her ability up to the present and promises to continue to show and teach to the best of her ability the merchandise of bookseller and all in which she is involved in this trade.

And to do this she has fed, and promises to continue to feed, treat, and house him gently and courteously, as is appropriate. And the apprentice has maintained himself up to this point, and promises to continue to maintain himself in all his clothing and things necessary to him during the said time. And this without either party paying out any money because of this present [contract], on one part or the other.

And making this [arrangement], the apprentice promises and commits himself to continue to learn well, to the best of his ability, the said merchandise of a bookseller, serve his said mistress in it and in all other lawful and honorable things that he is ordered to [do], work to her profit, avoid losses, and warn her of problems as soon as they come to his attention; without fleeing nor absenting himself from the said service during the time which remains of the said three years. And in case of flight or absence, he consents and agrees to be seized and apprehended anywhere, wherever he is found.

As thus has been agreed by and among the said parties. Promising, obligating, each in his own right, etc., the said apprentice his body and possessions, etc., renouncing on one part and the other. Done and passed in duplicate in the offices of the notaries, the year 1612, Friday, in the morning, the 17th day of February. And [Nivet] has declared that she does not know how to write or sign . . . and the said apprentice has signed.

2 A widow acts as a royal knight, Denmark 1554

Mogens Gyldenstjerne (1481–1569), a Danish knight, wrote this letter in May of 1554 to Sidsel Ulfstand (died c. 1575), the widow of Knud Gyldenstjerne of Ljungbygaard (c. 1480–1552). Upon the death of her husband, Sidsel Ulfstan inherited his estate and she also maintained one of the fiefs he had been entrusted with. It was usual practice that a widow remained in control of her husband's fief(s) for up to one year after his death, but in some cases the widow was granted control of the fief for her lifetime. This was the case with Sidsel Ulfstand. The letter reveals that she was not subject to special treatment because of her gender, but expected to fulfill the same obligations as any other landed and/or fief-holding person: to supply cavalry and men to the commander of the province within which she held land if or when an enemy attack was expected. The letter also shows that the commander, Mogens Gyldenstjerne, appears to have trusted her judgement regarding incursions into the country.

(The original letter is preserved in the Danish National Archives, Copenhagen. It has previously been published in *Breve til og fra Mogens Gyldenstjerne og Anne Sparre*, ed. by E. Marquard (Copenhagen 1929). Translated by Grethe Jacobsen and Pernille Arenfeldt.)

Kind and loving greetings now and forever sent with our Lord. Dear Lady Sidsel, my particularly good friend, I kindly inform you that I have received His Highness', my Gracious Lord's letter [stating] that there are a great number of soldiers gathered by the Elbe, and therefore I have been given command over Scania, Halland, Blekinge and Lister during the absence of my young Lord, Duke Frederik[.] I send you a copy of his Royal Majesty's letter, which will inform you of what to do. My request to you is that you will keep diligent watch over the castle and fief which is entrusted to you, and that you will inform and command all those who are free and noble that they should be prepared to leave with horses and armor when they are thus summoned; and if any peasants are assigned to your authority, then every tenth man must also be prepared [and] in the same manner the burghers within your fief so that they all are ready night and day when they are summoned. I also beg you on behalf of His Royal Majesty that, if you become aware of any incursions into the country, you send an accurately informed messenger, with whatever protection you can spare to our men wherever you find out they are gathered. Hereby you are commended to God. Hastily written at Elfsborg the 22 day of May, year etc. 1554.

Mogens Gyldenstjerne, Knight

[On the back of the letter: Seal and address:]

Kindly written to the honest and well-born woman, Lady Sidsel, the widow of Knud Gyldenstjerne of Ljungbygaard, my particularly good friend. Or her bailiff in her absence.

3 Petition to the king and queen, Denmark c. 1487

This petition was made to the Danish king and queen by an anonymous widow around 1487. The petitioner, the widow of the royal saddle maker, planned to carry on her late husband's workshop and explained that she needed some money and cloth for a cape, as she intended to travel to Germany in search of a journeyman. It was a regular practice of the royal court to import Dutch woollen cloth to use as partial payment of wages. This widow was not asking for charity, but rather a loan for

a reasonable purpose: a cape of this cloth would signal a respectable, well-off woman, making her journey easier and likely more productive.
(Original in the Danish National Archives, Copenhagen, Sign. RA. Reg. 108A. Pk. 1. 1487. Printed in *Danske Magazin*, ser. 4, vol. 1 (1864), p. 183. Translated by Grethe Jacobsen and Pernille Arenfeldt.)

I would like to beg you, gracious Lord, to lend me 30 marks, so that I may buy leather and other things I need for orders of Your Grace. Many of [the] saddles have to be repaired and your marshal has ordered a new saddle. Four new horse collars for my Gracious Lady's horses have been made and your marshal talked about two more collars. I will repay you the money if you would help me now. I have borrowed and pawned from good people, and I would like to pay them back, and I would like to travel to Germany with Your Grace's permission to inquire if I could get a good journeyman, one who can do all kinds of work. And I ask you, Gracious Lord, that you would consider my poverty and let me benefit from the fact that my poor husband has been your servant, so that you will give me five yards of cloth of the good kind for a cape. For God's sake, I ask your Grace to let me know . . .

4 Widows fight for their rights in court, Germany sixteenth century

Widows attempting to run a business after the demise of their husband often confronted particular obstacles. The widows featured in the two documents below took matters into their own hands by complaining to the authorities. Their technique consisted both of asserting their rights to practice their trades, and underlining their vulnerability as widowed women.
(Unpublished petitions in Frankfurt Stadtarchiv, Zünfte, Ugb. C-50, Ss, nr. 4; Ugb. C-32, R, nr. 1. Translated by Merry Wiesner-Hanks.)

(a) Widow's petition to the Frankfurt City Council, late sixteenth century

Distinguished and honorable sirs, I, a poor and distressed widow, wish to respectfully report in what manner earlier this year I spun some pounds of yarn, 57 to be exact, for the use of my own household. I wanted to take the yarn to be woven into cloth, but didn't know whom I should give it to so that I could get it worked into cloth the quickest and earliest.

Therefore I was talking to some farm women from Bornheim, who were selling their produce in front of the shoemakers' guild house, and they told me about a weaver that they had in Bornheim who made good cloth and could also make it quickly. I let him know   through the farmers' wives — that I wanted him to make my cloth. I got the yarn together and sent my children to carry it to him; as they were on their way, the weavers here grabbed the yarn forcefully from my children, and took it to their guild house. They said they had ordinances that forbade taking yarn to foreigners to weave, and told me they would not return it unless I paid a fine.

I then went to the lord mayors, asking them about this ordinance that would let people confiscate things without warning from the public streets. They said they didn't know about any such ordinance, and that my yam should have long been returned to me. I then went to the overseer of the guild, master Adlaff Zimmermann who lives by the Eschenheimer tower, who answered me with rough, harsh words that they would in no way return my yarn to me, and that the guild did have such an ordinance.

Therefore I respectfully request, if they do have such an ordinance, I didn't know anything about it, and so ask you humbly and in God's name to tell the weavers to return my yarn. If, according to this ordinance, I am supposed to pay a fine, they should take it from the yarn, and give the rest back. I ask this of your honorable sirs, as the protectors of widows and orphans, and pray that you will help me.

Your humble servant, Agatha, the widow of the late Conrad Gaingen.

(b) Widow's petition to the Frankfurt City Council, late sixteenth century

Most honorable and merciful gentlemen, you certainly know what a heavy and hard cross God has laid on me, and in what a miserable situation I find myself, after the much too early death of my late husband, with my young children, all of them still minors and some still nursing. This unfortunate situation is well known everywhere.

Although in consideration of my misfortune most Christian hearts would have gladly let me continue in my craft and occupation, and allowed me to earn a little piece of bread, instead the overseers of the woolweavers' guild came to me as soon as my husband had died, in my sorrow and even in my own house. Against all Christian charity, they began to order changes in my workshop with very harsh and menacing words. They specifically ordered that my apprentice, whom I had raised and trained at great cost and who had just come to be of use to me in the craft, leave me and go to them, which would be to their great advantage but my greater disadvantage. They ordered this on the pretense that there was no longer a master here so he could not finish his training.

Honorable sirs, I then humbly put myself under the protection of the lord mayors here, and asked that the two journeymen and the apprentice be allowed to continue on in their work as they had before unimpeded until a final judgment was reached in the matter. Despite this, one of the weavers began to shout at my journeymen whenever he saw them, especially if there

were other people on the street. In his unhindered and unwarranted boldness, he yelled that my workshop was not honorable, and all journeymen
who worked there were thieves and rascals. After doing this for several
days, he and several others came into my workshop on a Saturday, and,
bitter and jealous, pushed my journeymen out. They began to write to all
places where this craft is practiced to tell other masters not to accept anyone who had worked in my workshop.

I now humbly beg you, my honorable and gracious sirs, protect me and
my hungry children from such abuse, shame, and insult. Help my journeymen, who were so undeservedly insulted, to regain their honor. I beg you,
as the protector of humble widows, to let my apprentice stay with me, as
apprentices are allowed to stay in the workshops of widows throughout the
entire Holy Roman Empire, as long as there are journeymen, whether or
not there is a master present. Protect me from any further insults of the
wool-weavers' guild, which does nothing to increase the honor of our city,
which you, honorable sirs, are charged to uphold. I plead with you to grant
me my request, and allow me to continue my workshop.

WIDOWS AND WIDOWERS AS FINANCIAL ADMINISTRATORS

5 A widow makes arrangements for her daughters, England 1619

This is a will by a widow with two, probably teenaged, daughters. Eleanor Panton may
have been a Puritan, and was very well connected at the English Court (her husband
had been a courtier with a post under the Lord Chamberlain). Here, she is very
anxious that her daughters' inheritance transfer safely to them and that they be
married well, that is, to suitable gentlemen. Note that there is nothing here about the
daughters' wishes, but this does not mean that she would not have consulted them
if she were arranging the matches herself. Here, she entrusts her sister with the
custody of the girls, but cannot make her the legal guardian because of coverture,
the principle in English law under which married women could not act independently;
thus the girls' actual guardians are all male. Eleanor does not trust her own brother
or her brother-in-law, and instead rests her hopes, worriedly, on the integrity of male
friends who are the girls' guardians. As an extra precaution, Eleanor hoped that two
of her most influential contacts, a nobleman and a top-ranked lawyer, will serve as
overseers of the will and keep the guardian friends from cheating her daughters.
Guardians by custom got some benefits, at least in social connections, from arranging matches for their charges and she's fearful that her friends will abuse their
privileges. This will is not very different from that of a widower in the same circumstances: dying parents were keenly aware that children would be, as Sir Walter
Raleigh famously put it, 'hostages to fortune'.
(Public Record Office, Prerogative Court of Canterbury 117 Parker, November 24,
1619. Excerpted by Katharine Swett.)

[Eleanor Panton, widow of John Panton esquire, of St Clement Danes. 117 Parker. 24 November 1619.] '. . . and considering with myself that the greatest care I ought to take for things of this life, is the well disposing and government of my 2 daughters, the welfare and prosperity of whom although I know must come from God, and therefore do pray and beseech almighty God that he will bless my blessings and good wishes towards them, that he will be their father and mother, that his providence may watch over them and give them in godly life in this world even in all their ways and bring them at last to be saints in heaven, yet do I charge my executors of this my will hereafter named as they will answer me at the dreadful day of judgment, that they and every one of them do faithfully justly and truly perform the trust I do repose in them, that they do seek and labor for their good and preferment without expecting any gain or profit unto themselves any wise. And in hope thereof and of the good opinion I have of their honesties and love, [I appoint] John Williams doctor of divinity now Dean of Salisbury, Thomas Cook gentleman my old and true friend, and John Warburton gentleman, servant to Mr. Justice Warburton my cousin, all 3 executors of my will jointly. . . . They also to have the guardianship of my daughters Martha and Eleanor. My executors are to sue and labor to the King or Prince to whom they shall fall wards for their [the daughters'] wardship and tuition. But my sister Alice Bath is to have their [the daughters'] bringing up and breeding, she to have all reasonable funds, and I charge her to bring them up according to their degree and calling, and in fear of God and in all good nurture. Also executors are not to marry them to base or unworthy husbands for gain, nor contract for any reward or profit whatsoever from their matches. Executors are to buy 2 diamond rings of 100 pounds value each, and give 1 to my most honorable Lord the earl of Arundell, and the other to his Countess, humbly asking them to accept them [the rings] as a sign of my love and gratitude for their favors, or they [the Arundells] can choose to just have 100 pounds each. My sister Alice 100 pounds and a bed and bedstead with all bedding with it also the hangings and furniture which is in my chamber where I lie in my house at Westminster. All else to my 2 daughters. . . .

6 A remarrying widow, France 1549

Many women (and presumably men) were widowed more than once. This particular contract involves a widow, Geneviève Perquillon, who is planning to remarry, and whose mother has already survived two husbands. It is a marriage contract in which both parties act on their own behalf, and Perquillon brings a dowry in cash.
(Paris, Archives Nationales, Minutier central, Étude XI/29, October 4, 1549. Translated by Carol Loats.)

Were present in person Michel Mercier master fisher . . . living in Paris, rue de la Buscherie, for himself in his own name on the one hand, and Geneviefve Perquillon, widow of the late Olymier Rondeau, hosier, living at Paris, rue de la Buscherie, for herself in her own name, on the other part. These parties, in the presence of Michelle Mallart, widow of the late Loys de Puyrguyon, and previously widow of the late Jehan Perquillon, mother of the said Geneviefve, each willingly will affirm and here affirm that they have made, will make, and now make, together and each with the other, the arrangements of marriage, gifts, dower, promises, and customs which follow.

That is to say that they have promised and promise to take each other according to the name and law of marriage if God and our Holy Mother Church allow, as soon as they really are able and it is decided among them and their kin and friends; with the reputations, possessions, rights, and material interests that they have on one part or the other, that they promise, each in his own right, to put into their joint estate.

And further on behalf of the said marriage the said Perguillon has given and paid to the said LeMercier, who acknowledges having received it, the sum of 10 *écus d'or soleil*, given and receipted, etc.

And therefore and in consideration of the things said above, the said LeMercier has given and gives to the said Perguillon, his future spouse, the sum of 22 *livres* 10 *sous tournois* as preset dower, to be paid once, for her to have and take from all the possessions of the said LeMercier and [the possessions] of his heirs, etc., as soon as dower takes place, without restraint.

And also, Geneviefve will have and will take by first right the best gown which she has in use at the time of the end of the marriage without it being placed into the inventory nor divided up, etc.

Thus etc., promising, obligating, each in his own right, the one and the other renouncing, etc.. Done and passed in duplicate the year 1549, Friday, the fourth day of October.

7 Stipulations on a widower's raising his daughter, Germany 1569

Inventories taken at the time of death usually simply listed the property and goods that the deceased had owned, along with debts and financial obligations, but sometimes they included stipulations about the raising of children. Children who had lost one parent, as well as those who had lost both, were given guardians in many parts of Europe, who could intervene for the interests of the child even if the surviving parent was the father. Thus widowers' as well as widows' power over their own children was often limited.

(Nuremberg, Stadtarchiv, Inventarbuecher, Nr. 17, f. 112. Translated by Merry Wiesner-Hanks.)

Hans Maier must raise his little daughter, and provide her with the necessary food and clothing, until she has reached her twelfth year and reaches maturity. If however, Hans Maier does not support his child as she deserves, and because of her, truthful, basic grievances arise, the guardians shall have the power to take away the child (when it has not been reasonably cared for) from the father and send her elsewhere where she can be cared for according to her needs. This is with the stipulation that the father still provides the money for board, room, and upbringing, as he himself has offered and agreed to do.

8 Administering a son's will, Italy 1581

Bianca Zuchini lost virtually everything in the year of the plague, 1575–1576: her house burned down, and four of her children died. One of these, Ferigo, was old enough to make a will. Six years later, Bianca petitioned the Appeals Court to get the will read so that she could carry out her son's last wishes. She may also have hoped to receive some money or property herself.

(Archivio di Stato di Venezia, Pien Collegio, Suppliche di Dentro, filza 7, no. 35, June 1581. Translated by Monica Chojnacka.)

In the year of the contagion there was a fire in my house that caused extreme damage and ruin, as the city already knows, with the loss of my poor patrimony and the death of four of my children, among whom there died of the contagion my son Ferigo, who [before dying] called for witnesses and ordered his testament, which fell into the hands of Mr. Marco Franceschini, who is the notary of the Avogaria [State Attorneys General], from whom I have thus far not had information about it, and by grace I have learned that I may petition Your Serenity according to the laws, to open [the will], even though more than a year has passed, since Your Illustrious Lords had promised me at other times, and I, poor Bianca, widow of Mr. Evangelista Zuchini, wish to carry out what my above-named son ordered, and I recommend my soul to God's good grace, always praying to God that He keep the state [the Republic of Venice] in peace and tranquility.

WIDOWHOOD, AGE, AND POWER

9 A widow as mayor, Russia fifteenth century

Although women did not hold public office in Russia until the eighteenth century, they could openly wield power in their capacity as wives, mothers, and sisters of officeholders. The line between the public office and the private household of the

262

ruler was indistinct, and women of the elite could take advantage of their role in managing property to exercise great influence in governmental affairs. Thus women created political allies and political enemies for themselves. The former praised ruling women for their wisdom; the later condemned them for overstepping their place. In keeping with the religiously based culture of the day, these attitudes were expressed in Christian metaphors.

Among the most ambiguous examples of ruling women was Marfa Boretskaia, the 'mayoress' of Novgorod in the third quarter of the fifteenth century. She was the widow of a former mayor, Isak Boretskii, and the mother of a current one. It cannot be determined whether she herself held office officially, but she certainly spoke publicly at the Novgordian *veche*, or city assembly. Marfa was also the city's wealthiest citizen, and the largest landowner, holding vast tracts in Novgorod's extensive empire which stretched north to the White Sea and East across the Ural Mountains.

Novgorod was the primary commercial city of medieval Russia, standing at the head of its trade routes to Western Europe. Although part of the Russian state, it proudly proclaimed its autonomy. The archbishop of the city, the titular head of state, and a council of mayors, chosen from among the hereditary leading families, controlled the city. To supplement the small domestic militia, Novgorod contracted with Russian princes from other cities to provide military service, 'showing them the road' out of town when they failed to please. But by the mid fifteenth century, the growing centralization of the Russian state around the city of Moscow limited available choices of prince to those in Muscovite service. In a daring and internally divisive move, the Novgorodian leadership, led by the Boretskii family, extended an invitation instead to a prince from Poland-Lithuania, a Roman Catholic power and Russia's primary enemy. The Lithuanians failed to provide the promised military support and after a disastrous military loss, Novgorod surrendered. The city lost its autonomy; its assembly was closed down and its leading citizens were exiled or executed. Marfa herself was arrested and sent to Moscow as a prisoner in 1478. This account of Marfa's exploits is taken from a Russian chronicle composed in the late fifteenth century. Written under the aegis of the Muscovite victors, it magnifies the claims to the authority of the Grand Prince of Moscow and characterizes Marfa in an extremely hostile manner.

(Excerpted from the Sofia I Chronicle, *Polnoe sobranie russkikh letopisei*, vol. 39 (Moscow: Nauka, 1994), pp. 150–156. Translated by Eve Levin.)

. . . . Princes are beloved of God, and for that reason he is given the kingdom from God and power from the Highest, for he is the servant of God, and he loves justice and truth. Those Novgorodian men and the entire Novgorodian land were the patrimony of the sovereign Grand Prince Ivan Vasilevich of all Russia, but they forgot their great history . . .

. . . [t]he ancient Israelites, who did not obey the spoken words of the Lord and do them, for this reason were deprived of their promised land and were scattered among many lands So too these Novgorodian people revealed their pride in themselves . . . betraying their sovereign grand prince, and sought for themselves a Latin ruler as sovereign . . . ['Latin' referred generically to Roman Catholics. In fact, the terms of the agreement between Novgorod and Poland-Lithuania explicitly confirmed Novgorod's adherence to the Russian Orthodox faith, and required that the Lithuanian representative be Orthodox.] By that evil temptation many people were entangled in the toils of that hunter and proud murderer of human souls, the many-headed beast, the evil enemy, the Devil, and were sacrificed to evil by wicked advice, as though in a living hell. That tempter the Devil entered among them in the maleficent woman Marfa Isakova Boretskaia. That accursed woman wove wicked speech with the Lithuanian Prince Michael, and according to his promise, she wanted to marry a noble of the Lithuanian king. [There is no evidence that Marfa did, in fact, contemplate marriage to a Lithuanian, or to anybody else. She was quite elderly in 1471, the grandmother of adult grandchildren.] She thought to bring him to her in Great Novgorod, and to rule with him in the king's name the entire Novgorodian land. With this accursed idea, she began to tempt all the Orthodox people of Great Novgorod, wanting to lead them away from the grand prince, and bring them to the king. For that reason, she took on [the facade of] piety, like that ancient liar Jezebel. She killed many who prophesied in the name of the Lord, and was herself hung from the city walls and was trampled by horses, and so ended her wicked life, and dogs consumed her. So too [Marfa] was like another woman, the devilish Herodias, the wife of King Philip, whose lawlessness was revealed by John the Baptist. For that reason, she seduced the king, and convinced him, with her daughter's dancing, to cut off the head of the prophet . . . So too the Empress Eudoxia, who showed her evil, driving the patriarch of Constantinople, the great light to the world John Chrysostom, from his throne and imprisoned him in Armenia . . . So too the wicked Delilah tempted her husband Samson the brave . . . with tenderness and questioned him and learned his secret, cut his hair and gave him over to the barbarians like a plucked bird.

And this wicked Marfa, like them, wanted to tempt all the people, and divert them from the right path and turn them over to the Latin way. For the eyes of her soul were tempted and blinded by the Latin darkness, for the sake of the wicked Devil with her and the devices and ideas of the evil Lithuanian prince. With her in these ideas and plans, which came from Satan himself, the proud Devil, was the monk Pumin, the steward of the former archbishop, who was instigated by evil. That wicked man plotted in secret with her, and helped her in all evil, and wanted to elevate himself. But he did not receive his desire or his lot, for the Lord God did not permit it, and so he was not accepted by the Orthodox people for the highest rank. [The author is alleging that Pumin wished to become archbishop of

Novgorod. In Novgorodian tradition, the archbishop was not appointed by the metropolitan of Moscow, the head of the Russian Orthodox Church, but was instead chosen locally. Ecclesiastical and secular notables would identify three candidates, and then the final selection was made by lot.]. And this Pumin set his hopes on the great amount of gold that wicked woman Marfa gave him, and instructed her to give much to the people so that they would help them to their goal. And for that reason, that wicked, evil viper did not fear God and was not ashamed before human beings, and so introduced disorder and destruction to the entire Novgorodian land, causing the downfall of many souls.

About such mindless women the great John Chrysostom wrote, saying: 'There is nothing so evil on the earth as an evil and pagan woman. There is no beast so dissipated as a perfidious woman, proud and self-important.' On this topic, wise Solomon recounts, saying, 'There is no evil akin to feminine evil. It is better to live in the desert with a lion or a serpent than with an evil woman.' And this wicked woman not only destroyed herself and her own soul, but also brought her children with her into destruction, which became theirs also. For she brought temptation to the unseeing who embraced her, and benighted all who listened to her. And for that reason, many people at the assembly joined with her, and many listened to her tempting and God-rejecting words, not knowing that they were their downfall. Many of the people were confused by their temptation. But the reverend monastic priest Feofil, named to the archbishopric of his fathers, took good care of them, and taught them to avoid these evil ideas, and to desist from such an evil direction . . .

But they were mindless and hard-hearted, and they did not listen to scripture, but remained as described before, like a deaf asp, having stopped up their ears, so they could not hear the voices calling out to them. And so the men of Novgorod did not pay attention to the scripture that was told to them, nor to the demands of the episcopal blessing, and they did not desist from their wicked doings. For they harbored in themselves evil advice, and they could not stop . . .

[The account then describes Grand Prince Ivan III's invasion of Novgorodian territory and the defeat of the Novgorodian army.]

Then the men of Novgorod were brought from the battlefield to the grand prince, he, pious and wise, revealed how with wickedness in all matters and their treason, how they aposticized from the pious light and allied with the Latins, and being the patrimony of the grand prince, they gave themselves over to the Latin sovereign king – how on the copies of their treaty they listed the cities and villages of the grand principality of Moscow, the lands and waters, and all the tax income of Novgorod, which were written over to the king in their treaty with him. When the grand prince exposed all this, how the Novgorodians profited from wickedness, he ordered executed by sword the leading mayors and citizens, including that tempting woman Marfa's eldest son Dmitrii, the mayor of Novgorod, who was condemned . . .

10 Three letters from queen mothers, Ottoman Empire seventeenth century

From the time of the Ottoman's emergence as a state in the early fourteenth century, the mothers of Ottoman sultans and Ottoman princes and princesses had always played an important political role. But their political and cultural influence was particularly strong from the mid sixteenth century through the mid seventeenth century, a period popularly known as the 'sultanate of women'. During this period, the mother of the reigning sultan – the valide sultan, or queen-mother, frequently acted as regent for an underage ruler or even as a kind of de facto co-head of state. The following letters are among the many dispatches from the queen mother to the empire's grand vezir, the chief minister who was in charge of the day-to-day administration of imperial affairs. They were written by two prominent seventeenth-century queen mothers, Kösem and Turhan. The letters reveal the queen mother's dual responsibility in attending to affairs of state and in managing the affairs and relations of the dynastic family.
(Letters kept in the Topkapi Palace archives. Translated by Leslie Peirce.)

(a) This letter was written by Kösem some time between 1625 and 1627. Kösem was a brilliant politician who survived the ups and downs of the reigns of five sultans, the last two of whom were her sons. She wrote this letter five or six years into the reign of Kösem's eldest son Murat (IV), who is remembered for putting the empire back on an aggressive military footing after a period of internal and external troubles. Here we can see the fourteen- or fifteen-year-old Murat shaking off his mother's regency and Kösem's troubled resignation to this turn of affairs as she acknowledges that the empire will now be run without her tutelage. Two troublesome matters alluded to in the letter are the security of Yemen, which would break free of Ottoman control in 1636, and the chronic budgetary problem of meeting salary payments, especially to the Janissaries, the frequently unruly Ottoman infantry.

Greeting and prayers to his excellency the Pasha. And now, how are you and how are your affairs? Are you fine? May you enjoy good health and well-being. Should you ask after us, thanks to God (may his name be exalted) at present we are devoting body and soul and occupying ourselves night and day with the tranquility of Muhammad's community. And now it is declared: Letters have come from Egypt – apparently to you too – which describe the situation there. Something absolutely must be done about Yemen – it's the gate to Mecca. You must do whatever you can. You and my son must talk this over. I tell you, my mind is completely distraught over [the Yemen situation]. . . . You're going to have a lot of trouble with this, but service to Muhammad's community earns God's mercy. How are you getting along with salary payments? Is there much left? With the grace of God, may you take care of that obligation and then you can confer together over the Yemen situation.

My son leaves in the morning and comes back at night. I never see him. He won't stay out of the cold, he's going to get sick again. I tell you, this grieving over the child is destroying me. Talk to him, when you get a chance. He must take care of himself. What can I do? He won't listen. He's just gotten out of a sickbed and now he's walking around in the cold. All this has destroyed my peace of mind. All I wish is for him to stay alive. At least try to do something about Yemen. May God help us with this situation we are in. . . . You two know what's best.

(b) In this short letter, the first part of which appears to be an on-going conversation, Kösem arranges a political marriage between one of her daughters, Aisha, and the current grand vezir, Hafiz Ahmed Pasha. Such alliances between the dynasty and its leading officials were quite common. Since the husbands of princesses were usually considerably older than their wives and moreover subject to death in battle and occasionally execution, princesses often found themselves widowed and might remarry several times. Kösem was lucky to have several daughters and granddaughters whose marriages she was able to exploit to her advantage.

Greeting and prayers to his excellency the Pasha. I am informed of everything you said in your letter. People simply aren't aware of all the things that are going to get said over a handful of money. What's to be done? Perhaps [something can be done] after the holiday, God willing.

As for you, whenever you're ready let me know, and I'll act accordingly. We'll take care of you right away. The princess is ready. I'll do just the same as I did when I sent out my Fatma Sultan. Just write us when you want, and I'll arrange things accordingly. May God bless [the marriage].

(c) This letter dates from the early years of the regency of Turhan, who became valide sultan 1648, when the disastrous reign of Kösem's second sultan son, Ibrahim, ended in his death, the succession of his and Turhan's son Mehmed, and the transformation of Turhan into queen mother. Quite young (perhaps twenty-five years old), Turhan was thrust into the midst of state affairs since Mehmed was only six years old. In the following letter she is concerned with one of the most pressing problems of her regency: the long war with Venice over Crete and the readiness of the Ottoman navy. Turhan's many letters reveal a dynamic if at times uneasy relationship with her grand vezirs. In this early letter, the queen mother's ceaseless admonishing of the grand vezir was no doubt an attempt to impress him with her authority.

After greetings to the pasha it is declared: 'Why aren't you devoting our attention to the royal navy? In your audiences with us you deceive us by saying everything is taken care of, we are making sure that everything is perfectly in order.' I send someone to inspect – there is nothing in sight. You say 'we need one thousand two hundred oarsmen'. . . . I have checked, and we are more than three thousand oarsmen short. It is essential that we have them! We'll pay however many come, however many make it in time. You speak of [naval] provisions . . . if you had supplied funds, would there be such shortages? Everything should have been ready by now. You chatter idly in our presence, then you leave. What is the meaning of this? I swear by God, don't say you weren't aware of the problem. If you don't have the fleet ready to sail in ten or fifteen days, completely outfitted, you will suffer the consequences. Is this the way to guard the faith and the empire? Is this the way to serve Muhammad's community? If you don't perform your duties properly, may the sultan's bread be denied you and may all the sins of Muhammad's community hang on your plague-ridden neck! We entrusted all affairs to you on the grounds that you were a long-time, loyal official. How wonderful it would be if you brought honor upon yourself by serving well. Now, your duty is to keep us from chiding you. Why do you go and sit in the dockyard in vain, accomplishing nothing? May you take utmost care as we have instructed and be attentive, otherwise you will suffer the consequences. Your duty is to instruct the chief admiral by saying 'inform me of what you need and I'll supply it', and giving him the funds. Then, once you have acquitted your duty, any problems will be his responsibility.

11 Two letters from the dowager queen, Denmark
seventeenth century

Because of her great wealth, Dowager Queen Sophie (1557–1631) was able to exercise considerable influence on both Danish domestic affairs and the international politics of Northern Europe during the reign of her son, Christian IV (reigned 1596–1648). From the death of her husband, Frederik II, in 1588 until her death forty-three years later, she managed Nykøbing Fief, which she had received as dower lands in her marriage contract. During this period she was active in the political life of Denmark.

The first letter (a) is a request she made of her son, Christian IV, to change a levied tax for the peasants within her fief. By making this request she entered into the domain of the King and the influential Council of the Realm comprised of Danish noblemen.

The second source (b), is a letter from Christian IV to his mother in 1631. It reveals Sophie's role in international politics. During the Thirty Years' War (1618–1648), she lent money to several German Protestant princes as well as substantial sums to her son. Among her creditors was her grandson Frederick Ulrich, Duke of Brunswick-Wolfenbüttel (1591–1634), who owed her 300,000 thalers – a considerable sum. The commander of the Imperial Danish Army, Count Johan Tilly (1559–

1632), also made large claims against Duke Frederick Ulrich, and as a result Sophie intended to enter into direct negotiations with Tilly in the spring of 1631. Christian IV advised her to postpone the negotiations to the fall.

(Letter (a): preserved in Queen Sophie's letter book, which is kept in the Danish National Archives, Copenhagen. The letter book has been published as *Dronning Sophies Kopibøger* 1588–1617, ed. by S. Thomsen (Copenhagen, 1937). The second letter (b) is preserved in the University Library of Rostock. It has been previously published in *Kong Christian den Fjerdes egenhœnige Breve, vol. II, 1626–1631*, ed. by C.F. Bricka and J.A. Fridericia (Copenhagen, 1889–1891, reprint edition 1969). Translated by Grethe Jacobsen and Pernille Arenfeldt.)

(a) Nykoebing, 29 November, 1610.
Missive to the King of Denmark. The Dowager Queen informs him that the subjects in her dower lands on Falster have asked her to intercede with the king so that the tax in kind levied by him may be assessed in money for their part because it will, at present, be very difficult for them to render the required victuals in kind. Because it is laudable to stand by that which the King once and for all has commanded and prescribed, she only reluctantly requests changes, nonetheless she must adduce the following[:] a large number of cattle and all kinds of victuals are bought from her subjects not only for her own household, which she for years has maintained in Nykoebing fief, but also for her servants, for almost all of whom she provides [a] subsistence allowance. In addition, crops on Falster rarely succeed well enough for the subject to afford to pay in kind the manorial rent levied against them, but they most often have to pay it in money, for which they have to sell their cattle. Considering the aforementioned, the Dowager Queen must confess that it will be very difficult to render those victuals in kind particularly at this time of the year as they have already, before this food tax was levied, sold and disposed of everything which could be sold and done without. She kindly and motherly entreats the King to show mercy to her subject in Nykoebing fief, if it does not cause him inconvenience, and to assess the levied food tax in money for their part – as high as he wishes. In return, she will diligently ensure that this money will be collected from the peasants as soon as possible and delivered to the King's treasury at the determined time.

(b) Kindly, dear much beloved Mother, I have received the communication from my personal physician regarding the treaties the Our Dear [=you] intends to properly negotiate with Tilly concerning the Brunswickian [see introduction above] money, and upon [receiving] this, I willingly and with the respect of a son do not wish to hide that I owe my service to Our Dear in all possible ways. However, at this given time it does not seem advisable to me to enter into any treaties with the aforementioned Tilly before the coming summer has passed. If Our Dear could possibly detain [him] with good apologies towards

[the Feast of] St. Michael or St. Martin, then please do so, as it pleases you.
Hereby you are commended to loving God and I remain throughout my life
  Our Dear's obedient son
  Christian
At Frederiksborg [Castle] 25 March Anno 1631
By hand to my dear much beloved Mother.

12 Old age and good health, Spain sixteenth century

Despite the fact that the average life expectancy was no more than 40 years during the centuries covered in this book, this statistic can be deceiving. Those men and women who survived into adulthood had an excellent chance of living to ripe old ages. When King Phillip II of Spain asked every jurisdiction in his kingdom to report on the healthfulness of its site, the small village of Nombela in Spain boasted that its site was so healthy that its elderly lived long and active lives.

(*Relaciones histórico-geográfico-estadísticas de los pueblos de España hecho por iniciativa de Felipe II: Provincia de Madrid; Reino de Toledo; Ciudad Real*, eds. Carmelo Viñas y Mey and Ramón Paz (Madrid: CSIC, 1949–71), pp. 149–50. Translated and permission to reprint granted by David Vassberg, provided by Allyson Poska.)

This is a healthful location, because it has no [endemic] contagious diseases, and few ordinary illnesses. The residents by today's standards live long and healthy lives, and they get along very well despite their age, especially those over seventy years old. There are folks who walk eight or nine leagues behind a pair of animals. And if they live in the village they don't leave it. They can walk straight and perfectly well without a cane if they wish. And they have excellent memories undiminished by their age, and this can be seen every day. At present [in the village] there are elderly people of eighty and ninety whose faculties and memory are so good that they serve throughout the area as reliable eyewitnesses of past events and lineages. And there have been old people of a hundred and ten and a hundred and twelve so agile and with such good memories that they seemed no older than fifty. And [this village] is so healthful for the elderly that one oldster of over ninety was on his way to mass and fell into an open grave that had been dug for a burial, and he broke a leg. But he healed so completely that afterwards for many years he was as good as ever, and this same man later married a maiden of over sixty, and lived as a married man for another five or six years. It is reported that there was another fellow who reached a hundred and twelve, and was so healthy and agile and mentally alert that we used to go to him as an archive of information about the past. And it transpired that one Sunday while he was apparently healthy except for his age, when the mass was over, he stood up in the middle of the village church and removed his hat, and in the presence of the entire village he said, 'Gentlemen, for the love of God forgive me if I have offended you, because God forgives me and forgives you all.' Then he went home, and a few days later he died as a good Christian. And he had a brother who reached one hundred and ten. We recount this to demonstrate how healthy our old people are.

13 Old widow and young man, Germany sixteenth century

One of the most common stereotypes about older women, particularly widows, was that they were sexually voracious. This notion contributed to the pattern of witch

persecutions in much of Europe, in which older women were thought to seek sexual comfort as well as material gain and power from their associations with the devil. This idea was also reflected in poems, stories, and illustrations of older widows who married young men. This is a woodcut by the German artist Wolfgang Strauch; a corresponding woodcut of an old widower and a young bride – another common stereotype – has been lost.

(From Walter L. Strauss, *The German Single-leaf Woodcut* (New York: Abaris Books, 1975). Reproduced by permission.)

14 A widow reflects on her life, Serbia fifteenth century

Some widows chose to take vows as nuns in their later years. Although monastic life was characterized as a rejection of the secular world, these mature nuns often saw the religious life as an opportunity to continue their advocacy of their families, calling upon God to protect their families' interests. This original prayer by the nun Jevgenija reflects the emotions of the author. Jevgenija took vows late in life, after a tumultuous career. Born Milica Hrbeljanovic c. 1353, she was the daughter of the Serbian prince Vratko. Her husband, another Serbian prince Lazar, led the army defeated by the Ottoman Turks at the momentous battle of Kosovo in 1389. That battle marked the end of the medieval Serbian state. Lazar was executed, and Milica was left to rule as regent for her son under Ottoman authority. As part of making accommodation with the country's new suzerain, Milica sent her daughter Mara to become a wife of the Ottoman sultan Bayazid. When her son attained age of majority, Milica entered a convent, where she promoted the growing cult of her husband as a martyr to the Orthodox faith.

(Translated version published in *An Anthology of Medieval Serbian Literature*, ed. Mateja Matejic and Dragan Milivojevic (Columbus: Slavica, 1978), pp. 110–112. Excerpted by Eve Levin. Reprinted by permission.)

Who is this one?
Whisper into my ears!
Is this the one for whom I used to long,
my jewel, the gatherer of my dispersed children?
Is this the one whom enemies wanted to destroy out of envy
the light of my sight whom they wanted to incarcerate
and keep in the dark dungeon,
but could not?
Is this the bridegroom of my widowhood?

Come, O bridegroom,
Come and repay those who do evil to me
according to their deeds,
for they failed to understand
that you would come to my aid.
Take up arms and rise and do not tarry,

plunge into their hearts the sharp arrows
which they, the evil ones,
have sharpened against me.
I cannot stand their mockery.
Oh, with how many odious offences they plagued me.
Come, avenge me with your blood.
Come, O my helper, at the time of my failing.
Gather my dispersed children
who have been taken from me
by the envy of my enemies.
Gather them within my fence;
and guard my children
so that the wolf does not feed himself upon my flock
nor disperse them with his envy,
as he had done before when you were not with them.
Let your eyes not sleep,
let your feet not become weak,
guard my flock which I entrust to you.
Chase the barbarian infidels away from them.
Do not cease to fight them,
[defending] me and my flock.

Rejoice, O Lazar,
my never-sleeping eye.
And, to repeat what was already said at the beginning:
Lazar is the one who by his radiance
excels the brightness of the stars;
Lazar is the victim of invaders,
the confessor of the Trinity,
the liberator of the captives;
Lazar is the strong pillar of the Church,
a doctor to the sick, raiment to the naked;
Lazar is the mighty leader
and saviour of the monks,
and a firm [adversary] of demons
Rejoice, O Lazar,
I hymn you in the manner of apostles
and I repeat: Rejoice,
rejoice, O lily which sprang from a thorn,
O invincible weapon of soldiers;
rejoice, O teacher of hermits;

rejoice, O Lazar,
the rudder and the calm haven of seafarers.
Rejoice, O avenger of the wronged
and the reprimander of liars.
Rejoice, O comforter of mourners
and defender of the poor and raiment of the naked.
Rejoice, O beauty of the strong ones
and the protector of widows.
Blessed are you, indeed, Lazar;
bless me, the one who blesses you.
There is no praise of which you would not be worthy,
but my wit is getting tired . . .

HARDSHIP

15 A widow reflects on her misfortune, Denmark 1660

In 1660, Johanne Kaas wrote her autobiography, which gives insight into how fragile a widowed woman's status was in early modern Denmark. Although she was born into a noble family and married well, Johanne Kaas' widowhood was characterized by great hardship. It should be noted, that the difficult circumstances she describes most likely are overstated to emphasize her strong religious conviction. Nevertheless, it is evident that because she was without the protection of her husband and apparently unable to establish an alternative socio-economic network, her security and status were easily and almost entirely lost when unfortunate events, such as fire and raids by foreign troops, occurred.

(The autobiography has been published in *Personalhistorisk Tidsskrift*, ser. 5., vol. 1, Copenhagen and Christiania, 1904. Translated by Grethe Jacobsen and Pernille Arenfeldt.)

Notes by Johanne Kaas [wife of] Lave Urne.

Anno 1660 January 18th, did I, Johanne Kaas [wife of] the late, blessed Lage Urne, write the following to inform my children after my death and departure.

I, Johanne Kaas, was born on by fathers' estate here in Vendsyssel in the year 1602[,] on March 12th, which was a Tuesday[.] My dear, late, blessed parents let me to the [: my] holy baptism in the presence of many noble people as well as many other honest and good people.

[Her account of her upbringing which, after the death of her mother in 1660, was spent living with various relatives.] Meanwhile it happened by God's wise Providence that the honest and noble man Lage Urne of Bontofte asked for my hand, and then I was by God's Providence betrothed to him; later our wedding was held at Giollebo in Scania [in the] year 1630. After-

274

wards we lived together in a Christian and loving marriage for two years and a few weeks during which time our marriage was blessed with two children, a son and a daughter. The son Johan Urne, [and] the daughter Thalle Urne [wife of] Hans Wolff Mollhemes.

Since [the death of my husband] I have sat as a poor sorrowful widow and behaved myself in my widowhood after my blessed husband's death and departure [in a manner that] I will not be ashamed of in the face of God and the world. God has, according to his godly will and as he knows best what serves us in this miserable life, often sent me grief and sickness and sometimes loss of worldly possessions by damaging fire, which I have suffered by God's permission as well as by the unexpected incursion of enemies [during] which [they] stole [part of my] belongings. God has, though, at all times helped me until this day, so that I always have had a proper piece of bread, and in all my sorrows and hardships I found consolation in God and his blessed word and [I] made myself see that the hardship and sufferings of this brief life do not equal the glory that the son of God, my Saviour and salvation, has prepared for me and all true Christians in the happiness and bliss of the Kingdom of Heaven.

16 Widower's petition for assistance in supporting his elderly father-in-law, England 1706

Most of the sources about individuals whose spouses had died concern widows, for men were only rarely identified as widowers. Widowers faced many of the same problems that widows did, however, and they remarried at a faster rate than did widows. The following is a court case involving two parishes in England, Myddle and Preston Gubballs, about who was responsible to care for an elderly blind man, Andrew Weston. (The poor at this time in England were generally expected to seek assistance in their parish of residence if they had no family to support them.) Weston had earlier made a contract with his then son-in-law, Thomas Williams, arranging to be cared for, but Williams had been widowed himself and had recently remarried. The lawyer for the parish of Myddle argues that Williams has the obligation by law to care for his father-in-law, while the lawyer for Williams argues that he is too poor.

(Richard Gouge, *Antiquities and Memoirs of the Parish of Myddle, County of Salop* (London, 1875), p. 167. Spelling and orthography modernized.)

This was concerning Andrew Weston, who had lived some while in Marton, in a tenement [house] of above £10 per annum, under Mr. Thomas Harwood, who married the widow of Richard Atcherley. This Weston being aged, and his wife dead, went to Merrington to Thomas Williams, who had married his daughter and gave him all his goods and cattle on condition he would maintain him during his life. Not long after Thomas Williams's wife died, and Weston became blind, and altogether helpless. Upon this Thomas Williams prevailed with the Parish officers of Preston Gubballs [another parish near Myddle] to procure an order, and to send his father-in-law, Weston, into the Parish of Myddle, being the place of his last settlement, which was done accordingly. . . . We of the parish of Myddle . . . fetched a witness from Wrexham to prove the bargain between Andrew Weston and his son-in-law Williams; but Mr. Berkely [lawyer for Myddle] insisted upon the Statute of the 43rd of the Queen, cap. 2, whereby it is enacted that the grandfathers, grandmothers, fathers, mothers and children of any poor, lame, blind, &c., being of sufficient ability, shall make such allowance for the maintenance of such poor, &c., as the Justices at their Quarter Sessions shall allow. Here says Mr. Berkely, the grandfather-in-law, the grandmother-in-law, the father-in-law, the mother-in-law, the son-in-law, the daughter-in-law, though they be not named in the Statute yet by the equity of the Statute they are obliged, and so it had been resolved in that Court and in several other cases which he showed. Mr. Atkis [lawyer for Williams] did not gainesay [deny] any of this, but he insisted upon these words in the Statute, *being of sufficient ability*, and that Thomas Williams was a poor man and not able to do it. To which Mr. Berkley answered that Thomas Williams did hold a tenement of about £16 or £18 per annum, and had stock upon it . . . that he had lands in fee simple of about £8 to £10 per annum . . . that he had lately married a second wife with £100 portion [dowry] . . . Upon this the Court resolved that Weston's settlement was in Myddle parish, and that Thomas Williams ought to maintain him . . . This was accepted and he [Williams] took the blind man home with him.

17 Elderly man's petition for support, England 1648

Elderly people with no relatives to support them could obtain public assistance in some parts of Europe by the seventeenth century. The following is a petition presented to the Quarter Sessions of Walsingham, a regional court held four times a year, in the county of Norfolk in England. The justices ordered the petitioner's parish to support him with 12d. a week.
(Norfolk Record Office, C/S3/38. Cited in Tim Wales, 'Poverty, poor relief and the life-cycle', in Richard M. Smith, ed., *Land, Kinship and Life-Cycle* (Cambridge: Cambridge University Press, 1984), p. 388. Reprinted by permission. Spelling and orthography modernized.)

The said poor petitioner [Edward Messenger of Ashwicken] being aged fourscore [80] years, almost blind, and very lame of his ankles, by which infirmities he is made unable by labor to sustain himself any longer or to travel abroad [that is, out of his house] to gather relief from charitable people, and is allowed but six pence by the week [as poor relief] from the town wherein he inhabits, which in these hard times of dearth and scarcity will not buy any considerable or competent maintenance for his relief; also the house wherein he dwells for lack of repair (which he is utterly unable to bestow upon it) will not shelter and defend him from wind and rain . . . so that he perceives such distress coming upon him in his decrepit old age that he is likely to perish by hunger and cold, and sees no means left to him whereby to escape that imminent misery which otherwise will inevitably come upon him, but only by making known this his pitiful distressed condition to your Worships the Justices at this present Session, hoping that you will not turn away your eyes and ears from the cry of the poor, but rather cause them to whom it belongs to allow some more competent relief and provision for supply of these his great wants made known unto you.

18 Two ordinances about widows and property, Portugal early sixteenth century

The two ordinances featured here, in effect during the reign of King D. Manuel I (1495–1521), reveal some of the legal contradictions Portuguese widows faced. On the one hand, the law stipulated that family property belonged equally to the wife and husband, and that, upon his death, the widow was the head of the household and administered all assets. On the other hand, the law made allowances for authorities to move in and take control of an estate if the widow was shown to be squandering her money to the detriment of her dependants. No such fears have been found concerning widowed men.

(*Ordenações do Senhor Rey D. Manuel, Vol. IV*, (Coimbra: Na Real Impresna da Universidade, 1797), pp. 23–24 (a), pp. 32–33 (b). Translated by Darlene Abreu-Ferreira.)

Titulo VII. All marriages that take place in our Realms, and dominions, are considered to be split in half [common property], except for when something else is arranged and agreed between the two parties, because in that case what is settled between them shall be observed.

1. If a husband dies the wife is the head and takes possession of the household, if at the time of his death she lived in the house kept and maintained as husband and wife, and from her hand the heirs of her husband shall receive a portion of all the goods that are left from the death of her husband, and thus the legataries or legatees, in as much as that if some of the heirs, or legataries, or whoever else seizes possession of anything or the said inheritance after the death of the said husband without the consent of said wife, she can claim to have been robbed, and order it returned to her, for once the marriage is consummated by coitus, the wife has half a

share in all the goods that both possess, and the husband upon the death of the wife continues to hold the old tenure, that he formerly had, it appears just reason, that with the death of the husband she be provided with some expediency regarding the said tenure, it is worth knowing, that she be the head and takes possession of the household.

Titulo X. For since some women after the death of their husbands squander what they have, in such a manner that they then become poor and destitute, and those who should inherit her goods are harmed, and because it befits us to look after, that nobody misuse that which he has, wishing to reduce the scarcity in women, and look after her successors, we command that if it is proven that they [widows] maliciously or without reason waste, or entangle their goods, the justices of those places, where the said women have their goods, take all of them, and hand them over to whomever has charge of them, until receiving our orders, and to them [widows] provide their maintenance, according to who the persons are, and the charges they have, and inform us of it, for we command that these goods be looked after in such a manner, that those who ought to inherit them shall not be prejudiced.

1. However if such a widow was the wife of a nobleman or a knight of a manor, in such a case for the honor of the husband she had, and of her lineage, we command that if the justices of those parts have of her such information, do not disclose it right away, before doing something else, for we will order what is proper without scandal to her progeny.

19 Old age and senility, Spain 1588

Early modern society was very ambivalent about the elderly. Although they were respected as the heads of the household, they were also ridiculed for their traditional ways. As the Inquisition increasingly regulated the speech of its Spanish parishioners, some outspoken elderly unwittingly made heretical statements. In this blasphemy trial from 1588, the Spanish Inquisition decided not to punish a 90-year-old farmer despite the outrageousness of his ideas.
(Relaciones de Causas, Archivo Histórico Nacional, Sección Inquisición, legajo 2042, no. 22, fol. 1 (1588). Translated by Allyson Poska.)

Alonso López de Avelleyra, a farmer from Santa María de Duancos, 90 years old . . . During a conversation with others, he had said that he had had intercourse with twelve cleric's concubines, and having been reprimanded, he said that having intercourse with a cleric's concubine gained forty days of pardon and equaled a work of mercy. Because he was such an old man and confessed, he was reprimanded and condemned to pay six thousand maravedis in court costs.

20 A widow writes to her relatives for help, Russia seventeenth century

Although some Russian widows presided over large families and controlled significant property, others, especially childless ones, found themselves destitute and
vulnerable to pressure, even if they came from privileged social orders. In such
circumstances, widows depended upon their natal families for financial and legal
assistance. In this private letter, the widow Ustinitsa Saltykova seeks help from her
brother Mikhail and her nephew Ivan. Specifically, she asks for their help in over-
turning the petition of a rival who has asked state authorities to give him her widow's
portion of her husband's service land. The 'Stenka' mentioned here is probably a
slave or indentured house servant who found a more generous employer.
(Originally published in S.I. Kotkov, ed., *Gramotki XVII–nachala XVIII veka* (Moscow:
Nauka, 1969), pp. 57–58. Translated by Eve Levin.)

To my lord brother Mikhail Pamfilovich and to my lord Ivan Mikhailovich
the widow Ustinitsa petitions.

May our almighty master Christ God keep you in his mercy, my lords,
with your bride and children, and may you be pleased to remember in your
mercy my impoverished life. I, in my grief, find myself among the living on
November 3. In the future, God willing, please, my lord brother Mikhail
Pamfilovich, meet me in Moscow. I will go to Moscow for the first days of
the fast [the letter is dated November 7, so Ustinisa is probably referring to
Advent, which would begin later in the month], and you, my lord brother
Mikhail Pamilovich, do not forsake poor me. I am hoping for God's mercy
and for your charity, and apart from your charity, I, poor one, have no
friend. Iurii Ivanovich plagues me because Stenka, the Pole's son, has run
away from me and lives with him, and he is asking for release documents
for him, and I don't know how to give these release documents for him
without your charity. He, Iurii Ivanovich, told me to approach you if I
could a little about my work. So please, my lord brother, meet me in
Moscow. He, Iurii Zamytskoi, says that there are petitioners for the service
lands in Galich, and will soon go to Moscow for this with his sister, but
from my side there is nobody.

For this, my lord, I write just a little but I petition you greatly, with my
face to the ground.

21 A widow petitions for assistance, Italy 1566

This petition to the Pien Collegio of Venice, a sort of appeals court, was typical in
many ways. The petitioner, a widow, makes reference to past injustices, and also
emphasizes her vulnerable position as a widow and a mother caring for her family.
This petition also shows the murkiness of a widow's professional status. While some

widows did carry on their husband's trades, at least for a brief period, others found themselves bereft of financial resources, as Justina claimed to be. Note that she asserts that she is not practicing her husband's trade, and also that she is not supervising another artisan. Here, Justina was implicitly acknowledging that some widows did in fact function as 'silent' partners or owners of their deceased husband's business.
(Archivio di Stato di Venezia, Pien Collegio, Suppliche, filza 2, no. 17, April, 1566. Translated by Monica Chojnacka.)

I, Justina widow of Mr. Donato, a dyer, have begged for mercy from Your Serenity [the Appeals Court, representing the Republic of Venice], that you will concede to free me from the taxes placed on my husband for his occupation as dyer and other [occupational] activities in which he was involved leading up to his death. . . . I have found myself named as the debtor for the taxes leveled by the Decima [an office charged with leveling a head tax] and for taxes for practicing the art of dyer and other occupational activities that my husband practiced leading up to his death . . . and since I, a poor widow, have not practiced either dying or other commercial activity since his death, and since I have been named responsible for these debts even now, I humbly beg you to concede out of goodness to free me from this Decima tax [dating] from the death of my husband to the present, since I have neither practiced the craft of dyeing nor any other commercial activity, nor have I commissioned such activity, but I have only looked after my poor, numerous family. And I commit myself in God to these Lord Governors and with all due reverence recommend my soul.

22 Inventory of a very poor elderly man, Germany 1544

In many cities, inventories were to be taken at all deaths to prevent conflicts among heirs or creditors. Sometimes these inventories reveal great poverty among the elderly.
(Nuremberg, Stadtarchiv, Inventarbuecher, Nr. 4, f. 41 (1544). Translated by Merry Wiesner-Hanks.)

Absolutely nothing was on hand except for his daily clothes, specifically a tattered blouse and a pair of pants, and the same type of thing from his late wife. They had both been ill so long and had used everything for their necessities. There is therefore no need to take an inventory other than this.

23 Illustrations of the very elderly, Germany 1570s

Many artists chose to depict the ages of woman and man either as a single image or a series of images. These are the final woodcuts from a series made by the German artist Tobias Stimmer, showing men and women at ninety and one hundred. The verse under the men reads: Ninety years, children tease, One hundred years God is gracious. The verse under the women reads: Ninety years, the picture of a martyr, One hundred years, filling the grave.

(Walter L. Strauss, *The German Single-Leaf Woodcut* (New York: Abaris Books, 1975). Reproduced by permission.)

ꝛꝛ. Jar der kinder ſpot. | Jar genad dir Got.

Questions for discussion

1 What are some of the fears that govern legislation about widows?
2 How do social class and wealth affect a widow's or widower's options?
3 Do you find any geographic patterns in the status or options of widows or widowers?
4 What sorts of relationships – professional, familial – might a widow have?
5 What made a widow particularly vulnerable? Why were they more vulnerable than widowers?
6 When widows or widowers found themselves vulnerable, how did they defend themselves?

LIST OF CONTRIBUTORS

Darlene Abreu-Ferreira is a professor of women's history at the University of Winnipeg, and she is currently working on a book that highlights the lives of Portuguese women in the sixteenth and seventeenth centuries. Among her publications are 'From mere survival to near success: Women's economic strategies in early modern Portugal', *Journal of Women's History* and 'Fishmongers and Shipowners: Women in maritime communities of early modern Portugal', *Sixteenth Century Journal.*

Pernille Arenfeldt is currently a doctoral student at the European University Institute, where she is preparing a dissertation on the position of the female consort at the princely Protestant courts in sixteenth-century Germany. In 1998 she received her Cand.Mag. degree from Copenhagen University. She has previously published research on the Danish court in the sixteenth century and edited a collection of letters written by Countess Louise Danner (1815–1874), the morganatic wife of the Danish King Frederik VII (1808–1863).

Monica Chojnacka received her Ph.D. in history from Stanford University in 1994 and is currently Associate Professor of History at the University of Georgia. She has written articles on women, demography, and civic institutions in early modern Venice. Her book, *Working Women of Early Modern Venice*, was published by Johns Hopkins in 2001. Her current project is a book-length study of women and crime in early modern Italy.

Grethe Jacobsen is the head of the Danish Department at the Royal Library, Copenhagen. She received her Ph.D. in History from the University of Wisconsin, Madison in 1980 and was promoted to D.Phil. at Odense University, Denmark, in 1995. She has published numerous articles in English and Danish on urban women and guilds in Denmark 1400–1600, and the major study, *Kvinder, Køn og Købstadslovgivning 1400–1600* (Det Kongelige

Bibliotek, 1995). She is currently working on gender and power in late-medieval Danish society.

Allyson M. Poska is an Associate Professor of History at Mary Washington College in Fredericksburg, Virginia. She is the author of a book on local religious practice, *Regulating the People: The Catholic Reformation in Seventeenth-Century Spain* (E.J. Brill, 1998), and the editor of a new series on women and men in early modern Europe to be published by Ashgate. She is currently completing a manuscript on early modern peasant women's culture in north-western Spain.

Eve Levin is an Associate Professor of History at Ohio State University. She is the author of *Sex and Society in the World of the Orthodox Slavs, 900–1700* (Cornell University Press, 1989) along with numerous articles on various aspects of early modern Russian society, and translator and editor of Natalia Pushkareva's *Women in Russian History* (M.E. Sharpe, 1997). She is also the Editor of *The Russian Review*, a leading academic journal.

Carol Loats is Associate Professor of History at the University of Southern Colorado. Her research interests include women as artisans, gender and work, family networks, children and childhood, widows and never-married women, and work and community in early modern France. Her articles have appeared in *French Historical Studies* and the *Proceedings, Western Society for French History*.

Leslie Peirce is Professor of History at the University of California-Berkeley. She is the author of *The Imperial Harem: Women and Sovereignty in the Ottoman Empire* (Oxford University Press, 1993), *Making Justice: Women and the Moral Economy of an Ottoman Court* (University of California Press, forthcoming), and numerous articles on aspects of gender and sexuality in the Ottoman Empire.

Katharine W. Swett received her doctorate from Stanford University in 1991, and taught early modern British, European and women's history at Ohio State University for six years. She has published articles on widowhood, male friendship, and Welsh migration to London. She is currently an independent historian in Columbus, Ohio, writing a book on gender, patriarchy, and family dynamics in the Wynn of Gwydir family of Caernarfonshire, Wales.

Merry E. Wiesner-Hanks is Professor of History and Director of the Center for Women's Studies at the University of Wisconsin-Milwaukee. She is the author or editor of twelve books, including *Women and Gender in Early Modern Europe* (Cambridge University Press, second edition, 2000), *Christianity and Sexuality in the Early Modern World: Regulating Desire, Reforming Practice* (Routledge, 2000), *Gender in History* (Blackwells, 2001), and (with Lisa Di Caprio), *Lives and Voices: A Sourcebook on European Women* (Houghton Mifflin, 2001). She is the co-editor of the *Sixteenth Century Journal*.